George G. Evans

Visitors' Companion at our Nation's Capital

A Complete Guide for Washington and its Environs, with over One Hundred Photo Illustrations Made Expressly for this Work

George G. Evans

Visitors' Companion at our Nation's Capital
A Complete Guide for Washington and its Environs, with over One Hundred Photo Illustrations Made Expressly for this Work

ISBN/EAN: 9783337231309

Printed in Europe, USA, Canada, Australia, Japan

Cover: Foto ©Lupo / pixelio.de

More available books at **www.hansebooks.com**

AT OUR NATION'S CAPITAL.

A COMPLETE

GUIDE FOR WASHINGTON

AND ITS ENVIRONS,

WITH OVER ONE HUNDRED PHOTO ILLUSTRATIONS MADE EXPRESSLY FOR THIS WORK.

TO WHICH IS ADDED

An Appendix,

CONTAINING THE DECLARATION OF INDEPENDENCE, THE CONSTITUTION OF THE UNITED STATES, WASHINGTON'S FAREWELL ADDRESS, THE EMANCIPATION PROCLAMATION, LINCOLN'S SPEECH AT GETTYSBURG, AND MUCH OTHER INTERESTING MATTER CONNECTED WITH OUR NATION'S HISTORY.

EDITED BY THE PUBLISHER.

PHILADELPHIA:
GEORGE G. EVANS, 1314 FILBERT STREET.
1892.

PREFACE.

THE aim of this volume is to present to the reader, in attractive form, the interesting story of our Nation's Capital—how it has grown in the hundred years since its establishment to be the most magnificent city in America. With the history of the development and progress of the city it has been the purpose of the writer to give the latest and most authentic information of the different institutions of the Government. The illustrations have been carefully executed by the best artists, and embrace the Capitol and other Government buildings, and all the prominent features of the City of Washington and its environs. Special attention has been paid to the chapter on Mount Vernon and the Washington Family,—the portion relating to the English ancestry giving the results of the latest researches.

A noted writer has said: " The Nation has founded a city that bears and will transmit to posterity the name of Washington and his renown. It is a living, intelligent monument of his glory, and will reflect, as it grows in wealth and splendor, the inestimable consequences resulting to the country from his martial qualities and patriotic virtues," and it has been truly said by one of the great orators in Washington, that it is " a liberal education to go through its streets and public buildings." As the Capital of a great and enterprising people, its history illustrates the Nation's life, as well as the deeds of her greatest representative men, in the most critical periods of her existence. The name of Washington will be transmitted to posterity by the most magnificent city in the world

G. G. E.

MAY, 1892.

CONTENTS.

CHAPTER I.

THE CITY OF WASHINGTON—THE AVENUES AND STREETS—THE PARKS, SQUARES, AND CIRCLES—STATUES—THE WASHINGTON MONUMENT—CHURCHES—SCHOOLS—GOVERNMENT 17

CHAPTER II.

THE CAPITOL AND GROUNDS—MONUMENTS AND STATUES—THE ROTUNDA—THE LIBRARY OF CONGRESS—THE SENATE CHAMBER—THE NATIONAL STATUARY HALL—THE HALL OF THE HOUSE OF REPRESENTATIVES . . 37

CHAPTER III.

THE WHITE HOUSE—ITS HISTORY—DESCRIPTION OF THE BUILDING—THE GREAT STATE APARTMENTS—THE EXECUTIVE OFFICES 73

CHAPTER IV.

THE EXECUTIVE DEPARTMENTS OF THE GOVERNMENT—THE STATE, WAR, AND NAVY BUILDING—THE TREASURY—THE GENERAL POST-OFFICE—THE PATENT OFFICE—THE PENSION OFFICE—THE OFFICE OF THE ATTORNEY-GENERAL—THE AGRICULTURAL BUILDING 87

CHAPTER V.

THE NEW CONGRESSIONAL LIBRARY BUILDING—THE BUREAU OF ENGRAVING AND PRINTING—THE SMITHSONIAN INSTITUTION AND NATIONAL MUSEUM—THE CORCORAN GALLERY OF ART—THE ORDNANCE MUSEUM—THE NAVAL OBSERVATORY—THE SIGNAL OFFICE—THE GOVERNMENT PRINTING-OFFICE 111

CHAPTER VI.

MINOR OBJECTS OF INTEREST—FORD'S THEATRE—THE NAVY YARD—THE CONGRESSIONAL CEMETERY—BENEVOLENT AND EDUCATIONAL INSTITUTIONS—THE LOUISE HOME—W. W. CORCORAN—THE COLUMBIA INSTITUTION FOR THE DEAF AND DUMB—THE GOVERNMENT HOSPITAL FOR THE INSANE—HISTORIC HOUSES 129

CHAPTER VII.

THE ENVIRONS OF WASHINGTON—BLADENSBURG—THE CATHOLIC UNIVERSITY—THE SOLDIERS' HOME—ZOÖLOGICAL PARK—THE NEW NAVAL OBSERVATORY—OAK HILL CEMETERY—GEORGETOWN—THE COLLEGE—RESERVOIRS—CABIN-JOHN BRIDGE—THE GREAT FALLS OF THE POTOMAC—ANALOSTAN ISLAND—ARLINGTON AND ITS OWNERS—THE MILITARY CEMETERY—ALEXANDRIA 141

CHAPTER VIII.

MOUNT VERNON—THE TRIP DOWN THE POTOMAC—THE MOUNT VERNON LADIES' ASSOCIATION—THE TOMB OF WASHINGTON—THE OLD TOMB—THE MANSION-HOUSE—THE BANQUETING HALL—WASHINGTON'S LIBRARY—LAFAYETTE'S ROOM—THE ROOM OF NELLY CUSTIS—THE ROOM IN WHICH WASHINGTON DIED—MRS. WASHINGTON'S BEDROOM—THE OUT-BUILDINGS—THE GARDEN—THE HISTORY OF MOUNT VERNON—THE ANCESTRY OF WASHINGTON 159

APPENDIX.

FAMOUS STATE PAPERS, SPEECHES, ETC.—THE DECLARATION OF INDEPENDENCE—THE CONSTITUTION OF THE UNITED STATES—WASHINGTON'S FAREWELL ADDRESS—THE EMANCIPATION PROCLAMATION—LINCOLN'S SPEECH AT GETTYSBURG—HIS SECOND INAUGURAL ADDRESS—HIS FAVORITE POEMS 3
A SHORT HISTORY OF THE CITY OF WASHINGTON 49
LISTS OF THE PRESIDENTS, VICE-PRESIDENTS, JUSTICES OF THE SUPREME COURT, AND CABINET OFFICERS FROM 1789, AND THE DATES OF ADMISSION OF THE STATES 61
DIRECTORY OF THE CITY, AND GENERAL INFORMATION FOR VISITORS . 71

ILLUSTRATIONS.

	PAGE
Agricultural Building	107
Allen, Statue of Ethan	65
Arlington House	151
" Military Cemetery	152
Arms, Washington's	191
Asylum, Government Insane	135
Baltimore and Potomac Railroad Station	27
Blaine, Signature of James G.	Appendix 36
Bridge, Cabin John	148
Burgoyne, Surrender of	52

CAPITOL, THE 36
    Canopy of the Rotunda 48
    Corridor of the Senate 61
    Crawford Bronze Door 45
    Diagram of the Principal Story . . . 71
    Doors, Rogers and Crawford Bronze . . 44, 45
    Ladies' Parlor 63
    Library of Congress 55
    Lobby, House 68
    Mace, Speaker's 67
    Marble Room, Senate 60
    President's Room 60
    Representatives, Hall of the House of . 66
    Rogers Bronze Door 44
    Rotunda 47
    Senate Chamber 59
    Staircase, Senate 61
    Statuary Hall 64
    Supreme Court Chamber . . . 57

PAINTINGS:
    Burgoyne, Surrender of . . . 52
    Columbus, Landing of . . . 50

ILLUSTRATIONS. xi

PAGE

PAINTINGS:—*Continued.*

Cornwallis, Surrender of 53
De Soto Discovering the Mississippi 50
Independence, Signing of the Declaration of . 52
Perry's Victory on Lake Erie 62
Pilgrims, Embarkation of the . . . 51
Pocahontas, Baptism of 51
Washington Resigning his Commission . . . 53
"Westward Ho!" 69

STATUES:

Allen, Ethan 65
Discovery of America 42
Fulton, Robert 65
Garfield 65
Liberty 46
Lincoln 65
Settlement of America, First 42
Catholic University 144
Cemetery at Arlington, Military 152
Christ Church, Alexandria 156
"   "   , Interior of 158
Columbus, Landing of 50
"   , Statue of (Discovery) 42
Corcoran Gallery of Art 122
"   , W. W., Portrait of 136
Cornwallis, Surrender of . . . 53
Crawford Bronze Door 45
De Soto Discovering the Mississippi . . . 50
Discovery of America, Statuary Group of the . 42
Dupont, Statue of Admiral 23
Emancipation Proclamation, Signatures to . . Appendix 40
"   "   , Certificate of . . . " 36
"   , Statuary Group of . 29
Engraving and Printing, Bureau of 113
Farragut, Statue of Admiral 25
Ford's Theatre 130
Fulton, Statue of Robert 65
Garfield Monument 38
"   , Statue of 65
Greene, Statue of General 28

Greenough's Statue of Washington	40
Henry, Statue of Prof. Joseph	117
Houdon's Medallion of Washington	4
Independence, Signatures to the Declaration of	Appendix 9
" , Signing of the Declaration of	52
Insane, Government Hospital for the	135
Jackson, Statue of General	21
Lafayette Memorial	21
Liberty, Statue of	46
Library of Congress	55
" " , New Building of the	110
Lincoln, Signature of	Appendix 40
" , Statue of (Emancipation)	29
" , Statue of	65
Luther, Statue of	24
McPherson, Statue of General	26
Market, Centre	34
Marshall, Statue of Chief Justice John	40
Monument, Washington	30

MOUNT VERNON:

Banqueting Hall	165
Bedroom, Washington's	169
" , Mrs. Washington's	170
Dining Room, Family	167
Kitchen, Family	171
Mansion-House	163
Tomb of Washington	162
Museum, National	120
Naval Monument	39
Navy Building, State, War, and	86

PAINTINGS:

Burgoyne, Surrender of	52
Columbus, Landing of	50
Cornwallis, Surrender of	53
De Soto Discovering the Mississippi	50
Independence, Signing of the Declaration of	52
Perry's Victory on Lake Erie	62
Pilgrims, Embarkation of the	51
Pocahontas, Baptism of	51

ILLUSTRATIONS.   xiii

PAINTINGS:—*Continued.*

	PAGE
Washington Resigning his Commission	53
"Westward Ho!"	69
Patent Office	102
Payne Monument	146
Pennsylvania Avenue from the Treasury	20
Pension Building	105
" ", Interior of the	105
Perry's Victory on Lake Erie	62
Pilgrims, Embarkation of the	51
Pocahontas, Baptism of	51
Post-Office, The General	96
Prison, Old Capitol	131
Rawlins, Statue of General	26
Representatives, Hall of the House of	66
Rogers Bronze Door	44
Scott, Statue of General	23
Senate Chamber	59
Settlement of America, Statuary Group of the	42
Seward, Signature of William H.	Appendix 40
Smithsonian Institution	115
Soldiers' Home	142
State, War, and Navy Building	86
Station, Baltimore and Potomac Railroad	27
Statuary Hall	64

STATUES:

Allen, Ethan	65
Discovery of America, (group)	42
Dupont, Admiral	23
Emancipation Group (Lincoln)	29
Farragut, Admiral	25
Fulton, Robert	65
Garfield	38, 65
Greene, General	28
Henry, Prof. Joseph	117
Jackson, General	21
Lafayette	21
Liberty	46
Lincoln	29, 65
Luther	24

STATUES:—*Continued.*
    McPherson, General
    Marshall, Chief Justice
    Rawlins, General
    Scott, General
    Settlement of America (group)
    Thomas, General
    Washington
Supreme Court Chamber
Thomas Circle, View from
    " , Statue of General
Tomb of the Unknown Dead at Arlington
    " of Washington
Treasury Building
Trumbull Paintings, The
University, Catholic
War, and Navy Building, State,
View of the City of Washington

WASHINGTON:
    Coat-of-arms
    Medallion of (Houdon's)
    Monument
    Statues of
    Tomb of
"Westward Ho!"

WHITE HOUSE, THE:
    Bedroom, State
    Blue Room
    Cabinet Room
    Conservatory
    Dining-room, Family
        " , State
    East Room
    Green Room
    Library
    North Front
    Red Room
    South Front

VIEW OF WASHINGTON, FROM THE STATE, WAR, AND NAVY BUILDING.

CHAPTER I.

THE CITY OF WASHINGTON—THE AVENUES AND STREETS—THE PARKS, SQUARES, AND CIRCLES—STATUES—THE WASHINGTON MONUMENT—CHURCHES—SCHOOLS —GOVERNMENT.

THE City of Washington, the Capital of the United States of America, occupies a portion of the District of Columbia, a territory which is under the immediate control of Congress.

The District of Columbia comprises an area of about sixty-five square miles, and lies on the northern bank of the Potomac, one hundred and sixteen miles above its mouth. The greater part of this area is a plateau rising some four hundred feet above the level of the Potomac, and traversed by two streams, the Anacostia River, or Eastern Branch, and Rock Creek. Above the mouth of the Anacostia, the edge of the plateau recedes from the bank of the Potomac and leaves a comparatively low piece of land, about seven square miles in area. It is on this that the city is built. The suburbs occupy the hills to the north and west, the old city of Georgetown now forming a part of Washington.

The situation is an ideal one for a great city, and the founders were far-sighted men, L'Enfant's plan being adapted to a population of one million. The present number of inhabitants is about two hundred and forty thousand, but people are appreciating its advantages as a place of residence, and the growth is very rapid. Every year it is becoming more and more the centre of the political, literary, and social life of the country, and many people visiting the city become so fascinated by its many attractions that they make their homes there. The other great cities of the country, notwithstanding their many objects of interest, have a distinctly commercial aspect, but Washington shows a gayer spirit and commerce here is of secondary consideration. The Government, backed by the enterprise of private citizens, spares no pains and expense to make it year by year more worthy of its position as the capital of a proud and prosperous people.

Washington had the advantage, possessed by no other great city of modern times, of being planned entirely in advance by a skilful engineer. Thus the confusion and inconvenience arising from the presence of old buildings and narrow and crooked streets was avoided, nor is it necessary to go to vast expense to make the broad highways required in the great cities of to-day.

The plan of the city is symmetrical. The Capitol and White House are two centres, from each of which radiate broad avenues. The streets are laid out at right angles to each other and corresponding to the cardinal points. Three streets running from the Capitol, known as North, East, and South Capitol Streets, and a broad stretch of public gardens on the west, divide the city into four districts, known as North-East, South-East, South-West, and North-West. The streets running north and south are numbered, beginning at the Capitol, and the east and west streets bear the names of the letters of the alphabet, beginning at the same place. This system makes it easy to find any designated locality.

The streets vary in width from eighty to one hundred and twenty feet, and the avenues from one hundred and twenty to one hundred and sixty feet. Advantage has been taken of the intersections of the avenues with the streets to form miniature parks, square or circular in form, liberally planted with trees and flowers and adorned with statues. The same enlightened policy has been followed on the streets and avenues, and there is no city in the world that can compare with Washington in the beauty and convenience of its public highways. The tree-planting, though a detail of the original design, was practically begun in 1872 by the Shepherd Board of Public Works. More than seventy thousand trees have been planted, and the annual increase in the number exceeds three thousand. There are numerous varieties, such as the maple, elm, ash, poplar, buttonwood, tulip, oak, and others. Many of the streets are completely arched by trees throughout their entire length, and from the Capitol or the Monument Washington presents the appearance of a city in the midst of a forest. This liberal use of trees has had an important effect upon the general health of the people, for malaria, once so common, has almost entirely disappeared.

The majority of the streets are paved with asphalt, and there is a notable absence of the rattle and roar of vehicles, so common and annoying elsewhere.

More than one-half the entire area of the city was reserved for public purposes and is now used for the Government buildings and for parks and streets.

The most populous section is the North-West. Before 1870, it was dreary and unhealthy, abounding in swamps and mainly occupied by the tumble-down shanties of negro squatters. But the Board of Public Works, under the leadership of Governor Shepherd, began an extensive system of public improvements; the swamps were drained, streets laid out, and now the quarter is noted for the beauty of its highways and the elegance of its buildings. Here are the White House and the great department buildings, the theatres, the great hotels and stores, and the greatest number of churches and public institutions. In the portion known as the "West End" are the great mansions that have of late years so added to the beauty and fame of the city. The avenues cutting the streets obliquely have made many odd-shaped lots, and architects have taken advantage of the opportunity to make the buildings picturesquely irregular in their lines. There is no tolerance for the long rows of similar structures so common in other cities, and each house in a street seems to have a certain individuality.

The North-East is but slightly developed and has as yet but few inhabitants. As the population grows it will doubtless fill up, as the ground is high and the situation healthy.

The South-East was expected to become the chief quarter of the city, and some large and handsome buildings were erected here at an early date. But the development was retarded by the high prices demanded for land, and the tide of fashion and improvement set in to the North-West. Of late years, however, many fine buildings have been erected, and while it may never rival the West End in the way of fashion, it bids fair to become a beautiful and populous quarter.

The South-West is almost wholly given up to business, and is filled with manufacturing establishments, lumber yards, wharves, etc.

The great central thoroughfare is Pennsylvania Avenue. It is nearly five miles long, but is broken in two places by the Capitol and the Treasury. Between the two, its length of a mile and one-half forms the chief highway of the city. Its width is one hundred and sixty feet, and it is paved with asphalt. The smaller buildings are giving way to magnificent modern structures, and in a few years it will become the most splendid avenue in the world. A grand view is obtained by standing on the steps of the Treasury and looking towards the Capitol.

PENNSYLVANIA AVENUE FROM THE TREASURY.

The large area reserved for park purposes forms a very attractive feature of Washington life. West of the Capitol is the broad stretch of lands known as The Mall, extending to the river. The grounds nearest the Capitol form the Botanical Gardens, and contain great conservatories stored with rare plants. There is also a beautiful fountain designed by Bartholdi. To the west of the Botanical Gardens are the grounds of the National Museum and Smithsonian Institution, and of the Department of Agriculture, under whose charge are the great propagating gardens. At the end of The Mall, the Washington Monument rears its gleaming white shaft high towards heaven, and beyond are the grounds reclaimed from the river and laid out in beautiful parks.

On Pennsylvania Avenue, opposite the White House, is Lafayette

Square. It comprises about seven acres, and has many large trees and beautiful plants. Rare tropical flowers are set out in spring and make the square a very attractive place.

At the south-east entrance is a beautiful memorial erected by Congress to Lafayette and his compatriots who served during the Revolution. The figures are of bronze, the work of the French sculptors, Falquiere and Mercie. The total cost was $50,000.

The figure of Lafayette is ten feet high, and represents the gallant Frenchman in his uniform as a Continental general. At the sides are statues of Rochambeau and Duportail, of the French army, and D'Estaing and De Grasse, of the navy. In front is "America" holding up a sword to Lafayette.

LAFAYETTE MEMORIAL.

In the centre of the Square is the bronze equestrian statue of General Andrew Jackson, by Clark Mills. It is of heroic size, and the pose, as the horse is reared back while the general is giving a salute, is very striking. It was unveiled January 8, 1853, the thirty-eighth anniversary of the great victory of New Orleans. The material was obtained from cannon captured in Jackson's campaigns. This statue was the first piece of bronze casting of any magnitude undertaken in this country, and Mr. Mills met with great difficulties in his work, having to design his furnace himself. The cost was $50,000.

GENERAL ANDREW JACKSON.

North of the Square is the house occupied by Hon. William H. Seward, while Secretary of State, and where the assassin Payne attempted to kill him the same night that Booth shot President Lincoln.

At the north-east corner is the old mansion formerly occupied by Hon. Charles Sumner, while Senator from Massachusetts. It now forms a part of the Arlington Hotel.

At the north-west corner is the old Decatur mansion, built in 1819, the first private house on the Square. Subsequently, it became the residence of several foreign ministers. Later, it was occupied by Henry Clay, Martin Van Buren, and Daniel Webster, while Secretaries of State.

Washington Circle is at the intersection of Pennsylvania and New Hampshire Avenues and Twenty-third and K Streets, N. W. It contains Clark Mills's equestrian statue of Washington. The hero is represented as he appeared at the critical moment during the battle of Princeton. The American troops had given way before the onslaught of the foe, but Washington, with drawn sword, is rallying them to renew the fight. The likeness was taken from a bust by Houdon, executed during Washington's lifetime. The figure was cast from cannon given by Congress, and cost $50,000. It was unveiled in 1860.

WASHINGTON.

Dupont Circle is at the intersection of New Hampshire, Massachusetts, and Connecticut Avenues and Nineteenth and P Streets, N. W. It is handsomely laid out with trees and flowers. In the centre is the bronze statue of Admiral Samuel Francis Dupont, by Launt Thompson. The figure is of heroic size and the Admiral is represented as clad in full uniform and standing on the quarter-deck, with his marine glass in his hand. The pedestal is of granite, with a base of bluestone. The statue was unveiled with appropriate ceremonies,

December 20, 1884, Hon. Thomas F. Bayard, of Delaware, delivering the oration. The cost of the monument was $10,000.

Ten streets and avenues radiate from Dupont Circle, and some of the finest mansions of the city front upon it. Notable are the houses of Mr. Blaine, and "Stewart Castle," at present occupied by the Chinese Legation.

A short distance down Connecticut Avenue is the palatial mansion occupied by the British Legation.

Scott Square is at the intersection of Massachusetts and Rhode Island Avenues and Sixteenth and N Streets, N. W. It contains a small circular park, in the centre of which is an equestrian statue of General Winfield Scott. It was modelled by H. K. Brown, and cast in Philadelphia in 1874. The bronze was obtained from cannon captured during the Mexican War.

ADMIRAL DUPONT.

The General is represented in the full uniform of Lieutenant-General. The pedestal is of Cape Ann granite, and the five blocks are said to be the largest ever quarried in the United States. The lowest is twenty-six feet long, thirteen feet wide, and two feet thick, and weighs one hundred and twenty tons.

The cost of the statue was $20,000, and that of the pedestal $25,000.

Thomas Circle is at the intersection of Vermont and Massachusetts Avenues and Fourteenth and M Streets, N. W. It contains the equestrian statue of General George H. Thomas. It was modelled by J. Q. A. Ward. It is

GENERAL SCOTT.

sixteen feet high, and rests on a granite pedestal, on the sides of which are the insignia in bronze of the Army of the Cumberland.

GENERAL THOMAS.

The statue, costing $50,000, was erected by the comrades of the General, the members of the Society of the Army of the Cumberland. The pedestal, costing $25,000, was provided by Congress. In connection with the ceremony of dedication there was a grand military and civil parade, November 19, 1879. Hon. Stanley Mathews delivered the oration.

Four magnificent bronze lamps at the corners of the pedestal add greatly to the artistic effect of the monument.

North-west of Thomas Circle is the bronze statue of Martin Luther, erected by the members of the Lutheran Church. It was cast in Germany from the same moulds as the statue forming the centrepiece of the celebrated memorial at Worms. It is eleven feet high—a commanding figure. The Great Reformer is represented as he appeared before the famous Diet of Worms, 1521. In his left hand he holds a Bible, to which he points with his right; while his face, on which faith is admirably portrayed, is turned upward.

The statue was modelled by Rietschel, and cost, with the pedestal, $10,000.

Iowa Circle is at the intersection of Vermont and Rhode Island Avenues and Thirteenth and P Streets, N. W. It is proposed to erect here a statue of General John A. Logan, at the estimated cost of $40,000.

MARTIN LUTHER.

Farragut Square covers an area of a little more than one acre, at the intersection of Connecticut Avenue and I Street, N. W. In it

VIEW FROM THOMAS CIRCLE LOOKING NORTH.

stands the colossal bronze statue of Admiral David G. Farragut, modelled by Mrs. Vinnie Ream Hoxie. The figure is ten feet in height, and stands on a granite pedestal, which has a height of twenty feet. The material was taken from the propeller of Farragut's famous flag-ship, the "Hartford," with which he passed the forts below New Orleans and fought in Mobile Bay. The monument was unveiled April 25, 1881, Hon. Horace Maynard, of Tennessee, and Hon. Daniel W. Voorhees, of Indiana, being the orators of the occasion.

ADMIRAL FARRAGUT.

M'Pherson Square is at the intersection of Vermont Avenue and I Street, N. W. It contains a colossal equestrian statue of General James B. M'Pherson, erected by the Society of the Army of the Tennessee. It was designed by

Louis T. Robisso. The bronze was obtained from cannon donated by Congress, and the cost was nearly $25,000. It is fourteen feet high and stands on a massive granite pedestal, costing $25,000. The statue was unveiled October 18, 1876, and the ceremony was accompanied by an imposing military display and delivery of an oration by General John A. Logan.

GENERAL M'PHERSON.

Franklin Square is between Thirteenth and Fourteenth and I and K Streets, N. W. It comprises about four acres, and is prettily laid out, containing a large fountain in the centre. The spring supplying this fountain is excellent, and pipes convey water from it to the White House. Franklin Public School, the finest in the city, is opposite the north-east corner.

In the small triangular space made by the intersection of Tenth and D Streets with Pennsylvania Avenue, N. W., is a fine marble statue of Benjamin Franklin, presented to the city by Stillson Hutchins, in 1889. The figure is of heroic size, and rests on a granite pedestal eleven feet high. The great patriot and philosopher is represented in the dress he used while Minister to the Court of France during the Revolution.

Judiciary Square lies north of the junction of Louisiana and Indiana Avenues with D Street, N. W., and comprises about twenty acres. In the northern portion is the Pension Building, and in the southern the City Hall or District

GENERAL JOHN A. RAWLINS.

Court-House, in which the assassin Guiteau was tried for the murder of President Garfield. In front of the Court-House is a marble column twenty-seven feet high, on the top of which is a statue of Abraham Lincoln, made by Lot Flannery, a self-taught sculptor. The monument was erected by the subscriptions of the citizens of the District.

BALTIMORE AND POTOMAC RAILROAD STATION.

A bronze statue of General John A. Rawlins, Chief of Staff for General Grant, 1865, and Secretary of War in 1869, stands in a small triangular plot formed by the intersection of Pennsylvania and

Louisiana Avenues and Ninth Street, N. W. The figure is of heroic size, and was cast from cannon captured during the Civil War, which were donated by Congress. It was designed by J. Bailey, and cast in Philadelphia. The pedestal is of granite and is twelve feet high. The cost was $12,000, defrayed by the friends of the General. The statue was unveiled in 1874.

At the corner of Pennsylvania Avenue and Seventh Street, N. W., is a pretty drinking-fountain, presented to the city by Dr. Cogswell, of California.

At the corner of Sixth and B Streets, N. W., is the passenger station of the Baltimore and Potomac Railroad. It is connected with the history of the nation, as being the scene of a very tragic event. While walking through the ladies' waiting-room, on the arm of Secretary Blaine, President Garfield was shot by Guiteau, July 2, 1881. A silver star, set into the floor, marks the spot where he fell, and the company has placed a memorial tablet on the wall opposite the spot.

Stanton Place, formerly Greene Square, is at the intersection of Massachusetts and Maryland Avenues and Fifth and C Streets, N. E. It has an area of about three and one-half acres, and contains a colossal bronze equestrian statue of General Nathaniel Greene, the distinguished Revolutionary soldier and the hero of the battle of Eutaw Springs. It was modelled by H. K. Brown, and cast in Philadelphia. The cost was $50,000. The Continental Congress voted a statue to General Greene on account of his distinguished services, but lack of means and the apathy of succeeding Congresses caused a long delay. Finally an appropriation was secured and the statue erected in 1877.

GENERAL NATHANIEL GREENE.

Lincoln Park is on East Capitol Street, a mile east of the Capitol, and has an area of six and one-half acres. It contains the famous bronze group designated "Emancipation." It was designed by Thomas Ball, and cast in Munich in 1875. Lincoln is represented standing by a pillar, on which rests his right hand holding the Proclamation of Emancipation. His left hand is extended, as in blessing, over a slave kneeling at his feet. The shackles of the slave are broken, and he is gazing at the President as though giving thanks for his liberty. The group is ten feet high, and rests on a granite pedestal. A bronze tablet in the front of the pedestal is inscribed, "Freedom's Memorial. In grateful memory of Abraham Lincoln, this monument was erected by the Western Sanitary Commission of St. Louis, Mo., with funds contributed solely by emancipated citizens of the United States declared free by his proclamation, January 1, A.D. 1863. The first contribution of five dollars was made by Charlotte Scott, a freed woman of Virginia, being her first earnings in freedom, and consecrated by her suggestion and request, on the day she heard of President Lincoln's death, to build a monument to his memory." On the tablet at the back is an extract from the proclamation, "And upon this act, sincerely believed to be an act of justice warranted by the Constitution upon military necessity, I invoke the considerate judgment of mankind and the gracious favor of Almighty God."

EMANCIPATION STATUE.

The bronze cost $17,000. The dedication took place April 14, 1876, when Hon. Frederick Douglass delivered the oration.

THE WASHINGTON MONUMENT.

The original design of the Washington Monument contemplated a grand circular hall, two hundred and fifty feet in diameter, and one hundred feet high, surrounded by lofty colonnades. From the centre of the hall there was to rise a marble shaft six hundred feet high. The rotunda at the base was to be a National Memorial Hall, to contain statues of great Americans and paintings illustrating

THE WASHINGTON MONUMENT.

events in the Nation's history, while the crypt beneath would serve as a burial-place for those whom the people should especially honor.

The Monument stands at the western extremity of The Mall, so that it is at the same time west of the Capitol and south of the White House, from either of which a superb view of it can be obtained.

The foundation of the Monument is a mass of rock and concrete, one hundred and forty-one feet square and thirty-eight feet deep. From this rises the shaft, fifty-five feet square at the base, where the walls are fifteen feet thick, and gradually tapering, until, at the elevation of five hundred feet, it is about thirty-five feet square and the walls have a thickness of eighteen inches. At this point the pyramidal roof begins, rising an additional height of fifty-five feet, and ending in an aluminium tip. This metal was chosen because, on account of its freedom from oxidation, it always maintains its brightness. The tip is nine inches high and four and one-half inches square at the base. On the sides are engraved the names of the engineer and architect, the dates of the laying of the corner-stone and of the completion of the Monument, the names of the Commission at the completion, and " Laus Deo."

The total height of the Monument from the base-line to the point of the tip is five hundred and fifty-five feet four inches, thus making it the loftiest structure of masonry ever reared by man.*

The walls of the interior are lined with granite and contain a number of memorial stones sent from all parts of the world. Some are very beautifully carved, and all have inscriptions. Among these inscriptions are, "Greece," "Bremen," "From the Temple of Esculapius, Island of Paros," "The Free Swiss Confederation, 1870," "From Braddock's Field," "Cherokee Nation, 1855," "Brazil," "Arabia," "China." One block of sandstone has, "This block of stone is from the original chapel built to William Tell, in 1338, on Lake Lucerne, at the spot where he escaped from Gessler."

The interior is lighted by electricity, as there are no openings except the doorway at the base and the eight small windows at the top. Eight massive iron columns, extending from the base to the

---

* The Eiffel Tower, at Paris, has a height of nine hundred and eighty-four feet, but is built of iron. Of the other lofty buildings in the world, the spires of the Cologne Cathedral are five hundred and twenty-five feet high; the original height of the Great Pyramid was four hundred and eighty-five feet. Several European cathedrals have an altitude but little less; St. Peter's, at Rome, is four hundred and thirty-two feet high; and St. Paul's, at London, three hundred and sixty-one feet. Bunker Hill Monument is two hundred and twenty-one feet high. The City Hall, at Philadelphia, will be five hundred and thirty-seven feet high.

top, support the iron staircase and the elevator. The strength of the latter was severely tested during the progress of construction, as all the marble blocks were raised by it, and it was constantly bearing a greater weight than it will ever carry again. The time required for a trip to the top is seven minutes. There are nine hundred steps in the staircase, and at every fifty feet are platforms giving the climber a chance for rest, or, if he desire it, access to the elevator.

A magnificent view is obtained from the top of the Monument. There are two windows on each side, five hundred and seventeen feet above ground. The City of Washington appears spread out like a grand cyclorama, the broad avenues, the parks, and public buildings presenting a beautiful spectacle. The surrounding hills to the north and east form a grand amphitheatre, while to the west the course of the Potomac can be seen as it winds its way through picturesque scenes, and far in the distance lies the haze indicating the Blue Mountains.

The construction of the Monument was begun by the Washington Monument Society, and the corner-stone was laid July 4, 1848. Hon. Robert C. Winthrop made the address. In the course of his remarks he said, "Build it to the skies, you cannot outreach the loftiness of his principles; found it upon the massive and eternal rock, you cannot make it more enduring than his fame; construct it of the peerless Parian marble, you cannot make it purer than his life; exhaust upon it the rules and principles of ancient and modern art, you cannot make it more proportionate than his character."

Work was continued until 1854, when it ceased from lack of funds. Endeavors were made to induce Congress to appropriate the money necessary for the completion, but nothing was accomplished until 1876, when the "Centennial feeling" prevailed and the requisite amount was voted. Work was recommenced and pushed rapidly until it was finished, the capstone being set December 6, 1884, and the Monument was dedicated, with imposing ceremony, February 21, 1885.

The total cost was $1,187,710, of which $200,000 was furnished by the Society and the balance by Congress.

Long Bridge extends from the foot of Maryland Avenue across the Potomac, and is more than a mile long. It is an unsightly-looking structure in these days of great engineering feats, but shows thorough and honest workmanship. Though built of wood, as far back as 1835, it is still in very good condition and sustains a very heavy traffic. One side is used by the railroads, the other by vehicles and foot-passengers. It cost about $100,000. It possesses a peculiar interest from the fact that across it marched hundreds of thousands of Union soldiers on their way to the battle-fields of the South, and many a veteran recalls to-day the thrill he felt when, in 1865, on his homeward march, he placed his foot upon Long Bridge.

Many of the small parks and squares are unimproved and as yet unadorned with statues. But Congress is not oblivious of the Nation's heroes, and nearly every year is marked by the erection of some new tribute to the brave and wise men who are gone. In a few years no city in the world will be able to vie with Washington in the number and beauty of its memorials. And these will have been erected not by the will of a monarch, but by a loving and grateful people, who desire thus to testify their affection and respect for their faithful fellow-laborers in the cause of human equality and freedom.

The churches of Washington are very numerous, and the religions of nearly all civilized peoples are represented by their congregations. Some of the edifices are very beautiful and costly, and compare favorably with the temples of any city in the world. There are nearly two hundred churches, and the number of communicants exceeds sixty thousand. The average attendance is about one hundred thousand—nearly one-half the population—a very good showing for any large city.

The oldest church in the District is St. Paul's, Rock Creek Parish, near the Soldiers' Home. Thomas Bradford gave the land, and the church was erected in 1719 of bricks brought from England. Christ Episcopal Church, at Sixth and G Streets, S. E., was built in 1795, shortly after the laying-out of the city, and was doubtless expected to become the fashionable place of worship. The trend of population, however, set in the opposite direction, and the handsome and costly churches are in the North-West. St. John's, at H and Sixteenth Streets, N. W., was designed by Latrobe, the architect of the Capitol, and erected in 1816. President Madison worshipped in this venerable church, and other Presidents have been regular worshippers. All through his official term President Arthur attended the morning service here. The Church of the Christian Disciples, better known as the Garfield Memorial Church, is on Vermont Avenue between N and O Streets, N. W. It stands on the site of a small chapel where Garfield worshipped for many years while a member of Congress and when President. The pew he occupied has been placed in the church and is draped in black and bears a silver memorial tablet.

The public schools of the city are admirably conducted. There are many large and handsome buildings in use. The Wallach School, on Pennsylvania Avenue between Seventh and Eighth Streets, S. E., is a fine brick building. The most imposing is the Franklin School, at Thirteenth and K Streets, N. W. It is one of the finest school buildings in the United States, and a model of it took the First Prize at the Paris Exhibition, 1889. The annual appropriation for the support of the schools exceeds $700,000. Nearly eight hundred teachers are employed, and there are more than thirty-eight thousand pupils.

The importance of good market facilities has not been overlooked, and Washington is very well supplied in this respect. There are five market houses, all of them large and convenient, but the Centre Market is probably the finest structure of its kind in the country.

THE CENTRE MARKET.

It lies south of Pennsylvania Avenue, between Seventh and Ninth Streets, N. W. In its construction the most improved modern methods were followed, and in the facilities offered to the public and the dealers it is unsurpassed. There are four large buildings

THE DISTRICT GOVERNMENT.

forming a square, the length of each being four hundred feet, with an average width of eighty-two feet. The surface available is more than nine thousand square yards, and there are six hundred and sixty-six stalls. The market was built in 1873, and has cost $500,000. Many articles besides food-products can be purchased, there being an extensive variety of household utensils and a great display of flowers and plants. Washington is admirably situated for obtaining choice supplies of all things good to eat. It is in the centre of a fine agricultural region and near Chesapeake Bay, the best place in the world for ducks, terrapin, fish, and oysters. Anyone fond of good living needs but to take a walk through the market in the early morning to make him wish to settle in Washington for the rest of his days.

The water-supply of Washington is very abundant, and is obtained from the Potomac above the Great Falls. It is conveyed to the city by an aqueduct which has been considered a triumph of engineering. It is nearly twelve miles long, and during its course passes over six bridges and through twelve tunnels. The reservoir is west of Georgetown, and the water is conveyed thence to the city by means of huge mains. They are carried over Rock Creek by a fine bridge which sustains a wide roadway.

The government of the District of Columbia is in the hands of three Commissioners, appointed by the President. They have full control of all matters, subject to the supervision of Congress. One-half of the current expenses and of the cost of public improvements is borne by Congress, the balance being provided for by local taxation. The assessed valuation of real estate exceeds $150,000,000, and the rate of taxation is one and one-half per cent.

THE CAPITOL, EASTERN FRONT.

CHAPTER II.

THE CAPITOL AND GROUNDS—MONUMENTS AND STATUES—THE ROTUNDA—THE LIBRARY OF CONGRESS—THE SENATE CHAMBER—THE NATIONAL STATUARY HALL—THE HALL OF THE HOUSE OF REPRESENTATIVES.

IN beauty of design, skill in execution, and advantage of situation the Capitol can challenge comparison with any public building in the world. In the midst of a beautiful park, standing on the crest of a hill ninety-six feet above the level of the Potomac, its lofty dome and stately columns are visible at a distance of many miles, and present to the eye of the beholder a picture of majestic beauty that can never be forgotten. Other public buildings of ancient and modern times may excel it in some particulars, but none give such an impression of grandeur and majesty.

THE GROUNDS.

The park surrounding the Capitol has an extent of forty-six acres, and has been artistically laid out under the supervision of Mr. Frederic Law Olmstead, of New York. It is surrounded by a low wall of granite, but the drives and pathways have been skilfully planned to give easy access to the building, whose beauties are veiled, but not hidden, by the luxuriant masses of foliage. The grounds afford many delightful spots for rest and retirement, and the Government has done much to make them attractive to the people. Pretty arbors and drinking-fountains and wide, comfortable seats are scattered in shady nooks, while the many varieties of trees from all parts of the world excite the admiration of the visitor. Several trees were planted by President Washington, and one of these, north of the Capitol, known as the Washington Elm, is still flourishing luxuriantly.

In the southwestern portion of the grounds is a pretty tower erected at the mouth of the tunnel through which is drawn the supply of pure air for the Hall of the House of Representatives. It is covered with ivy and looks as though it were part of some ancient ruin. A similar tower northwest of the Capitol is used for ventilating the Senate Chamber.

The slope of the hill west of the Capitol has been beautifully terraced, and the view obtained from this side is much finer than that

THE GARFIELD MONUMENT.

from the east. The terraces seem part of the building, and the effect is that of a massive mountain of white marble crowned by the glistening dome. Magnificent double flights of steps, forty-eight feet wide, lead to the upper terrace, which is nearly nine hundred feet long and sixty feet wide. It is enclosed by a marble balustrade adorned with elegant bronze vases for flowers.

At the southwestern entrance to the grounds is a magnificent statue of President Garfield. The figure is of bronze, resting on a granite pedestal. The martyred President is represented as he appeared when delivering his inaugural address. At the base of the pedestal are three recumbent bronze figures representing a Student, a Warrior, and a Statesman, typical of the three periods of Garfield's life. The monument was erected by his comrades of the Army of the Cumberland, and unveiled May 12, 1887. The artist was J. Q. A. Ward, and the total cost was $65,000.

THE NAVAL MONUMENT

Is on Pennsylvania Avenue near the western entrance to the Capitol grounds. It bears the inscription, "In memory of the officers, seamen, and marines of the United States Navy who fell in defence of the Union and liberty of their country, 1861–1865." The upper figures are nearly nine feet in height and represent America weeping for the loss of her brave sons, while History is inscribing on a tablet the record of their illustrious deeds. On the front is a statue of Victory, holding aloft a laurel crown, and at her feet are figures of Neptune and Mars, typifying the Navy and the Marine Corps. On the back is a statue of Peace, extending an olive branch, while around her are emblems of her conquests. The monument is of Carrara marble resting on a granite pedestal, and is forty-six feet high.

THE NAVAL MONUMENT.

It was executed in Rome by Franklin Simmons from a design by Admiral Porter, and was unveiled in 1877. It was erected by the contributions of the Navy, amounting to $21,000, the pedestal, costing $20,000, being provided by Congress.

Immediately west of the Capitol is the large bronze statue of Chief Justice John Marshall. The great jurist, clad in his robe of office and seated in the chair he used for so many years, is represented as delivering a judicial opinion. The pedestal is of Italian marble, and bears on its front the inscription, "John Marshall, Chief Justice of the United States. Erected by the Bar and Congress of the United States. A.D. MDCCCLXXXIV." Panels on the sides, with figures in low relief, represent Minerva dictating to Young America the Constitution of the United States, and Victory leading Young America to swear fidelity on the altar of the Union.

CHIEF JUSTICE JOHN MARSHALL.

Facing the grand central portico is the colossal statue of Washington, executed in Rome by Horatio Greenough, and placed in position in 1842. It is of Carrara marble, resting on a granite pedestal, and cost $45,000. Washington is represented as seated in a curule chair, his left hand holding a sheathed sword, while his right is extended toward heaven. The figure is partially nude, a mantle draping the body below the waist and extending over the right shoulder. The chair is adorned with statuettes of Columbus and an Indian chief and with lions' heads and acanthus leaves. On the sides are designs representing Hercules strangling the serpents, and Apollo driving the chariot of the Sun.

WASHINGTON.

On the back is a Latin inscription, "*Simulacrum istud ad magnum Libertatis exemplum, nec sine ipsa duraturum,*" which may be translated, "This statue is for a great example of Liberty, nor without Liberty will the example endure." On the pedestal is the famous extract from the eulogy delivered by Governor Henry Lee, of Virginia, "First in war, first in peace, first in the hearts of his countrymen."

THE CAPITOL

Consists of a central building connected by corridors with two wings or extensions. It has a rustic basement, a principal story, and an attic story surmounted by an entablature and a balustrade. Its total length is seven hundred and fifty-one feet four inches and its breadth varies from fifty-six feet to three hundred and twenty-four feet, including the porticoes and steps, and it covers an area of nearly four acres. Its extreme height from the ground to the top of the statue of Liberty on the summit of the dome is three hundred and seven feet six inches.

The central portion, or the original Capitol, completed in 1827, is three hundred and fifty-two feet four inches long and one hundred and twenty-one feet six inches wide. It is constructed of Virginia sandstone, painted white. The connecting corridors, forty-four feet long and fifty-six feet wide, and the wings, one hundred and forty-two feet eight inches long and two hundred and thirty-eight feet ten inches wide, are constructed of Massachusetts marble.

The Capitol faces the east, while the rear overlooks the most populous and fashionable quarter of Washington. It was originally believed that the city would develop toward the east, but the extension has been almost entirely in the opposite direction, and, like the Irishman's shanty, the Capitol has its "front door on the back side." Of late years efforts have been made to have the central portion rebuilt of marble, and the opportunity will doubtless be taken to make the western front conform to the eastern.

The grand central portico at the eastern entrance is one hundred and sixty feet wide and has twenty-four massive monolithic columns, thirty feet high. On the tympanum is an allegorical group, designed by John Quincy Adams and executed by Persico, a distinguished

Roman sculptor. It represents the "Genius of America." The central figure is America with spear and shield, at her feet an eagle with an olive branch. The shield rests on an altar inscribed with the date, July 4, 1776. Hope, resting on an anchor, is addressing America, who points to Justice. Justice is holding the Constitution of the United States, and is watching her scales.

On the buttresses at the top of the steps are two colossal marble groups. The southern one is entitled the "Discovery of America," and represents Columbus holding the globe, while an Indian maiden, amazed and terrified, crouches at his feet. The armor was copied from a suit worn by Columbus and still preserved at Genoa. The group was executed by Persico in 1846 and cost $24,000.

DISCOVERY OF AMERICA.   FIRST SETTLEMENT OF AMERICA.

The northern group is entitled "Civilization, or the First Settlement of America," and represents a struggle between a pioneer and an Indian. The wife of the pioneer, holding her babe to her bosom, is terrified at his danger, but is waiting to share his death or victory. The group is the work of Greenough and cost $24,000.

Colossal statues of Carrara marble, representing War and Peace, stand in niches on either side of the entrance. They were executed by Persico and cost $12,000 each.

Over the entrance is a sculpture, in low relief, by Capellano, representing Washington being crowned with laurel by Fame and Peace.

On the grand central portico the Chief Justice of the Supreme Court has administered the oath of office to the Presidents of the United States since the inauguration of Andrew Jackson in 1829. Before a vast multitude of their fellow-citizens from all parts of the land the Chiefs of the Nation have vowed, by the help of God, to be faithful in the performance of the duties of their high office. To their honor be it said that their oaths have never been violated. No other country in the world can show such a succession of rulers. Great statesmen and victorious soldiers are to be found in the list, but in every case personal ambition has given way to the desire to serve the country.

At the main entrance of the Capitol is the famous bronze door, designed by Randolph Rogers and cast in Munich in 1860. It is within a bronze casing, is nineteen feet high and nine feet wide, weighs ten tons, and cost $28,000. On the casing are emblematic designs and at the top a bust of Columbus. On the nine panels are designs in high relief representing scenes in the life of Columbus and in the discovery of America. Taken in order, beginning at the lowest left-hand panel, they show: "The Examination of Columbus before the Council of Salamanca;" "The Departure of Columbus from the Convent of La Rabida for the Spanish Court;" "Columbus before the Court of Ferdinand and Isabella;" "The Departure of Columbus from Palos on his First Voyage of Discovery;" "Columbus Landing at San Salvador;" "First Encounter of Columbus with the Indians;" "Triumphal Entry of Columbus into Barcelona;" "Columbus in Chains;" "The Death-bed of Columbus." Between the panels are ten heads of the historians of the voyages of the great discoverer, and at the sides are statuettes of prominent contemporaries.

The House and Senate extensions have each twenty-two massive monolithic columns on their eastern porticoes and ten similar columns on their northern and southern projections and on their western fronts. On the tympanum of the northern, or Senate, extension is a magnificent marble group, designed and executed by Thomas Crawford, representing "American Civilization and the Decadence of the Indian Races." The central figure represents America; on the right are Pioneers and Indians; on the left, War, Commerce, Education, and the Mechanical Arts.

THE ROGERS BRONZE DOOR.

At the entrance of the Senate extension is a bronze door modelled by Thomas Crawford and cast at Chicopee, Mass. It is fourteen

THE CRAWFORD BRONZE DOOR.

feet six inches high and nine feet six inches wide, and weighs seven tons. It cost $57,000, and was placed in position in 1868. Its eight panels contains scenes in high relief representing incidents in the early history of the United States. Beginning with the uppermost right-hand panel, are the " Battle of Bunker Hill and the Death of General Warren, June, 1775 ;" the " Battle of Monmouth and Washington's Rebuke of General Charles Lee, the Traitor, June, 1778 ;" the " Battle of Yorktown, 1781, the Gallantry of Hamilton ;" " A Hessian Soldier in a Death-struggle with an American ;" an allegory of the " Blessings of Peace ;" the " Ovation to Washington at Trenton, 1789 ;" the " Inauguration of Washington as First President of the United States ;" and the " Laying of the Corner-stone of the Capitol of the United States." On the framework are designs of the acanthus, maize, grape, and cotton-boll. The door is one of the finest specimens of bronze-casting ever made in the United States, and compares very favorably with the Rogers door.

THE CRAWFORD BRONZE DOOR.

The huge dome, rising in its classic beauty far above the main building, is a fitting crown to the noble edifice. It is of cast iron and weighs nearly four thousand tons. Large sheets of iron, securely bolted together, rest on iron ribs, and by the plan used in its construction the changes of temperature make its contraction and expansion merely " like the folding and unfolding of the lily." It was built from designs of Thomas U. Walter, of Philadelphia, and cost $1,250,000. Eight years were required in its construction, so carefully was the work done, and as it is thoroughly protected from the weather by thick coatings of white paint, renewed yearly, it is likely to last for centuries. Its base consists of a peristyle of thirty-six fluted columns surmounted by an entablature and a balustrade. Then comes an attic story, and above this the dome proper. At the top is a gallery, surrounded by a balustrade, from which may be

LIBERTY.

obtained a magnificent view of the city and its environs. Rising from the gallery is the "lantern," fifteen feet in diameter and fifty feet high, surrounded by a peristyle. Over the lantern is a globe, and standing on the globe is the bronze statue of Liberty, designed by Thomas Crawford and cast at Bladensburg, Md. It is nineteen feet six inches high, weighs seven and one-half tons, and cost more than $24,000. It was placed in position December 2, 1863, amid the salutes from guns in Washington and the surrounding forts and the cheers of the thousands of soldiers.

THE ROTUNDA.

The Rotunda of the Capitol is a magnificent circular hall, ninety-five feet in diameter and one hundred and eighty feet in height. Above are the thirty-six windows of the peristyle, then the curving dome, and at its top the "eye," an opening fifty feet in diameter. Suspended over the eye is an immense iron canopy on which is Brumidi's celebrated allegorical painting, "The Apotheosis of Washington." Washington, with Freedom and Victory at his right and left, and thirteen female figures, representing the original States, occupy the centre; around the border are six groups representing the "Fall of Tyranny," "Agriculture," "Mechanics," "Commerce," the "Marine," and the "Arts and Sciences." The figures are large and most carefully finished. The painting occupied Brumidi for several years and cost nearly $50,000. While it presents a fine appearance from the floor of the Rotunda, the best point of view is obtained by ascending to the gallery immediately beneath it. This gallery has the peculiar property known as "whispering," a whisper spoken on one side being distinctly heard on the other, although the diameter of the dome at this point is sixty-five feet.

Above the architrave is a frieze, ten feet wide, containing frescoes

THE ROTUNDA. 47

by Brumidi and Castigini, illustrating important events in American history.

THE ROTUNDA.

Over the four entrances are stone panels, cut in high relief, by distinguished Italian sculptors. They represent scenes in the early history of the country. The panel over the western door is by

Capellano, and shows Pocahontas saving the life of Captain John Smith. That over the northern entrance is by Gavelot, representing

THE CANOPY.

William Penn making his famous treaty with the Indians. Over the eastern and southern doorways are panels by Causici showing the "Landing of the Pilgrims" and "Daniel Boone in Conflict with the Indians." The cost of these groups was $3500 each.

HISTORICAL PAINTINGS. 49

On the walls are arabesque designs and panels containing medallion heads of Columbus, Raleigh, Cabot, and La Salle. They are by Causici and Capellano, and were placed in position in 1827.

Eight large paintings, each eighteen by twelve feet, are set in panels around the walls. They are all by American artists. Four of them represent scenes in the early history of America. The first shows "Columbus Landing at San Salvador." The great discoverer is displaying the banner of Spain, and taking possession of the new country in the name of his sovereigns. John Vanderlyn was the artist, and the painting cost $10,000.

The second painting was executed by William H. Powell at a cost of $12,000. It is supposed to represent "De Soto Discovering the Mississippi." The central figure is De Soto, mounted on a spirited horse, and accompanied by cavalry and artillery. Indians, having offered gifts for the acceptance of the stranger, are earnestly watching his approach, while some monks are attending to the setting up of a crucifix. Although showing skill in design and carefulness in finish, the painting cannot be considered as historically accurate.

The third painting represents the "Baptism of Pocahontas." The young Indian princess is kneeling at the font; behind her stands her husband, John Rolfe. Sir Thomas Dale, and others prominent in the history of Virginia, and several Indian chiefs are also represented. The Randolphs and several other prominent Virginia families trace their descent from Pocahontas. The painting is the work of John G. Chapman, and cost $10,000.

The fourth painting represents "The Embarkation of the Pilgrims" at Delft. The little company, kneeling on the deck of the "Speedwell," are invoking the blessing of God on their journey and His guidance in their undertaking to establish a State where there should be religious liberty. The central figure holding the Bible is Elder William Brewster; the pastor, William Robinson, is offering prayer; kneeling between them is Governor Carver, and kneeling in the right foreground is Miles Standish with his wife. It was painted by Robert W. Weir, and cost $10,000.

The other four paintings are by Colonel John Trumbull, son of Jonathan Trumbull, Governor of Connecticut during the Revolution, and an aide-de-camp to General Washington. Trumbull spent nearly thirty years in studying art in Europe and in collecting materials for these paintings. They are considered as especially valuable historically, since Trumbull obtained sittings from all the

THE LANDING OF COLUMBUS.

THE DISCOVERY OF THE MISSISSIPPI.

prominent actors in the Revolution, and the faces are faithful likenesses of the people they represent. The artist received $32,000 for the series.

The first shows "The Signing of the Declaration of Independence." John Hancock, the President of the Congress, whose famous signature is so well known, is seated at the table. In front

THE BAPTISM OF POCAHONTAS.

THE EMBARKATION OF THE PILGRIMS.

of him stand Thomas Jefferson and his fellow-members of the committee, Benjamin Franklin, John Adams, Roger Sherman, and Robert L. Livingston. The Members of Congress are seated in rows around the hall. On the wall may be seen banners with the cross of St. George, thereafter to be replaced by the stars and stripes. Trumbull obtained his ideas for the details of the painting from

SIGNING THE DECLARATION OF INDEPENDENCE.

THE SURRENDER OF GENERAL BURGOYNE.

Jefferson, Adams, and others who were present at the time, and has given us a faithful picture of the historic scene.

The second painting is "The Surrender of General Burgoyne." Trumbull was present and made a sketch at the time. General

Burgoyne, accompanied by General Phillips and officers of his staff, is offering his sword to General Gates, who refuses to receive it

THE SURRENDER OF LORD CORNWALLIS.

WASHINGTON RESIGNING HIS COMMISSION.

and invites the British officers to partake of refreshments in his tent.

The third painting is entitled "The Surrender of Lord Cornwallis at Yorktown." General Lincoln is conducting the British officers, who are on foot, between the lines of the American and French armies, drawn up to receive them. Washington refused to allow the British to march out with colors flying and the usual honors of war in retaliation for the treatment Lord Cornwallis accorded General Lincoln at the surrender of Charleston, one year before.

The fourth painting represents one of the grandest scenes in history: "General Washington Resigning his Commission to Congress." At the head of a victorious army, he had had it in his power to overthrow the newly acquired liberties of his country and make himself an absolute monarch. We see him here returning to Congress the authority it had given him and preparing to resume the life of a private citizen. Many famous people are represented. In the front row on Washington's right are Thomas Jefferson and James Monroe, and standing behind is James Madison—the three Presidents from 1801 to 1825. A few feet behind Washington stands Charles Carroll of Carrollton with his two daughters, while in the gallery are Mrs. Washington and her three grandchildren.

The floor of the Rotunda is of sandstone, supported by brick arches resting on peristyles of columns. It was designed to place the body of Washington in the crypt formed by these columns, but the heirs decided that it must remain at Mount Vernon.

THE LIBRARY OF CONGRESS.

Passing through the western doorway of the Rotunda we come to the main hall of the Library of Congress, or the National Library, as it may perhaps more properly be called. It is a large and elegantly finished room, ninety-one feet long, thirty-four feet wide, and thirty-eight feet high. Two other halls, to the north and south, are of nearly the same dimensions. Taught by the experience of 1851, when a fire destroyed nearly thirty thousand books and pamphlets and a number of valuable paintings, Mr. Thomas U. Walter, the architect of the Capitol, constructed the present halls thoroughly fire-proof. They are lighted by windows and glass roofs and have tessellated marble floors. The book-cases and galleries are of iron, and are painted in light, delicate shades and gold. It is estimated that the shelves have a total length of five miles, yet notwithstanding that the books are arranged in double rows the space afforded is greatly inadequate, and the floors and recesses are covered with books and pamphlets. There are more than six hundred thousand books and two hundred thousand pamphlets at present in the Library, and as the yearly increase is more than twenty thousand, the pressing need of more ample accommodations has led Congress to appropriate $3,000,000 for a new building.

The Library was begun in 1802 with about three thousand books purchased in London by order of Congress. John Randolph, of Roanoke, was one of its most ardent supporters in its early days. When the British invaded Washington in 1814 they used the books

THE LIBRARY OF CONGRESS.

of the Library and many of the archives of the Government to kindle the fire which destroyed the Capitol. In 1815 Congress purchased the library of Thomas Jefferson, consisting of about seven thousand books, as the nucleus of a new Library. In 1851 the number of books and pamphlets had risen to sixty thousand, but half of them were destroyed by the fire of that year. In 1866 the scientific library of the Smithsonian Institution was added to the Library, which has since that time been the place of deposit of all the publications and exchanges of the Institution. In 1867, chiefly through the efforts of Rutherford B. Hayes, at that time Chairman of the Library Committee of Congress, the Peter Force collection was purchased at a cost of $100,000. By the operation of the Copyright Law two copies of each book, pamphlet, engraving, etc., copyrighted in the United States, must be deposited in the Library.

The Library is one of the great libraries of the world, and in some departments—notably in literature relating to America—it stands unrivalled. In addition to many rare and ancient books and manuscripts, every important work issued by American and foreign presses since the beginning of the century may be found on the shelves. There are files of all the principal American newspapers from 1735 to 1800, and the collections of magazines and newspapers since 1800 are without equal.

The Law Collection, a portion of the Library, is kept in the basement. It contains over seventy thousand volumes, and is the finest of the kind in the world. Every volume of American, English, Scotch and Irish court reports is to be found here, and also the statutes of all countries from 1649 until the present time.

The room containing the Law Collection was used by the Supreme Court until 1860. In the vestibule can be seen Latrobe's celebrated "corn-stalk" columns, the capitals being formed of ears of corn.

It was in this chamber that Clay and Webster, those giants of a former age, made argument before the Supreme Court, and here Chief Justice John Marshall rendered the decisions that have remained the highest law in the land to this day.

THE SUPREME COURT CHAMBER.

North of the Rotunda is the chamber formerly occupied by the Senate, but used by the Supreme Court since 1860. The Court is composed of a Chief Justice and eight Associate Justices, appointed by the President with the consent of the Senate, and holding their offices during "good behavior." The Court is in session from October until May, and during the rest of the year the Justices act as Circuit Justices in the nine judicial circuits into which the territory of the United States is divided.

The Supreme Court Chamber is a beautiful specimen of classic architecture. It is semicircular in form, its greatest length being seventy-five feet and its greatest width and height forty-five feet. The ceiling is a portion of a low dome. The Judicial Bench is at the eastern end, and behind it is a row of pillars of variegated marble with white marble capitals. Overhead a wide arch spans the Bench, and around the walls are marble pilasters. On the walls are marble busts of the deceased Chief Justices. The central portion of the chamber has mahogany tables and chairs for the use of the lawyers and others having business with the Supreme Court. At the sides are rows of seats upholstered in red velvet for the convenience of spectators. Fine portraits of Chief Justices Jay, Marshall, Taney, and Chase are in the robing-room, west of the corridor.

THE SUPREME COURT CHAMBER.

The sittings of the Court begin promptly at noon, when the crier requests all persons to rise, and announces, "The Honorable the Chief Justice and the Associate Justices of the Supreme Court of the United States." The Justices, clad in long silken robes with voluminous sleeves, advance from the robing-room and take their places on the Bench, the Chief Justice in the centre and the others in the order of their appointment. They bow to the members of the Bar and the spectators, and then seat themselves. The court Crier opens the session by speaking the ancient formula: "Oyez! Oyez! Oyez! All persons having business with the Supreme Court of the United States are admonished to draw near and give their attention, for the Court is now sitting. God save the United States and this Honorable Court!" The business begins as soon as the crier has finished his announcement. Then decisions, if there are any, are read by the Justices, after which the first case on the day's docket is taken up. The intercourse between the Justices and the members of the Bar is very pleasant and courteous, and patient attention is paid to the arguments, no matter how long or tedious they may be. Promptly at four the Court is adjourned for the day, and the Justices retire to the robing-room, where their silken gowns are removed by colored attendants. The sessions are held five days in the week, Saturdays being occupied by the Justices in consultation.

In accordance with the provisions of the Constitution, Congress created the Supreme Court by Act of September 24, 1789. President Washington appointed John Jay, of New York, as the first Chief Justice. The business of the Court at that time required the appointment of but five Associate Justices. On Jay's resignation in 1795 he was succeeded by John Rutledge, of South Carolina. Rutledge presided for one year, and his commission not having been confirmed by the Senate, was succeeded by Oliver Ellsworth, of Connecticut. Ellsworth resigned in 1799. In 1801, John Marshall, of Virginia, was appointed Chief Justice, and continued to execute the duties of his high office until 1835. It has been said: "It was he who established the power of the Supreme Court as we recognize it at the present day. It was he who, more than any other man of his time, carried forward the work of the Constitution in welding the loose league of States into a compact, powerful nationality."

Notwithstanding Marshall's greatness in great things, he was sometimes puzzled by very trivial matters. An amusing anecdote is told of him. While driving one day near Fredericksburg, a small sapling growing along the side of the road became entangled between the wheel and the body of his wagon. It was impossible to drive on, and the Chief Justice was in a dilemma. Observing a negro near by, he called to him to come and cut it down. The negro, observing the situation, backed the horse until the wagon was free of the sapling, and the learned jurist went on his way wondering.

On the death of Marshall, in 1835, President Jackson appointed Roger B. Taney, of Maryland. Taney was a man of marked ability, but was unfortunate in having to render decisions on questions connected with the subject of slavery at a time when political passions were very bitter, and he became the object of much undeserved obloquy.

Chief Justice Taney died in 1864, and was succeeded by Salmon P. Chase, of Ohio, who had been Secretary of the Treasury under President Lincoln. Chase died in 1873, and President Grant appointed Morrison R. Waite. Chief Justice Waite died in 1888, and President Cleveland appointed the present Chief Justice, Melville W. Fuller. The salary of the Chief Justice is $10,500; that of an Associate Justice is $10,000. By an Act of Congress, passed in 1869, a Justice may retire on full pay if he has reached the age of seventy and has been on the bench ten years.

THE SENATE CHAMBER.

The Senate Chamber is in the northern extension of the Capitol. It is one hundred and twelve feet long, eighty-two feet wide, and thirty feet high. The ceiling is formed of iron girders and cross-pieces enclosing glass panels adorned with paintings representing Union, Progress, the Army and Navy, and the Mechanical Arts. Hundreds of gas-jets above these panels shed a soft, diffused light

THE SENATE CHAMBER.

during the night sessions. Around the walls are marble pilasters arranged in pairs, and panels adorned in buff and gold.

The Vice-President of the United States is the President of the Senate. His seat is on a daïs at the northern end of the chamber. On his right sits the sergeant-at-arms, on his left the assistant door-keeper, while in front are the desks of the clerks and the tables of the official reporters. Arranged in semicircular rows in front of the President's chair are the mahogany desks and chairs of the Senators. Some were brought here from the old Senate Chamber, and were used by famous Senators of former times. On each desk is a silver plate engraved with the name of the occupant. Over the President's chair is a gallery for the reporters of the press, and directly opposite is that reserved for the members of the Diplomatic

THE MARBLE ROOM.

THE PRESIDENT'S ROOM.

Corps. The eastern gallery is for ladies and the western for gentlemen.

Behind the Chamber is the Lobby, and north of it the "Marble Room," the walls, floor, and ceiling entirely of polished marble. It is used by the Senators for consultation and for the reception of special visitors.

West of the Marble Room is the "Room of the President of the United States." The President comes to this room during the hurried closing hours of the session to sign the bills passed at the last moment. A bill passed by Congress within ten days of the time of adjournment, must be signed by the President before the session closes, or it fails. The room is one of the handsomest in the Capitol, being elaborately decorated with frescoes by Brumidi. On the walls are portraits of President Washington and the members of his first Cabinet, Thomas Jefferson, Alexander Hamilton, General Knox, Edmund Randolph, and Samuel Osgood, and at the corners of the ceiling are pieces representing Discovery, Exploration, Religion, and History, while between the corner-pieces are representations of Liberty, Legislation, Religion, and Executive Power.

East of the Marble Room is the Vice-President's Room, containing Rembrandt Peale's celebrated painting of Washington and also a marble bust of Vice-President Henry Wilson, who died in this room November 22, 1875.

The Senate Reception Room is north of the vestibule leading to the eastern entrance. It is sixty feet long, and has a vaulted ceiling

THE CORRIDOR.

THE STAIRCASE IN SENATE WING.

divided by an arch into two parts. Frescoes by Brumidi, entitled Liberty, Plenty, Peace, War, Prudence, Justice, Temperance, and Strength adorn the walls. There is also a painting by the same artist showing Washington in consultation with Hamilton and Jefferson.

Magnificent staircases with massive pillars and balustrades lead from the main floor to the galleries. In a niche at the foot of the eastern staircase is Powers's marble statue of Benjamin Franklin, and on the wall above the first landing is Powell's painting of "Perry's Victory on Lake Erie." The battle was a most desperate one. The American fleet was outnumbered both in guns and vessels by the British, and early in the action Perry's flag-ship, the "Lawrence," became disabled and was in a sinking condition. Finding he could do nothing further in his own ship, he immediately abandoned it for the "Niagara," and continued the fight. The picture

PERRY'S VICTORY.

shows him making the perilous transfer. His young brother was with him, and the boat was exposed to a furious cannonade, but the passage was made in safety, and his daring act, inspiring his followers with renewed courage, enabled them to gain the victory. It was on this occasion he sent the famous dispatch, "We have met the enemy, and they are ours."

In the hall east of the Ladies' Gallery are two famous pictures of the Cañons of Colorado and Yellowstone. They are by Moran, and cost $10,000 each. There are also portraits of Clay, Webster, and Calhoun. In the ante-room of the Ladies' Gallery there is a painting showing the first fight between ironclads, and a picture of the Electoral Commission. There are also portraits of General Dix and Charles Sumner. A very handsomely furnished room north of the gallery is for the use of lady visitors.

THE LADIES' PARLOR.

At the foot of the western staircase is a marble statue of John Hancock by Horatio Stone. Over the landing is a painting by James Walker of the "Storming of Chapultepec" by the American forces under General Scott.

THE NATIONAL STATUARY HALL.

South of the Rotunda is the National Statuary Hall, formerly occupied by the House of Representatives. It was designed by Latrobe, and is considered a perfect specimen of classic architecture. Its beauties did not, however, fit it for its purpose, as its acoustic properties are probably the worst in the world. It is semicircular in form, ninety-five feet long, and the height to the top of the domed ceiling is sixty feet. At the southern end is a magnificent arch supported by beautiful columns of variegated Potomac marble, with white marble capitals sculptured in Italy. A colonnade of similar columns surrounds the chamber. Under the arch is an American eagle, sculptured in stone by Valperti, and over it a plaster figure, by Causici, representing the Goddess of Liberty.

The clock over the doorway leading from the Rotunda was designed by Franzoni. History is represented standing in a winged chariot and writing on a tablet the record of the Nation. The wheel of the chariot forms the face of the clock.

This hall was used by the House of Representatives from 1808 until 1814, when it was destroyed by the British. On its reconstruction, in 1817, it was again devoted to its original purpose until 1857, when the House assembled in its new hall in the southern extension. A memorial of a sad event recalls its former use. Let into the floor near the southwest corner is a brass tablet, marking the spot where John Quincy Adams was stricken with apoplexy, February 21, 1848.

At the suggestion of Senator Morrill, of Vermont, the hall was devoted to its present use, and in 1864 the President was authorized

STATUARY HALL.

to invite each State "to send the effigies of two of her noblest sons, in marble or bronze, to be placed permanently here." Rhode Island was the first to respond to the invitation, sending marble statues of Roger Williams, her founder, and General Nathaniel Greene, the Revolutionary hero. Connecticut sent marble statues of Jonathan Trumbull, the last Colonial Governor and the original of the *sobriquet* "Brother Jonathan," and Roger Sherman, one of the committee

THE NATIONAL STATUARY HALL. 65

appointed to draft the Declaration of Independence. New York sent bronze statues of Vice-President George Clinton, "one of the

ROBERT FULTON.

ETHAN ALLEN.

LINCOLN.

GARFIELD.

signers," and Chancellor Robert R. Livingston, who administered the oath to President Washington in 1789. Massachusetts sent marble statues of Governor John Winthrop and Samuel Adams, the

"Father of the Revolution." Vermont sent marble statues of Colonel Ethan Allen and Jacob Collamer. Maine sent a marble statue of William King, her first Governor. Pennsylvania sent marble statues of Robert Fulton, who made steam navigation practicable, and William Muhlenberg, the heroic minister. Ohio sent statues of Garfield and Governor William Allen. New Jersey sent a marble statue of Richard Stockton, a signer of the Declaration, and a bronze statue of General Philip Kearney, killed at Chantilly, Va., 1862. The other States will doubtless soon respond, so that all may see in the National Capitol the statues of the men whom the people delighted to honor.

Besides the contributions of the States, there are a number of statues, busts, and portraits purchased by the National Government. There is a plaster cast of Houdon's statue of Washington, taken from the original at Richmond; a statue of Lincoln by Vinnie Ream Hoxie; marble statues of Hamilton and of Colonel Edward D. Baker, killed at Ball's Bluff, October 21, 1861, by Horatio Stone, and a bronze statue of Jefferson, by D'Angers. There are also busts of Lincoln, Kosciusko, and Thomas Crawford, and portraits of

THE HALL OF THE HOUSE OF REPRESENTATIVES.

Washington, Jefferson, Lincoln, Charles Carroll of Carrollton, Benjamin West, and others.

The Hall of the House of Representatives.

The Hall of the House of Representatives occupies the southern extension of the Capitol, and is one of the largest and finest legislative halls in the world. It is one hundred and thirty-nine feet long, ninety-three feet wide, and thirty-six feet high. The ceiling is similar to that of the Senate Chamber, but the glass panels are adorned with the coats-of-arms of the States. Fifteen hundred gasjets placed above the ceiling give light during night sessions. On a platform four feet high at the south is the chair of the Speaker, and in front of it a large marble table. At the Speaker's right, on a marble pedestal, is his symbol of authority, the time-honored mace. The mace was adopted by the House in the First Congress, and has been in use ever since. When it is placed on its pedestal it signifies that the House is in session and under the Speaker's authority; when it is placed on the floor, that the House is in committee of the whole. The mace is a bundle of black rods fastened with transverse bands of silver, like the Roman *fasces*. On its top is a silver globe surmounted by a silver eagle. When the sergeant-at-arms is executing the commands of the Speaker he is required to bear aloft the mace in his hands. Close by sits the sergeant-at-arms. On the Speaker's left is the chair of the assistant door-keeper. In front of the Speaker's table are marble desks for the clerks and official reporters. Arranged in semicircular rows around the Speaker's table are the desks and chairs of the members.

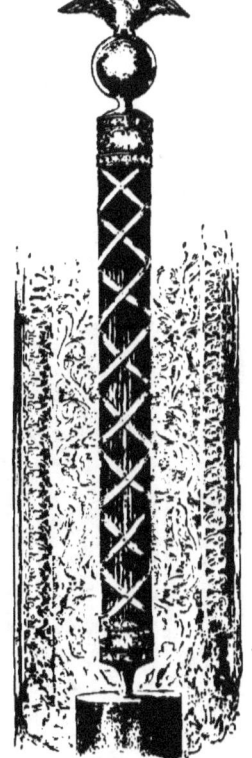

THE SPEAKER'S MACE.

A large full-length portrait of Washington by John Vanderlyn is on the wall to the east of the Speaker, and one of Lafayette by Ary Scheffer is on the west. To the east of the Washington picture is a panel containing a painting by Bierstadt representing the "Settlement of California," and on a corresponding panel on the west "The Discovery of the

Hudson River," by the same artist. There is also a panel containing a fresco by Brumidi, entitled "Washington at Yorktown." Over the main entrance is a large clock supported by the figures of an Indian and a pioneer and surmounted by an eagle. This clock has acquired a wide notoriety, since it is the habit of the sergeant-at-arms to turn back the hands toward the close of the last day of the session. Above the Speaker's chair is the Press Gallery. Portions of the galleries are reserved for the Diplomatic Corps and for the wives and friends of the Representatives. The rest is for the accommodation of the public.

South of the Hall is the Members' Lobby, the walls adorned with portraits of past Speakers. Opening from this are the members' retiring-rooms. Around the Hall are rooms for the officials of the House and for the most important committees. The room of the Committee on Ways and Means is very richly frescoed. A fine collection of paintings of the principal forts of the United States is in the room of the Committee on Military Affairs.

Grand staircases, similar to those of the Senate wing, lead to the galleries. At the foot of the eastern staircase is a marble statue of Jefferson, by Hiram Powers, costing $10,000, and over the landing is

LOBBY.

a large painting, by Frank B. Carpenter, of "Lincoln Signing the Proclamation of Emancipation," September 22, 1862. It was purchased from the artist for $25,000 by Mrs. Mary E. Thompson, and by her presented to the Government. Over the lower landing is an equestrian portrait of General Scott by Troye.

At the foot of the western staircase is a bronze bust of a Chippewa chief. Over the landing is an immense chromo-silica entitled "Westward Ho!" showing a party of emigrants crossing the Rocky Mountains. It was painted by Emanuel Leutze, and cost $20,000. The painting beneath, "The Golden Gate," is by Bierstadt.

The basement story of the Capitol is taken up by the post-offices of Congress and by numerous committee rooms. Some of these are richly adorned and frescoed. In the Senate wing a fresco by Brumidi showing the "Signing of the Treaty of Ghent" in 1814, is over the entrance to the room of the Committee on Foreign Affairs. Another by the same artist of Robert Fulton is over the door of the room of the Committee on Patents. The room of the Committee on Indian

"WESTWARD HO!"

Affairs was intended originally for the Committee on Agriculture and is beautifully decorated with American vines and fruits.

There are some very fine frescoes in the room of the Committee on Military Affairs. They represent "The Boston Massacre," "The Battle of Lexington," "Death of Wooster," "Washington at Valley Forge," and "The Storming of Stony Point."

The Crypt is beneath the Rotunda, and a star in the floor marks the exact centre of the Capitol. Beneath the Crypt is a chamber called the "Undercroft."

In the basement of the House wing are several beautiful rooms. That of the Committee on Agriculture contains the best frescoes in the building. They are by Brumidi, and represent Cincinnatus called from his plow to be dictator, and Putnam called from his plow to be a general in the Continental army. There are also representations of harvests of ancient and modern times, and medallions of

Washington and Jefferson. On the ceiling are figures of Flora, Ceres, Bacchus, and Boreas, emblematic of the seasons of the year.

Man's physical wants are amply provided for by two very good restaurants, open to the public. Whether Senatorial "cold tea" can still be obtained is a matter of grave doubt, but there is no lack of substantial and appetizing viands to revive the energies of the exhausted legislators.

The sub-basement contains the ventilating and heating apparatus. There is a labyrinth of gloomy vaults, dangerous to venture into without a guide. They were once the scene of a sad incident. The young wife of a Congressman ventured alone to explore their mysterious recesses. Soon losing her way, she wandered bewildered throughout a whole night. In the morning she was found by her friends; but the horror of that night had caused her hair to turn white and had overthrown her reason, nor was it for several years that her mind was restored to its normal state.

No visitor should fail to ascend to the dome, for though the journey is toilsome, the magnificent view well repays the labor. The finest prospect is obtained from the gallery, directly below the lantern. From this point the city of Washington, the silvery Potomac, the hills of Maryland and Virginia, lie spread out before the spectator in a picture of surpassing beauty. The great public buildings loom up in all their grandeur, and the streets and parks, with their masses of luxuriant foliage, remind one of some rare Florentine mosaic. Off to the west are the hills of Georgetown and stately Arlington, its pillared front showing like the façade of some ancient temple. On the north is the park surrounding the Soldiers' Home and Howard University. To the east and south the Anacostia and gleaming Potomac stretch away until lost behind the hills.

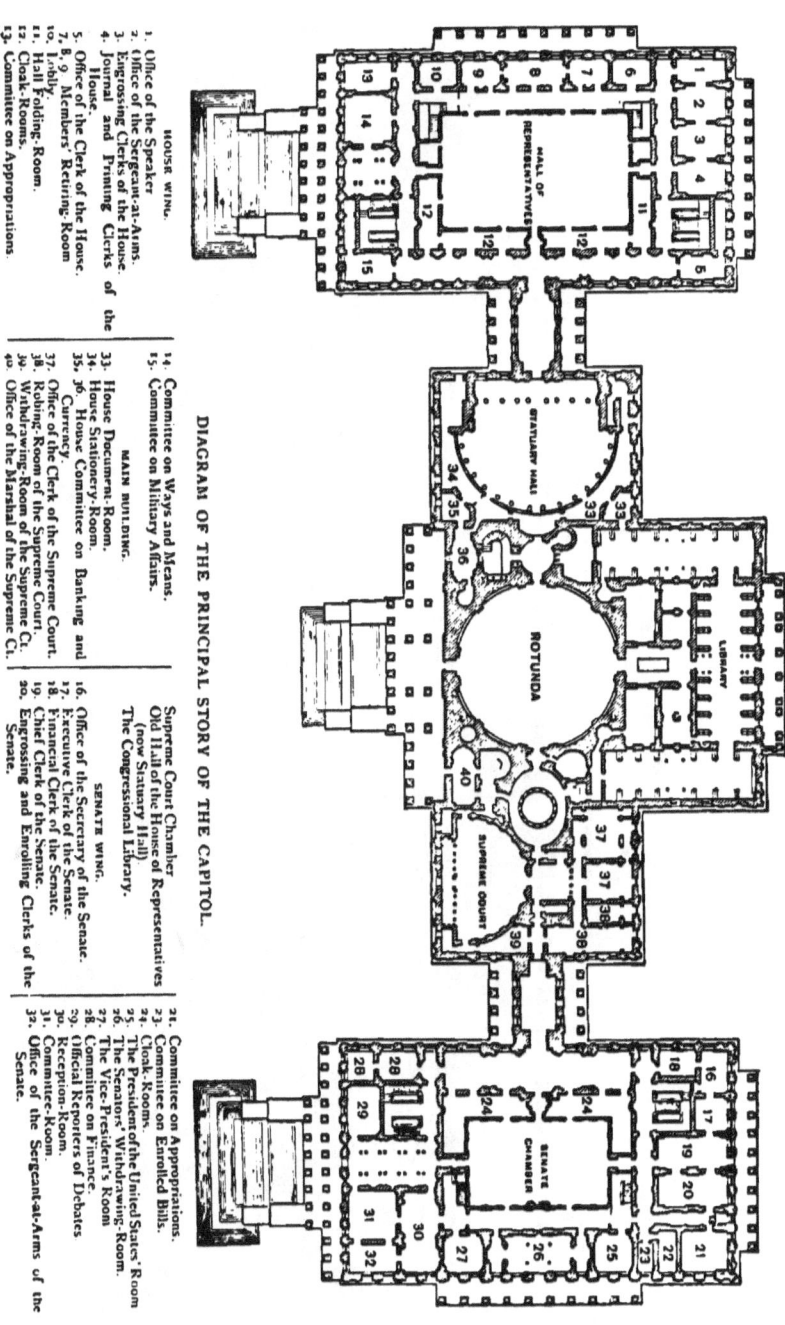

DIAGRAM OF THE PRINCIPAL STORY OF THE CAPITOL.

HOUSE WING.

1. Office of the Speaker.
2. Office of the Sergeant-at-Arms.
3. Engrossing Clerks of the House.
4. Journal and Printing Clerks of the House.
5. Office of the Clerk of the House.
7, 8, 9. Members' Retiring-Room.
10. Lobby.
11. Hall Folding-Room.
12. Cloak-Rooms.
13. Committee on Appropriations.
14. Committee on Ways and Means.
15. Committee on Military Affairs.

MAIN BUILDING.

33. House Document-Room.
34. House Stationery-Room.
35, 36. House Committee on Banking and Currency.
37. Office of the Clerk of the Supreme Court.
38. Robing-Room of the Supreme Court.
39. Withdrawing-Room of the Supreme Ct.
40. Office of the Marshal of the Supreme Ct.

Supreme Court Chamber
Old Hall of the House of Representatives (now Statuary Hall)
The Congressional Library.

16. Office of the Secretary of the Senate.
17. Executive Clerk of the Senate.
18. Financial Clerk of the Senate.
19. Chief Clerk of the Senate.
20. Engrossing and Enrolling Clerks of the Senate.

SENATE WING.

21. Committee on Appropriations.
23. Committee on Enrolled Bills.
24. Cloak-Rooms.
25. The President of the United States' Room.
26. The Senators' Withdrawing-Room.
27. The Vice-President's Room.
28. Committee on Finance.
29. Official Reporters of Debates.
30. Reception-Room.
31. Committee-Room.
32. Office of the Sergeant-at-Arms of the Senate.

THE WHITE HOUSE, NORTH VIEW.

CHAPTER III.

THE WHITE HOUSE—ITS HISTORY—DESCRIPTION OF THE BUILDING—THE GREAT STATE APARTMENTS—THE EXECUTIVE OFFICES.

THE residence of the President of the United States is officially styled "The Executive Mansion," but is universally known as "The White House." As the home of the chief executive officer of the nation, it is an object of absorbing interest to all citizens. There is a personality about it that is lacking in the Capitol, for the work of Congress is the result of the deliberations of bodies of men, and no one person can be held accountable for good or evil consequences. But the acts of the President are done on his own individual judgment, and he alone must receive the praise or bear the blame. In the White House dwells the one man whom the whole people unite in selecting, and whom, as their chosen chief, they delight to honor. The President is the embodiment of the power and sovereignty of the nation, and represents it among the powers of the world.

The White House was the first public building erected at Washington. As soon as Congress had determined the site of the Capital, the Commissioners issued a call for the submission of designs for the "President's House," offering "a premium of $500, or a medal of that value, at the option of the party." Of the many plans submitted, the one selected was that of James Hoban, a talented young Irishman, who had been for some time settled at Charleston, South Carolina, and he was charged with the construction of the building. Hoban's plan followed very closely that of the Duke of Leinster's palace, at Dublin; and this, together with the fact that the building would far exceed in size and splendor any private dwelling at that time existing in the country, created considerable opposition to it. The ideas of the French Revolutionists in regard to "Republican simplicity" were beginning to have a strong influence on America, and many sarcastic remarks were made about the "President's Palace." Appropriations were frequently refused by Congress, and it required all the influence of President Washington to enable the Commissioners to obtain the funds necessary to complete the building.

The corner-stone was laid October 13, 1792, amid imposing Masonic ceremonies, and in the presence of President Washington, the Commissioners of the District, and a large number of eminent men. Notwithstanding the various delays, the building was so far finished by 1799 as to be ready for occupancy, and President Washington had the satisfaction of knowing that his successors in office would be suitably accommodated.

THE WHITE HOUSE, SOUTH VIEW.

The White House may be said to have made Hoban's fortune, for his success with it led to his employment as the architect of some of the largest and handsomest buildings erected during the early days of the city. He was a man of admirable social qualities, and was greatly esteemed by all who knew him. He died in 1831.

The vast supply of fine white marble, since so much used in the construction of public buildings, was at that time unsuspected, and Hoban selected Virginia sandstone as his building material. To preserve the stone from the injurious effects of the climate, and to prevent it acquiring a dingy appearance with age, the building has always been covered with heavy coats of white paint. It is doubtless from this fact that the popular name has been derived, although some have attributed it to the circumstance that the home of Mrs. Custis, before her marriage with Colonel Washington, was known as the White House. As Lady Washington never lived in the present Executive Mansion, the tradition has very little foundation.

On the removal of the seat of government from Philadelphia to Washington, in 1800, President John Adams and his family took up their abode in the mansion. Although the building was finished it was but partially furnished, and Mrs. Adams has left in some of her letters a graphic account of the inconveniences the family experienced. There was not a bell in the whole house, and the great East Room, since the scene of so many brilliant festivities, was bare and desolate. As no attempt had been made to lay out the grounds and no grass was to be seen anywhere, Mrs. Adams used the East Room for drying the family washing. During Jefferson's administration the furnishing was completed and the house became a suitable home for the President.

The White House suffered the fate of the other public buildings when the British captured Washington in 1814, being set on fire, but, owing to a heavy rain, the damage done was not very great. The advance of the enemy was very sudden, and there is a ludicrous story told of an interrupted dinner party. Mrs. Madison had made arrangements for a grand dinner, and although the President had cautiously retired to a place of safety, she determined to have her dinner, not expecting the British until next day. At the moment the guests were sitting down to the table, word came that the invading forces were at the Capitol. Away rushed the guests, but Mrs. Madison refused to leave until she had cut from its frame the large painting of Washington now hanging in the East Room, and made arrangements for its conveyance to some secure place. When the British arrived they found the dinner ready on the table and the wines cooling on the sideboard—a very pleasing sight to hungry soldiers. No doubt they did full justice to the banquet before they fired the building. The Federalist wits made great merriment over the incident, and all connected with the Administration came in for a share of the ridicule, but Mrs. Madison certainly showed great presence of mind and carried off all the honor there was.

The reconstruction of the White House was finished in 1817, Presidents Madison and Monroe occupying meanwhile a building known as the "Octagon House," still standing at the corner of New York Avenue and Eighteenth Street. It was in this house that President Madison signed the Treaty of Ghent in 1815.

The portico of Ionic columns, on the north of the White House, was added in 1829, and internal improvements have been made at various times since, notably during the administration of President Arthur, when the house was completely refurnished and fitted with all the conveniences of a modern mansion. Under President Harrison great improvements have been made in the decorations, and the interior now presents a very artistic appearance.

The immense increase in the amount of business devolving upon the President, as well as his social duties as the chief of official society at Washington, has rendered the White House far too small for the present needs of the Executive. It is proposed to make large extensions to the present building, and plans designed by Mrs. Harrison have met with great approval. When these additions have been finished, the President will have a building wherein he can live comfortably and at the same time discharge effectively his duties as Chief Executive of the Nation and head of society at the Nation's Capital.

The White House is situated on a Government reservation, known as the President's Grounds, fronting on Pennsylvania Avenue opposite Lafayette Square. A broad semicircular drive-way sweeps from the two gateways on the Avenue past the main entrance. The grounds are very beautiful with their stately trees and well-kept lawns. The reservation extends southward to the river, and with the lands there reclaimed and The Mall will form a beautiful park of several hundred acres. To the south of the White House the ground slopes gently towards the river, and this rear lawn is the scene of the annual "egg-rolling," a pretty custom of unknown origin. On Easter Monday, the whole place is swarming with gaily-dressed children busily engaged in rolling their brilliantly-colored eggs down the grassy slope.

During the pleasant afternoons and evenings in spring and summer the famous Marine Band gives open-air concerts on the lawn, and the grounds become a favorite resort for all. No restriction is placed on the visitor, but everyone is allowed to wander at will, and freely enjoy the delight and beauty of the scene.

The White House has a frontage towards the north of one hundred and seventy feet and a depth of eighty-six feet. There are two stories and a basement, and the whole is surmounted by a balustrade. In the centre of the north front is a square portico of lofty Ionic columns. A semicircular colonnade adorns the rear. The building is almost entirely devoid of ornament, but its very simplicity of design gives it a severe yet classic beauty. On the west are extensive conservatories, filled with rare and beautiful plants, the source of the brilliant floral displays at the state dinners and receptions.

CONSERVATORY.

The main entrance opens into a spacious room, forty by fifty feet, termed the "Vestibule." This formerly presented a very shabby appearance, but little attention having been given to its decoration. President Arthur succeeded in having the old wooden partition, separating it from the central corridor, removed, and in its place was put a magnificent screen of jewelled glass, made by Tiffany, of New York. Appropriations made in 1891 made further improvements possible, and now the room is very beautiful.

The ceiling is laid out in an "oval," with a circle inside containing twenty-four small panels, richly decorated with ornaments and blended in colors from a cream to an old red. The oval is ornamented with a medallion and a liberty cap at either end. From the borders of the oval panels extending to the side walls contain small circles decorated with stars. The artistic use of colors and shading produce the effect of high relief. Upon the mantel wall towards the East Room is a panel formed of flags, trophies, and other emblems, containing in the centre a medallion of Washington, encircled by a wreath of laurel. A similar panel on the west wall contains a medallion of Lincoln. The four doors are crowned with heavy scroll work, and in the centre of each is the "fasces," symbolical of union. The entire coloring is cream and old red, richly illuminated with gold leaf. The columns are a rich blending of old metal effect, and ornamented from the capital downward with shield and battle axe.

A small corridor on the east of the Vestibule gives access to the official stairway and leads to the famous East Room.

This is the largest apartment in the building, and is a magnificent chamber, eighty feet long, forty feet wide, and twenty-two feet high.

THE EAST ROOM.

It is richly ornamented in the Grecian style, the prevailing colors being white and gold. The lofty walls are adorned with eight large mirrors over carved mantel-pieces. From each of the three panels of the ceiling hangs a magnificent crystal chandelier. A full-length portrait of Washington, by Gilbert Stuart, and one of Martha Washington, by E. F. Andrews, occupy panels in the walls. The portrait of Washington is the one saved by Mrs. Madison. The dress in which the artist has represented Martha Washington was one made in Paris to be worn at the Martha Washington Centennial Tea Party, at Philadelphia, in 1876, and is considered a very fine reproduction of the style of dress during Revolutionary times. Two other panels are filled by full-length portraits of Abraham Lincoln and Thomas Jefferson; the latter, by Gilbert Stuart, being the best-known portrait of the great statesman.

The East Room was formerly used for state banquets, but is now used only for receptions. On these occasions it presents a very brilliant appearance. The windows are screened by rare tropical plants and the mantels are heaped with masses of roses and other flowers. All the brightness is not monopolized by the ladies and the flowers, for the gleam of gold and silver lace and the flashing of jewelled orders show the presence of members of foreign legations and officers of the Army and Navy.

Next the East Room on the southern front is the Green Room. As is the case with the other "color" rooms, it takes its name from the prevailing color of the decorations. The ceiling is beautifully ornamented with medallions containing representations of musical instruments and cherubs, and garlands of flowers. The woodwork is in imitation of old ivory, richly adorned with gold. There is a full-length portrait of Mrs. Hayes, by Huntingdon, presented to the Government by the Women's National Temperance Union. There are also fine portraits of Mrs. Tyler and Mrs. Polk.

THE GREEN ROOM.

The Blue Room is of oval form and occupies the centre of the southern front of the building. The decorations and furniture are light blue and gold. When holding receptions, the President stands in this room and the guests are introduced to him here before passing to the other parlors. The room is of especial interest, as it was here that President and Mrs. Cleveland were married, standing just north of the centre of the room.

West of the Blue Room is the Red Room, the private or family parlor, as it is called. The walls and curtains are of Pompeiian red and the furniture is upholstered in red plush. There are pictures of Presidents John Adams, Van Buren, and Taylor. Used, as this room is, by the President and his family, it has a cosy, home-like look, far different from the stately grandeur of the other parlors.

THE BLUE ROOM.

The State Dining Room, in the southwestern corner of the building, is a spacious apartment, thirty by forty feet, and is magnificently ornamented in the Colonial style, the prevailing color being a rich creamy-brown. The ceiling is surrounded with a frieze of garlands, about three and one-half feet wide, with medallions at intervals. From these, wreaths and vines run to the chandeliers. Beneath the cornice is a heavy frieze about four feet in width, which blends into the wall with garlands of native vines, leaves, and fruits. Over the door is a large medallion, in the centre of which is a shield of the United

States. On each side of the medallions is a horn of plenty, with Indian corn and native fruits. These medallions are connected with ornamental wreaths and festoons, in Colonial style. There is a dado about four feet high with representations of shells, seaweed, and coral. The general character of the work in the whole room is in what is known as "applique relief," which is produced by blending transparent colors on a light ground, producing a wonderfully lustrous result when lighted up, as the State Dining Room usually is, when used. The effect is greatly increased by the fact that the various colors and figures are "edged up" in relief to imitate the corded or raised work in applique, hence the name of this new and very effective style of ornamentation. State dinners are usually given once or twice a week during the winter, and are very brilliant affairs. Lavish use is made of the plants and flowers from the conservatories, and the table, laden with a rare display of plate, porcelain, and cut-glass, presents a beautiful appearance, forming an effective setting for the gay toilets of the ladies and their glittering jewels. The table service is exceedingly beautiful, and is adorned with various representations of the flora and fauna of America. The new set of cut-glass was made at White Mills, Pennsylvania, and is regarded as the finest ever produced in this country. It consists of five hundred and twenty separate pieces, and

THE RED ROOM.

was specially ordered by the Government for the White House. On each piece of the set, from the mammoth centre-piece and punchbowl to the tiny salt-cellars, is engraved the coat of arms of the United States. The execution of the order occupied several months, and cost $6000. The table can be made to accommodate as many as fifty-four persons, but the usual number of guests is from thirty to forty.

THE STATE DINING ROOM.

The Family Dining Room, on the north side, is used by the President and his family on ordinary occasions, when they are alone or with intimate friends. Though lacking the magnificence of the State Dining Room, it is a very cheerful apartment, and much more home-like than the former.

A grand corridor extends from the East Room to the entrance to the conservatories. It is used as a promenade by the guests at receptions, and contains a fine collection of portraits of the Presidents.

On the second floor are the Executive offices and the private apartments of the family, the latter occupying the western half.

The "Ante-room" is at the head of the official stairway. Here visitors to the President enter and hand their cards to the usher. The Library is a large oval room corresponding to the Blue Room below. Low book-cases, lining the walls, contain a choice collection of more than seven thousand volumes, selected mainly by Mrs.

Fillmore. The massive oaken table was presented by the British Government in 1881, and is of historic interest. It was made from

THE FAMILY DINING ROOM.

THE LIBRARY.

timbers of the British ship "Resolute," sent to the Arctic Ocean in 1852 in search of Sir John Franklin. The vessel was abandoned, but afterwards recovered by an American whaler. Fine portraits of the first five Presidents are on the walls, and artistic bronzes are displayed in various places.

THE CABINET ROOM.

STATE BED-ROOM.

Next is the Cabinet Room, where the heads of the Departments meet the President for consultation. At the head of the long table is the chair of the President, the Secretary of State sitting on the right and the Secretary of the Navy on the left. Though the room is handsomely decorated, it is not of its appearance that the visitor thinks. It is of the many matters of vast importance, not only to America but to all mankind, that have here been determined. Jefferson's purchase of Louisiana in 1803, acquiring for the United States the Mississippi Valley and the outlet to the Gulf of Mexico; the Florida purchase of 1819; the Mexican War, with its subsequent cession of California, were discussed and settled here. Within these walls President Lincoln consulted with Seward, Stanton, and Chase on questions concerning the very existence of the nation, and here he first read to the Cabinet the draft of the Proclamation of Emancipation.

There are two handsomely furnished State Bed-Chambers, used for the accommodation of distinguished guests.

The President is "at home" to visitors on Wednesdays, Thursdays, and Saturdays, from 10 A.M. to 1 P.M. Persons desiring to see him, call between these hours, and present their cards to the private secretary. Each is introduced in turn, and has the opportunity of speaking with the Chief Officer of the Nation.

The East Room is open to the public at ordinary times, but special permission is usually necessary to visit the other state parlors.

STATE, WAR, AND NAVY BUILDING.

CHAPTER IV

THE EXECUTIVE DEPARTMENTS OF THE GOVERNMENT—THE STATE, WAR, AND NAVY BUILDING—THE TREASURY—THE GENERAL POST-OFFICE—THE PATENT OFFICE—THE PENSION OFFICE—THE OFFICE OF THE ATTORNEY-GENERAL—THE AGRICULTURAL BUILDING.

THE eight Executive Departments of the Government have their chief offices in the City of Washington, and are as follows: The Department of State, the Treasury Department, the War Department, the Navy Department, the Post-Office Department, the Department of the Interior, the Department of Justice, and the Department of Agriculture. The heads of these Departments constitute the President's Cabinet, and each has the title of Secretary, except the heads of the Post-Office Department and the Department of Justice, who bear respectively the titles of Postmaster-General and Attorney-General. Each member of the Cabinet receives a salary of $8000 per annum. Besides these Departments, there are some minor institutions, such as the Smithsonian Institution, the Government Printing-Office, etc., which are managed by superintendents or commissioners, and are not directly responsible to any of the Executive Departments.

THE STATE, WAR, AND NAVY BUILDING,

In which are the offices of the three Departments, stands west of the White House. It is a large and magnificent building, constructed of granite and thoroughly fire-proof. The style is the Italian Renaissance. Above a sub-basement and basement rise the three principal stories of the structure, crowned by an artistic mansard roof. At the centre of each façade is a handsome pavilion adorned with columns and rising a story higher than the rest of the building.

On the roof of the eastern one is the time-ball, dropped every day at noon by the officials at the Naval Observatory.

The building is five hundred and sixty-four feet from north to south, and three hundred and forty-two feet from east to west. The greatest height is one hundred and forty-five feet. There are five hundred and sixty-six rooms and more than two miles of corridors. The building was begun in 1871, from designs of A. B. Mullett, and completed in 1887, at a cost of nearly $12,000,000.

The interior is in keeping with the exterior in its handsome yet substantial construction. The grand staircases are of granite and have beautiful bronze balusters. The corridors are beautifully frescoed and paved with tessellated black and white marble, and the chief apartments are adorned and furnished with great taste and elegance.

THE DEPARTMENT OF STATE

Was the first of the Executive Departments to be created by Congress in 1789. Thomas Jefferson was the first Secretary. The business is in charge of the Secretary, who is aided by several assistant secretaries, chiefs of bureaus, etc., and numerous clerks. The Secretary is always the first of the Cabinet officers to receive his appointment, and his signature must accompany that of the President on the commissions of all the other members. He has charge of all matters pertaining to the intercourse of the United States with other nations and the several States of the Union. His relations with the President are very intimate and confidential, and should the President and Vice-President be, for any cause, removed from office, he would succeed as President.

The State Department has its offices in the southern portion of the building. On the third floor is the Library, founded by Thomas Jefferson, containing over fifty thousand volumes in many different languages. But of far greater interest to the visitor are the numerous relics deposited in the Library. Here may be seen the original draft of the Declaration of Independence, the desk on which it was written, and also the original engrossed copy bearing the signatures of members of Congress, notable among them those of John Hancock, Charles Carroll of Carrollton, and Stephen Hopkins. The signature of the latter looks as though he had heard Franklin's famous remark, that if they did not all hang together, they would all hang separately, but there is evidence to show that palsy, not fear, made his hand shake. The original draft of the Constitution is also carefully preserved, together with Washington's commission as Commander-in-Chief and his war sword. Hundreds of volumes contain the papers of Washington, Jefferson, Madison, Monroe, and some of the other Presidents. One hundred and seventeen volumes are filled with the Washington correspondence, and here can be seen letters to his overseer, giving minute directions about the cultivation of his farms, side by side with letters from the crowned heads of Europe and all the great men of his time.

Many curious and instructive things are to be found among the archives of the Department. All the treaties of the United States with foreign governments, from the earliest one, made by the infant nation with France in 1778, are carefully preserved. Those made with Oriental nations are very grand indeed, one with Turkey being resplendent with golden lettering, the signature or "cipher" of the Sultan being magnificent. A treaty with Japan was brought into the Department in a beautifully lacquered box, suspended from a pole carried by two officials, who were answerable for its safety with their lives. Diplomatic intercourse with the Oriental nations is marked by much magnificence and state, and costly presents are expected to be given and received. Several Japanese swords have been thus given to the State Department, and present a very grand appearance with their golden scabbards and jewelled hilts.

In charge of the Department is the Great Seal of the United States. It must be affixed to all executive proclamations, to pardons, and to all commissions of ministers and consuls to foreign countries. It is very carefully guarded, and is never impressed upon a document unless by the express order of the President.

The Bureau of Indexes and Archives has charge of all the correspondence of the Department. Many hundred letters and documents are received daily and carefully indexed by name and subject before being sent to the various officials. Notwithstanding the hundreds of thousands received since the foundation of the Government, so complete is the system and so careful the practice, that any paper may be found by a five minutes' search.

The office of the Secretary, and the Diplomatic Reception Room, in which the Secretary receives the officials of foreign governments, are on the second floor. The furniture of the Reception Room is of ebony, upholstered in brocade. The walls are painted in the Egyptian style, and the floor of tessellated marble is covered with Oriental rugs. Magnificent chandeliers hang from the ceiling, and the walls are adorned with busts and paintings of Secretaries Jefferson, Webster, Seward, Washburn, Fish, Evarts, Blaine, and Frelinghuysen. There is also a portrait of Lord Ashburton. A collection of portraits of all the Secretaries from 1789 may be seen in the anteroom at the west end of the corridor.

The War Department,

Which has charge of all the military affairs of the Government, was established in 1789, General Knox being the first Secretary. Besides matters strictly military, many other subjects come under its supervision, such as the improvement of rivers and harbors, to which the Government devotes annually many millions of dollars, explorations and surveys, and the national asylums and cemeteries. The total annual expenditure of the Department is nearly $50,000,000.

The Department occupies the northern and western portions of the building. The offices of the Secretary are on the second floor in the central portion of the western wing. They are spacious apartments and are very handsomely furnished. There are some fine portraits of former Secretaries and paintings of great battles. On the walls of the stairway are other portraits of the Secretaries. In the corridor, three portraits especially deserving attention are those of the three great generals of the Civil War—Grant, Sherman, and Sheridan. There are also cases containing figures showing the uniform and equipments of the various branches of the service at the different epochs of the nation's history. Probably the most interesting are Morgan's famous riflemen and Washington's bodyguard. Other cases contain specimens of the fire-arms used, from the old flint-lock musket to the latest magazine rifle. An interesting exhibit is that showing the means of army transportation, both of the ordinary baggage and provision service and of the hospital corps. There is also a case containing specimens of the flags carried by the various branches of the service. Specimens of the armor-piercing projectiles used by the modern high-power guns are grimly suggestive of the havoc that would be wrought in war.

The Library of the Department contains more than twenty thousand volumes, besides the many special collections scattered among the various bureaus. All the publications relating to modern methods of warfare are on the shelves, and no pains are spared to keep the collections up to date. The Department has charge of the publication of the Records of the Civil War, a work of great magnitude and value.

The rooms occupied as Headquarters of the Army are in the northern wing and form an elegant suite of apartments. They contain portraits of all the Commanders-in-Chief of the Army of the United States.

In the rooms of the Bureau of Military Justice are preserved several relics of Lincoln's assassination. Here is the pistol used by Booth and the fatal bullet that ended the life of the martyred President.

THE NAVY DEPARTMENT

Occupies the eastern front of the State, War, and Navy Building. The Secretary of the Navy has charge of all matters pertaining to the Navy, and, in addition, has the direction of the Naval Observatory and the work of the Hydrographic Office. The business of the Department is conducted by the various Bureaus, such as those of Yards and Docks, Navigation, Ordnance, Steam Engineering, etc.

The office of the Secretary is on the second floor opposite the grand staircase. It is a large apartment, handsomely decorated in the Grecian style and beautifully furnished. It contains fine portraits of some of the later Secretaries of the Navy. In the corridor opposite the entrance and on the floor above are beautiful models of some of the recent additions to the "New Navy." The model of the "Vesuvius" shows the peculiar arrangement of its dynamite guns. The monitor "Miantonomoh" and the "Monterey" illustrate the modern type of coast-defence vessels. The great change that has taken place during the last fifty years in the construction of naval vessels is strikingly shown by comparing these new types with the old line-of-battle ship "Pennsylvania," a model of which can be seen in the Secretary's office. Though the "Pennsylvania" carried one hundred and twenty guns, the weight of her entire broadside was not much greater than that from the four great guns of the "Miantonomoh," while between the destructive energies of the two vessels, no comparison can be instituted.

The Reception Room of the Library of the Department is on the fourth floor. It is the handsomest room in the building, being beautifully panelled in costly foreign and domestic marbles and adorned with bronze symbolic figures. Over the door is a piece of verd-antique, brought from the ruins of the Temple of Jupiter at Pompeii. The collection of works pertaining to naval matters is very complete, and numbers more than twenty thousand volumes, many of them works of great rarity and value.

The Hydrographic Office is under the direction of the Bureau of Navigation. It supplies the Navy and mariners generally with charts of all the navigable waters of the world except those of the United States. The Coast Survey, a bureau of the Treasury Department, has charge of the latter.

The Bureau of Navigation has also charge of the Naval Observatory and of the publication of the Nautical Almanac. The calculations for the Almanac are made by the best astronomers in the country, and the value of their labors is highly appreciated both at home and abroad. The Almanac is published three years in advance, and no vessel is allowed to leave port without a copy of this or a similar publication issued by some other of the great maritime nations.

The Treasury Building

Is east of the White House. The southern portion lies across the line of Pennsylvania Avenue and intercepts the view from the White House to the Capitol. Tradition makes President Jackson responsible for the selection of the site, and the story—whether true or false—is very characteristic of his quick, imperious temper. The building in use by the Department since 1814 had been destroyed by fire in 1833, and, as late as 1836, the new building had not been begun. Wearied at the long delay, the President one morning walked over from the White House, and, striking his cane on the ground, exclaimed, "Here, right here, I want the corner-stone laid."

THE TREASURY BUILDING.

(93)

Possibly it was not his business to determine the matter, but few people would have cared to tell him so.

The Treasury is an immense building, four hundred and sixty feet long and two hundred and sixty-four feet wide. The style is an adaptation of the Ionic order of Grecian architecture. There is a rustic basement and three upper stories surmounted by a balustrade. The older or eastern portion is of sandstone and has a façade of thirty columns, thirty-one and one-half feet high. It was designed by Robert Mills and completed in 1841. The rest of the building is of granite, completed in 1869, after designs of Thomas U. Walter. On the three fronts are porticoes of lofty monolithic columns. The total cost was nearly $10,000,000.

The Secretary of the Treasury is in charge of the financial affairs of the Government, and is one of its most important officials. The vast business under his direction is subdivided among the various bureaus and requires the services of a whole army of clerks and minor officials. Much of the business is transacted at the sub-treasuries and custom-houses throughout the country, but the most interesting matters are to be found in Washington. The chief objects of interest in the Treasury Building are open to the inspection of visitors.

The Cash Room is a very beautiful apartment. It is two stories in height with a balcony around the second story. The walls are panelled with fine specimens of various foreign and domestic marbles, highly polished. Vast sums of money are paid out here daily, as much as $10,000,000 having been paid on one order.

The rooms of the Secret Service Division, on the second floor, contain a curious collection of objects pertaining to the various frauds attempted on the Government. There is a "rogues' gallery," consisting of the photographs of counterfeiters. While the majority of these "crooks" have most repulsive faces, showing unmistakable traces of vicious natures, there are others whose appearances would deceive the most wary, and these are generally the ones who have been most successful and have given the officials the greatest trouble. There are many dies, moulds, and plates used by the counterfeiters, quite a collection of weapons taken from them, and specimens of their work imitating the money and securities of the Government. One of the most interesting objects is a counterfeit $20 note. So well is it executed that it would defy any but the most careful scrutiny, but on close inspection it is seen to be done with pen and ink. The maker has never been detected, and it would seem that his object cannot be to get money, for he could make far more by spending his time and talents in some lawful pursuit.

The Bureau of Redemption is in the northwestern corner. Here the worn-out notes are brought from all over the country to be cancelled and redeemed. They are carefully counted and their face value returned to the owners. After they have been made up in packages about one-half inch in thickness they are placed under a machine which quickly punches four holes in them. They are then taken to a room in the basement containing the macerating machine. This is a huge steel vessel inside of which there is a grinding apparatus revolving in water. The opening through which the notes are introduced is secured by three locks, and the keys are in the custody of the Secretary, the Treasurer, and the Comptroller. Unless all three of these officials or their representatives are present the macerator cannot be opened. After the notes are reduced to a fine pulp, a valve, secured by three other locks, is opened in the presence of the same officials, and the mass allowed to escape into a tank underneath, from which it is pumped out into one of the court-yards and then sold, at the price of about $40 a ton, to the manufacturers of coarse paper. Small portions are made up into little souvenirs of various designs and sold to curious visitors. The average face value of the notes thus destroyed at one time is about $400,000, but sometimes rises as high as $2,000,000.

The final operation in making the notes of the Government is performed in the basement. As they come from the Bureau of Engraving and Printing they lack the red seal of the Department. When this has been put on they are taken to the vaults.

The vaults for the storage of the gold and silver coin are very interesting, not so much from their construction, which seems simple enough, but from their contents. The large vault shown to visitors contains what looks like a huge cage, formed of cross-bars of steel. A passage about two feet wide separates this from the walls. Through the bars one can see rough wooden boxes piled up to the ceiling. In one place is a table on which are piled one thousand silver dollars. The visitor follows the guide in his walk around the cage, and can then have the happy consciousness that he has been around, and almost within reach of, nearly $100,000,000. The money stored here is nearly all held for the redemption of the silver certificates, but it is only a portion of the whole amount in the possession of the Government. The remainder is kept in the various sub-treasuries.

The total value of the coin, notes, and securities in the vaults of the Treasurer's Office at Washington is generally about $650,000,000.

A most careful supervision is maintained over all the employés while on duty, and at night a force of sixty watchmen, most of them veteran soldiers, patrol every part of the building.

THE POST-OFFICE DEPARTMENT.

The Post-Office Department building occupies the entire square bounded by Seventh, Eighth, E and F Streets, N. W. It is constructed of white marble from New York and Maryland. Above a

THE GENERAL POST-OFFICE.

rustic basement rise the two principal stories, adorned with monolithic columns and pilasters with rich Corinthian capitals. The building extends three hundred feet from north to south, and two hundred and four feet from east to west, and is seventy feet high. It was begun in 1839, from designs by Robert Mills, and finished in 1855, by Thomas U. Walter. The entire cost exceeded $2,000,000.

The Post-Office Department was established in 1789, Samuel Osgood being appointed Postmaster-General. The business of the office was not very great. People in those days were not generally given to writing letters, and postage was high and the mails slow and infrequent. Even as late as 1839, when the Federal Government had been in existence fifty years, the entire business of the Department was not so great as that of the New York office is to-day. Some interesting statistics, furnished by the Postmaster-General, show its condition at three periods of the nation's history.

	1790.	1839.	1892.†
Number of post-offices	75	12,780	65,094
Number of employés and agents	130*	17,000*	184,431
Number of pieces of mail matter	500,000*	Unknown	4,351,844,845*
Revenue	$37,935	$4,481,657	$65,908,909.36
Expenditure	32,140	4,636,536	72,069,114.55

* Estimated. † February.

The workings of the Post-Office are peculiarly interesting to the people. It is the one department of the Government in which every man, woman, and child has a personal interest. The vastness of its business can be appreciated by the consideration of some statistics from the report of the Postmaster-General. The transportation routes number over twenty-eight thousand, with a total length of four hundred and thirty-nine thousand miles, and an aggregate of three hundred and twenty-six million miles travelled. The "Star routes" number over sixteen thousand, with a length of two hundred and thirty-eight thousand miles, and aggregating one hundred million miles travelled. These are for the benefit of the rural and sparsely settled districts, off the lines of railroads and steamboats, and have received their name from being marked with an *asterisk* in the records. The railroad routes number nearly twenty-three hundred, with a length of one hundred and fifty-nine thousand miles, and the number of miles travelled annually is nearly two hundred and twenty-nine million.

The Dead-Letter Office

Proves very interesting to the visitor. Here come all the waifs and strays of the business. The "dead mail" sent to the office is opened by the clerks by means of sharp, thin knives, and if any address is found by which the pieces can be returned to the sender, they are at once re-directed and sent off. If no means of doing this can be discovered, all pieces containing anything of value are laid aside, after a record of their contents has been made, and at the end of six months any money is turned into the Treasury and the packages are disposed of at auction as "unclaimed mail matter."

The Dead-Letter Office has been called. a "monument to the stupidity of the people;" and the title seems a true one. The Superintendent reports that in 1891 more than six million eight hundred thousand pieces of original "dead mail" matter were treated, besides more than seven million imperfectly addressed letters which were withdrawn by the Railway Mail Service to be supplied with correct addresses by the post-offices at the railway centres, and which never came to the Office.

Of the opened letters more than thirty thousand contained $48,000 in money; of these, twenty-one thousand, or seventy per cent., containing almost $38,000, were returned, and the rest were made over to the Treasury. Of this last $9000 or more, $4400 were comprised simply in blank envelopes containing coins found loose in the mails.

The most of the undelivered money turned into the Treasury comes from the dupes of the "green-goods" swindlers; and, as these remittances are usually under fictitious names, the identification of the senders is impossible. Thirty thousand letters were found to contain papers aggregating in value $1,800,000. Ninety-five per cent. of these were restored. Forty-one thousand contained photographs; of these, thirty thousand were restored. Of the one hundred and forty thousand letters containing stamps, one hundred and twenty-five thousand were returned to the writers.

Eighty thousand domestic parcels were received. Six thousand and five hundred were misdirected, and seventeen thousand having been insecurely wrapped, had no addresses at all. Nineteen thousand were not transmissible as parcels. Thirty thousand of the domestic parcels were either forwarded to their destinations or to the senders.

One hundred and seventy thousand letters which were returned to the writers failed of delivery and again came to the Dead-Letter Office. Of the unclaimed and undelivered matter four hundred and twenty thousand were letters misdirected, or only partially directed.

Five million seven hundred thousand letters contained inclosures of no value. Of these, one million seven hundred and forty thousand were returned to the writers; ten per cent. of these failed to reach the addresses given in the correspondence of the writers, and the number of letters of this class actually restored, therefore, was one million five hundred and seventy thousand. Fully one-half of these five and three-quarters millions of letters contained nothing by which the writers could be identified. Unaddressed letters gone wrong are a class of mail which shows no possible fault on the part of the service. Of these letters, bearing no superscription whatever, the last three decades show the following increase: the number in 1870 was three thousand; in 1880, nine thousand; in 1890, almost twenty-eight thousand.

Nine letters out of every ten that go wrong, go wrong because of the carelessness of the senders. Persons mailing letters might with excellent effect put something on the inside or outside by which the sender or the addressee might be found. Care might be taken, in sending letters to cities, to put on streets and numbers, for experience teaches that three-fourths of the letters addressed "general delivery" never reach the addressees, because the addressees trust the free delivery so much that they never think of going to the general delivery. The return request printed or written in the corner of the envelope is a convenience to the Department and a double convenience to the sender of the letter, for a letter so marked, if not called for, is returned at once to the sender, who knows as quickly as possible that his message has not reached its destination.

The public often write addresses imperfectly or illegibly. They are careless about writing the names of towns and States. They seal letters insecurely, or put on additional mucilage and cause letters to stick together. They use dark-colored envelopes and then pencils or light ink. There is frequently too much printing on the face of the envelope

In the "Museum" of the Office are preserved some of the articles found in the mails. The collection excites wonder. Lucifer matches, percussion caps, cartridges, gunpowder, and all sorts of explosives one would think even bad enough, but in addition are specimens of rattlesnakes, tarantulas, and other venomous creatures which were found alive.

A curious and interesting relic is the set of accounts kept by Franklin while Postmaster-General for the Colonies, twenty years before the Revolution.

The Postal Museum

Contains a very interesting exhibit of the management of postal affairs in this and foreign countries.

Among the most interesting foreign exhibits are models of German mail wagons, showing the arrangements for carrying mails and passengers alike. From Austria come letter-boxes of unique patterns, photographs of public buildings, and portfolios showing the blanks, books, and forms of the Austrian postal savings-bank system and of the Austrian collection service. There are an Austrian posthorn and Hungarian mail-boxes. From Australia is contributed a handsomely framed photograph of the public buildings in Victoria, bordered by a complete set of genuine Victoria postage stamps uncancelled. From England there are post-marking instruments, photographs of parcel-post wagons, wagons used in the royal mail, and tandem tricycles.

Canada contributes specimens of its letter-boxes; a box for the conveyance under seal of valuable mail matter; a complete set of letter-carrier's uniforms, the carrier's helmet for summer and his cap for winter, his heavy clothing for one season and lighter for the other, the Astrakhan cap and collar, leather legging, chamois vest, and storm coat.

From India there are models which exhibit in a most life-like way, even to the reproduction of the features and forms, the Calcutta letter-carrier, the stamper in the post-office, the mail wagon driver, and the native mail runner, who also carries with him a spear as a weapon of offence and defence. One of these spears has been sent, containing around the shank a string of sleigh-bells which jingle as the runner goes, the purpose being to frighten off poisonous reptiles. There is also a model of the camel post and of the native runner crossing a stream with his mail bag, on a raft of earthenware pots, and a model of the tonga, a wagon used on hill roads.

From our own country have been received scores of relics of the postal service. Hundreds of photographs of post-offices and postmasters, ancient books, a ball of twine made from waste scraps which a postmaster was years in putting together, a specimen of a mail chute for high office buildings in cities, from the Treasury Department photographs of all the principal public buildings in the United States, a photograph of the oldest postmaster, and a copy of the first post route map, constructed at a time when the whole postal service of the United States could be described in a half-dozen lines.

The transactions of the Money Order Office are very large and extensive. There are more than ten thousand of these offices. Nearly twelve million domestic money orders are issued during the year, and their value amounts to nearly $120,000,000. As showing the care exercised, out of all this immense business there were but two hundred and twenty-six cases of alleged erroneous payment, amounting to $6982, which, on being examined, proved the Department to be to blame only to the extent of $1627, which amount was paid. The ratio of wrong payment is one to every one hundred and forty thousand.

The revenue derived from the money orders exceeded $866,000.

The Office is located in the large brick building, opposite the Post-Office, at the corner of Eighth and E Streets.

THE DEPARTMENT OF THE INTERIOR.

The Department of the Interior was created by Congress in 1849, Thomas Ewing, of Ohio, being the first Secretary.

Its work is very extensive and important, and for the convenience of transacting business is divided among several divisions and bureaus. The chief of these are the Patent Office, the Pension Office, the Bureau of Indian Affairs, the Bureau of Education, the Census Office, and the General Land Office.

The Patent Office

And some of the other divisions of the Department occupy the building extending from Seventh to Ninth Streets and from F to G Streets, N. W. It is a huge structure, measuring two hundred and seventy-five feet from north to south and four hundred and ten feet from east to west, and is seventy-five feet high. The main building is of granite and freestone, the east and west wings of marble, and the northern extension of granite. The style of architecture is Doric. The columns of the porticoes are huge monoliths. The main

THE PATENT OFFICE.

entrance on F Street is an exact reproduction of the front of the Parthenon at Athens. A fine court-yard gives light and air to the two hundred rooms.

The building was begun in 1837 and completed in 1860, at a cost of $2,700,000.

The Patent Office is under the direction of the Commissioner of Patents, and the business is very large and profitable, and is increasing rapidly every year. Many thousand patents are issued annually, and the receipts exceed $1,200,000.

The Patent Office issues weekly "The Official Gazette," containing a record of the patents issued, together with illustrations and designs.

The Library, on the first floor, contains a fine collection of works relating to inventions, and is largely increased every year.

The halls of the Museum of Models contain the chief attraction for the visitor. They are four in number, and are each two hundred and forty-two feet long and sixty-three feet wide. They contain one hundred and fifty thousand models, but none of an earlier date than 1836. In that year the entire collection accumulated by the Government was destroyed by the burning of the Post-Office building. Another fire, in 1877, destroyed more than eighty thousand models then stored in the north and west halls of the present building. As reconstructed, the building is thoroughly fire-proof, and there is no fear of any similar catastrophe.

An interesting object is the model of an invention of Abraham Lincoln, made while he was a flat-boatman on the Western rivers. It was designed to assist the boatmen in getting their vessels over the bars and shallows that form such an obstruction to navigation, and also to prevent them from sinking in case of running on a snag. He proposed to do this by the use of huge air-bags, to be inflated like bellows when necessary.

The Bureau of Indian Affairs has charge of all matters pertaining to the Indians. There are about two hundred and fifty thousand of these troublesome wards of the Nation, and great care must be constantly exercised to see that they get their proper allowance of food and clothing. Neglect in the past has caused immense expenditure and serious loss of life in the numerous Indian troubles of the last twenty years. The Bureau has also charge of the schools established of late years, notably at Hampton and Carlisle, where the young Indian children are taught various useful trades. The Government is gradually buying from the Indians their vast reservations, so that these may be thrown open to settlement.

The total annual appropriation on account of the Indians is about $16,000,000.

The Bureau of Education was established in 1867 in order to collect and transmit information in regard to educational matters in this and foreign countries. Its reports are widely circulated, both at home and abroad, and are greatly appreciated at the various centres of learning. On its staff are some of the best-educated men in the country, and it has as volunteer assistants the teachers of all the schools and colleges. Its work is very quietly done, but is of immense importance to the community, since in its reports are given the latest ideas of the best educators of all parts of the world. From the teacher of the humble district school to the president of the great university, all in the profession are vitally interested in the work of this Bureau.

The General Land Office is a very important bureau of the Department of the Interior, having charge of all the public lands of the United States. The vast domain belonging to the Government was acquired at different times and in various ways. Much was ceded by the original States. The Louisiana purchase in 1803, and the explorations immediately following it, more than doubled the then area of the Union, extending its dominion over the whole of the Mississippi Valley and to the Pacific Coast. The result of the Mexican War was a further increase of territory, including all the lands from Texas to California. As the various Western States were admitted to the Union, much of the public domain was ceded to them, and a large amount has been occupied by settlers or given to railroad companies to aid in the construction of their lines.

By the laws of the United States any citizen can acquire title to land by actual settlement or by purchase. The lands near the railroads are held at a minimum price of $2.50 per acre; those more remote at $1.25 per acre. Title to one hundred and sixty acres, known as a quarter-section, will be given to any citizen who will settle on and cultivate it for five years, and who will pay the necessary fees. Special arrangements are made whereby the land may be purchased after having been cultivated for a shorter period. About ninety million acres have been acquired by settlers, since 1865, under the homestead laws.

The Pension Office.

The Pension Office is the largest and most important division of the Interior Department. It has charge of all the rolls of the soldiers and sailors engaged in the various wars of the United States, and of all matters relating to pensions. When it is remembered that there were more than two million persons enlisted in the service during the Civil War, and that applications for pensions have been made on

THE PENSION OFFICE. 105

behalf of more than one million of these, some idea may be obtained of the vast work of the office.

THE PENSION BUILDING.

INTERIOR OF THE PENSION BUILDING.

The Pension Building is in the northern part of Judiciary Square, between Fourth and Fifth and F and G Streets. It is a handsome structure four hundred feet from east to west, two hundred feet from north to south, and seventy-five feet high. The style is the Italian

Renaissance. The material is pressed brick relieved by terra-cotta mouldings. A broad band of terra-cotta, extending around the building, depicts incidents in the life of the soldier. The interior is a magnificent court-yard, rising the whole height of the building and covered by a roof of iron and glass. Tiers of galleries give access to the surrounding rooms. It was occupied in 1885, and the opening was signalized by the Grand Ball given in honor of the Inauguration of President Cleveland, March 4, 1885, when eighteen thousand people were present.

The cost of the building was $500,000.

The Department of Justice.

The Attorney-General, the head of the Department of Justice, has been a Cabinet officer since the foundation of the Federal Government, when Edmund Randolph was appointed, but the Department, as now organized, has existed only since 1870. It has charge of all the law business of the Government, and all the law officers are part of its staff. One very important function of the Attorney-General is to act as the legal adviser of the President and the members of the Cabinet. Many difficult questions of law are constantly arising in the ordinary course of business, and the proper course to pursue is often difficult to determine. The decisions of the Attorney-General are not law, and the various Courts may afterwards rule otherwise if the matter in dispute be brought before them, but his opinions have great value as coming from one who is an expert. He is always selected on account of his abilities as a lawyer, and many of the most learned counsel in the land have occupied the position.

The chief offices of the Department are in the large building on Pennsylvania Avenue opposite the north front of the Treasury. It was formerly occupied by the Freedmen's Saving and Trust Company, and was purchased by the Government, in 1882, for $250,000. The building is handsomely constructed of brownstone, and is four stories high, with a mansard roof.

The first floor is occupied by the Court of Claims. The apartments of the Attorney-General are handsomely furnished and contain a fine collection of portraits of all the Attorneys-General since the foundation of the Government.

The Department of Agriculture

Occupies a building on the southern side of The Mall, west of the Smithsonian Institution and facing Thirteenth Street. It is a handsome structure of pressed brick with brownstone facings. There are three stories and a mansard roof. It is one hundred and seventy feet long and sixty-one feet wide, and was erected in 1868, from designs by Adolph Cluss, at a cost of nearly $150,000.

There are many objects of interest in the building. The Library contains nearly twenty thousand volumes and is the finest collection

THE AGRICULTURAL BUILDING.

of works relating to agriculture in the world. Besides all the important domestic publications there are many rare and valuable works from foreign presses.

The Museum consists of an immense collection of specimens and models of agricultural products, together with objects illustrating their cultivation and the articles manufactured from them. There are splendid models of the many fruits and vegetables grown in the United States, and many specimens of minerals and forest growths. The effects of the variations of climate on the different productions are finely illustrated.

There is also a fine collection of poultry and game-birds. The

Entomological collection shows specimens of all the insects that play such havoc with the farmer's crops, together with the progress of their destructive work, and the means taken to counteract it.

The building is open from 9 A.M. to 4 P.M.

The Agricultural Grounds comprise about thirty-six acres, and contain many objects of beauty and interest. South-east of the main building is Industrial Hall, with part of the exhibits of the Museum. East is the Seed House, where a large number of persons is employed in packing the many varieties of seeds and in distributing them throughout the country. The Department raises vast quantities of seeds, and also makes large purchases from reliable firms both at home and abroad, so that it is enabled to send supplies to farmers who, from various causes, have lost their own supply. It is constantly on the lookout for new varieties and for such foreign plants as may possibly be profitably grown in the United States.

On the west are immense conservatories, three hundred and twenty feet by thirty, where all kinds of rare and beautiful plants and fruits are grown. There are specimens of the orange, pineapple, olive, grape, and many others. To the north is an extensive Arboretum, containing a choice collection of trees.

The Department of Agriculture was formerly in charge of a Commissioner, but the growing sense of its immense importance to the country caused it to be made a Cabinet Department, Jeremiah M. Rusk being appointed as first Secretary in 1889.

Although the work is carried on in a very quiet manner, and at an expense that is trifling compared with that of some of the other Departments, it is, nevertheless, of vast importance to the whole country. The object of the Department is to assist the farmers—the food-growers of the nation—and increase their knowledge by supplying them with the latest discoveries in the science of agriculture. Talented specialists are constantly engaged in making careful investigations of agricultural matters, and much valuable work is done and many important discoveries made. Examinations by the Microscopical division are made with a view to discover the causes of diseases of plants and animals and to provide remedies. Plants are frequently discovered to possess valuable medicinal properties previously unknown. The Entomologists make investigations of insects injurious to grains, fruits, and vegetables, and frequently gain important information in regard to their habits, development, and the best means for their destruction.

The Department makes exhaustive investigations into all diseases of farm animals, such as pleuro-pneumonia in cattle and cholera in hogs and chickens, diseases that entail immense loss upon the farmers. Much has been done to lessen the ravages of these dread diseases, and the gain to the country through the increased value of the product far exceeds the cost of the Department.

The Department has a number of reliable correspondents in the agricultural districts of the country who make simultaneous reports each month on the condition of the crops, the result of local agricultural experiments, and other valuable matters. From the information thus obtained, the Department makes up its monthly bulletin and crop report, which is sent all over the country and widely published by the newspapers. These reports are of the greatest practical value to those dealing in agricultural products.

The correspondence of the Department is enormous, thousands of persons writing about agricultural matters from all sections of the country. In addition to letters come packages containing strange birds and insects, with the request for information as to their destructive powers. Peculiar grasses and plants, supposed to be poisonous, are sent on for examination, and in general, the Secretary is supposed to be an Oracle that can give the correct answer to any question concerning the soil.

The results of the labors of the Department and its advice in regard to them are given in its annual report, probably the most widely circulated and best read of all the Government publications. Though very bulky, it is eagerly sought for by the farmers, who probably wonder how their fathers ever did without it.

The total annual appropriation for the Department is about $3,000,000. The Agricultural Experiment Stations cost over $700,000, the Weather Bureau about $900,000, and the Bureau of Animal Industry $500,000.

THE NEW CONGRESSIONAL LIBRARY BUILDING.

CHAPTER V.

THE NEW CONGRESSIONAL LIBRARY BUILDING—THE BUREAU OF ENGRAVING
AND PRINTING—THE SMITHSONIAN INSTITUTION AND NATIONAL MUSEUM—
THE CORCORAN GALLERY OF ART—THE ORDNANCE MUSEUM—THE NAVAL
OBSERVATORY—THE SIGNAL OFFICE—THE GOVERNMENT PRINTING-OFFICE.

BESIDES the great department buildings, there are numerous other institutions in Washington that present many objects of great interest to the visitor. Some of these are either entirely or partially under Government control, while others represent the enterprise or benevolence of private citizens.

THE NEW CONGRESSIONAL LIBRARY BUILDING.

The growth of the Library of Congress has been so great that the halls in the Capitol used for its accommodation are entirely inadequate. To meet present and future needs for more space and better quarters, Congress has already appropriated $2,400,000 towards the erection of a new building, now rapidly approaching completion, which will be the finest structure of its kind in the world.

The new Congressional Library building stands in the centre of a plot of ten acres, lying on the south side of East Capitol Street, between First and Second. It is four hundred and seventy by three hundred and fifty feet, and covers an area of three and three-quarters acres.

The style of architecture is the Italian Renaissance, the original designs being made by Smithmeyer & Pelz. There is a basement, in rustic style, a principal story, and a second story surmounted by a balustrade. Pavilions at the corners and on the eastern and western fronts, surmounted by attics, are adorned with beautiful Corinthian columns, and on the keystones of the arched windows of the first story are elegantly carved heads, thirty-three in number,

(111)

representing the various types of the different races of mankind. The main entrance is through a magnificent central pavilion on the western front, leading to the grand staircase giving access to the second story.

The central portion is formed by a great octagonal building, one hundred and forty feet in diameter, with an extreme height of one hundred and seventy-five feet. Within this is the Reading Room, one hundred feet in diameter and one hundred and twenty feet high, well lighted by large windows in the clere-story. A gallery runs around this, and two tiers of alcoves give opportunity for retired study and research. Great book-stacks, or repositories, each containing nine tiers of cases, connect the central rotunda with the north, east, and south sides of the building, and form four court-yards seventy-five to one hundred by one hundred and fifty feet. The walls of these court-yards are lined with ivory-white enamelled brick, which reflect light through the windows of the book-stacks.

The material of the exterior walls is granite, and the building is constructed entirely of this stone and brick and iron, rendering it completely fire-proof. The boilers and pumps for the heating, ventilating, and power apparatus are in a prettily designed building east of the Library, under ground.

The connecting repositories, with their many tiers of cases, will give shelf-room for two million volumes, while the outer rooms can accommodate some five or six million more. Should future needs require, additional repositories could be erected in the court-yards.

The Library is being erected under the direction of General Casey, Chief of Engineers, U. S. Army, by Mr. Bernard R. Green, Superintendent and Engineer. It is expected to be completed in 1896, and the estimated total cost is $6,000,000.

THE BUREAU OF ENGRAVING AND PRINTING.

The national currency, bonds, checks, and internal revenue stamps are made in the building of the Bureau of Engraving and Printing, at the corner of Fourteenth and B Streets, S. W. The building is a handsome brick structure in the Romanesque style, two hundred and twenty by one hundred and thirty-five feet. There are three stories and a basement, and a high tower at the north-eastern corner. It was erected in 1878, at a cost of over $300,000.

The printing division occupies the third floor and employs about five hundred persons. Six hundred printed sheets is the daily task allotted to each pressman, and as all imperfect sheets are rejected by the examiners and a record made of the number and pressman, much defective work will result in a speedy dismissal from the service. Steam-power is not used for the presses, as it is found that the delicate nature of the work and the care required to obtain perfect impressions requires hand labor. Each pressman has a woman to assist him, her work being to place the sheet on the press and

THE BUILDING OF THE BUREAU OF ENGRAVING AND PRINTING.

remove it when printed. After each impression the plate must be carefully cleaned and polished with whiting, then inked, and wiped to remove the superfluous ink. As it has been found that the hand is the best medium that can be used for wiping the plate, the necessity of an assistant to handle the paper is obvious. When they have received the first impression the sheets are carefully dried, and after some days are given to another set of pressmen, who print the other side. No one person is allowed to attend to more than one operation. When the sheets have been printed they are subjected to a rigid scrutiny by the examiners, and such as are satisfactory are sent to be numbered and lettered. The final operation is the stamping with the red seal of the Treasury, done in the basement of the Treasury building.

There is an elaborate system in use to prevent error or fraud on the part of the employés. The sheets of special paper are delivered by the officials of the Treasury to those of the Bureau, and must be receipted for, not only as to their number and proposed use, but also the value they will have when printed. They are carefully counted before being given to the pressmen, each of whom places a private mark on every sheet he prints. They are counted again at every subsequent stage of their manufacture, counted again before being sent to the Treasury, and counted again when received there. From the time a piece of paper comes from the manufacturer until it is placed, a finished note, in the Treasury vaults, it has passed through the hands of over fifty persons, and each person handling it is known and is held accountable. The workmen are separated from the public by a high wire screen and are under the constant surveillance of watchmen stationed in all the rooms. Finally, before anyone leaves the building at the close of work, every printed sheet and piece of paper and every plate and die must be accounted for and locked away in the safes.

The time required for completing a sheet is about thirty days, each sheet consisting of four notes.

Specimens of the work of the Bureau are shown to visitors. A large case in the hall contains fac-similes of the various notes and bonds. In the waiting room are collections of the engravings used, and testimonials from the Vienna and Berlin Exhibitions of the excellence of the work of the Bureau.

THE SMITHSONIAN INSTITUTION.

The Smithsonian Building stands on a part of the public reservation denominated The Mall, situated between Seventh and Twelfth Streets and North B and South B Streets, the site being about twenty feet above the average level of Pennsylvania Avenue. The style of architecture is that of the last half of the twelfth century, and is generally known as the Norman. The semicircular arch, stilted, is employed throughout in doors, windows, and other openings. It is the first edifice in the style of the twelfth century ever erected in this country, and is universally conceded to be one of our finest specimens of architecture. The entire length of the building, from east to west, is four hundred and forty-seven feet, its greatest breadth one hundred and sixty feet. The east wing is eighty-two by fifty-two feet, the west wing eighty-four by forty, the main building two hundred and five by fifty-seven, and fifty-eight feet high. There are nine towers, the highest of which reaches an elevation of one hundred and fifty feet. The material employed is a red sandstone, found near the mouth of Seneca Creek, about twenty-three miles

THE SMITHSONIAN INSTITUTION.

north of Washington. The corner-stone was laid May 1, 1847, and the building completed in 1855. In January, 1865, a fire destroyed the interior of the upper story of the main building and the interior of the large north and south towers. These were, soon after, reconstructed in a fire-proof manner; and, in 1883, the entire interior of the east wing and range was removed and replaced with fire-proof materials.

The Smithsonian Institution, the chief American scientific establishment, known throughout the world by its researches, its publications, its collection and distribution of specimens of natural history, and its interchange of the works of scientific men, owes its name and origin to an Englishman, James Smithson, who died in Genoa,

Italy, in 1829, and who bequeathed the whole of his property "to the United States of America to found at Washington, under the name of the Smithsonian Institution, an establishment for the increase and diffusion of knowledge among men."

The first announcement made to the American Government of this bequest was in 1835, and it was communicated to Congress by President Jackson. After considerable discussion as to the propriety of the acceptance of the trust, an Act was passed in June, 1836, authorizing the President to appoint an agent to proceed to England to secure the gift for the United States. Hon. Richard Rush, of Pennsylvania, was appointed, who succeeded in 1838, after protracted litigation, in procuring a decree from the English Court of Chancery, by which the United States came into possession of the estate of Mr. Smithson, amounting to £104,960 8s. 6d. This amount was shipped in gold to the United States Mint in Philadelphia, where it was recoined into American money, yielding $508,318.46, and made a part of the funds of the Government. In 1864 a residuary legacy of Smithson was received amounting to $26,210.63. By savings of income, profitable investments of interest, etc., in 1867 an addition of $108,620.37 was made to the principal, which was still further increased in 1881 by the sale of Virginia stock, and in 1891, by a gift of $200,000 from Thomas G. Hodgkins, of Setauket, New York, so that the permanent fund now amounts to about $900,000. The principal of the bequest remains intact, the building, furniture, etc., having been paid for out of the income.

The proper disposition of the Smithson bequest was discussed by Congress for eight years, and various schemes were considered for accomplishing the words of the will—"The Increase and Diffusion of Knowledge among Men." Finally, in 1846, a bill was passed and the Institution organized.

It has an Honorary Board—"The Establishment"—consisting of the President, Vice-President of the United States, members of the Cabinet, the Chief Justice of the Supreme Court, and the Commissioner of Patents—which visits the Institution annually. The control and management of the Institution, however, is entrusted to a "Board of Regents," composed of fourteen persons—the Vice-President, the Chief Justice, three Senators, three members of the

THE SMITHSONIAN INSTITUTION. 117

House of Representatives, and six persons elected by Congress, no two being chosen from one State.

The administration of the Institution was entrusted at the outset, in 1846, to its Secretary, Professor Joseph Henry, of the College of New Jersey, who continued its chief executive officer till his death in 1878, when he was succeeded by Professor Spencer F. Baird, and on his death, in 1887, by Professor Samuel P. Langley.

As a testimonial of the high appreciation of the people of the United States for the great scientific achievements of Professor Henry, Congress, in 1880, voted an appropriation of $15,000 to erect a statue in his honor. It is a bronze figure of heroic size, and stands in the Smithsonian Grounds north of the western wing of the building. It was designed by the celebrated sculptor, William W. Story, and was unveiled on April 19, 1883, with appropriate ceremonies.

PROFESSOR JOSEPH HENRY.

The policy of the Institution is to initiate original plans for abstruse research, especially in lines not occupied by other organizations. It freely gives its publications and specimens without requiring an equivalent in return, and places its books, apparatus, and collections at the disposal of investigators and students in any part of the world. It has been the chief promoter of scientific exploration and investigation of the climate, products, and antiquities of the continent by the United States and State Governments, societies, and individuals.

The publications of the Institution consist of three series: "Contributions to Knowledge," "Miscellaneous Collections," and "Annual Reports."

It has a library of nearly one hundred thousand volumes deposited in the Library of Congress, to which large additions are made annually by means of its international exchanges with several thousand learned societies in all parts of the world.

On the first floor of the Smithsonian building, the main hall is devoted to the collection of Birds, and includes sixty thousand specimens, many of them to be found in no other museum in the world.

In this hall is also to be found the Conchological department, very extensive and important.

The Coral collection is one of great value and beauty, and represents many faunal regions. All the species from the fishing banks of eastern North America are represented. The Sponges include those from Florida, the Bahamas, and the Mediterranean, etc.

The colossal group "America," in terra-cotta, modelled by John Bell, Esq., is a full-sized reproduction of one of the corner-pieces of sculpture in marble which form part of the Albert Memorial in Hyde Park, London. It was presented by Henry Doulton & Co., London.

The celebrated panel of "Limoges faience," presented by Haviland & Co., composed of over nine hundred tiles, was designed and painted by M. Bracquemond. The picture is allegorical, and represents the genius of man utilizing the waters of the rebellious stream and storm, the fires of the volcano, and lightning, and making them the willing slaves of Progress. In the background is the town of Limoges, with its numerous potteries. The coloring of these tiles resembles that of an oil painting, and their effects are different from any heretofore produced with the same materials.

In the grand hall on the second floor, two hundred feet by fifty, are arranged the Archæological collections, without doubt the largest and most interesting in this country, and so far as relates to America the most extensive in the world. Here are to be seen all that illustrates the customs of early man, as shown by implements and other objects of stone, metal, bone, and earthenware, exhumed from graves, mounds, etc.

In the south hall are numerous relics of James Smithson, the Founder of the Institution.

THE NATIONAL MUSEUM,

Situated in The Mall, south-east of the Smithsonian Institution, was established by the Government, in 1846, by the Act of Congress transferring to the Smithsonian Institution the custody of the specimens collected by the Wilkes Exploring Expedition, which were on exhibition in the Patent Office. The transfer was not made, however, until 1858. The means for the support of the Museum are furnished by Congress.

The additions to the Museum consist of five classes : *First*, Those from the different Government expeditions, in accordance with the law of Congress. *Second*, Donations from private individuals, made either spontaneously or in response to special invitations and requests. *Third*, Results of exchanges with various establishments or individuals at home and abroad. *Fourth*, From explorations made at the expense of the Smithsonian Institution. *Fifth*, From purchase (which is very limited). It is in this that the National Museum differs from similar establishments throughout the world, which depend very largely upon purchases to secure desired materials.

All specimens of natural history, geology, mining, metallurgy, objects of aboriginal workmanship, ancient or modern, etc., belonging to the United States, are contained in this collection.

The Museum, however, is not merely a place of deposit for scientific material, but, by means of a thorough classification and the illustration of the history of human culture, it is destined to become the most comprehensive and instructive educational exhibit in the world.*

The building, commenced in April, 1879, and occupied in 1881, is in the form of a square, with sides of three hundred and twenty-seven feet extreme length and a central rotunda or dome. It contains underground basement rooms for a steam-heating apparatus, a steam-engine, coal vaults, etc.

On the main floor there are seventeen halls which freely communicate with one another by wide and lofty archways, furnishing eighty thousand three hundred square feet of floor space.

The centre of the building is octagonal on the ground, surmounted

---

* Some faint idea of the magnitude and importance of the collection may be gained from an estimate of the number of specimens in the different departments: Antiquities and ethnology, 650,000 ; mammals, 10,000 ; birds and eggs, 100,000 ; reptiles, 30,000 ; fishes, 100,000 ; mollusks, 425,000 ; insects, 600,000 ; ores and metals, 50,000 ; rocks and building stones, 50,000 ; minerals and metals, 70,000 ; marine invertebrates, 500,000 ; fossil invertebrates and plants, 500,000 ; **arts and industries,** 40,000.

by a sixteen-sided polygon of sixty-seven feet diameter, containing large windows, surmounted by a slate roof and lantern crowned by a decorated finial. This dome is seventy-seven feet high on the side walls, or one hundred and eight feet to the top of the finial.

The main entrances are in the centres of each façade between two towers eighty-six feet high which act as buttresses for the naves. Between the towers, above and receding from the doorways, are large arched windows set with ornamental glass. Over the gable of the north nave is an inscription stone—"National Museum, 1879,"

THE NATIONAL MUSEUM BUILDING.

and an allegorical group of statuary designed by C. Buberl, of New York, representing "Columbia as the Protectress of Science and Industry."

Pavilions are placed at the corners. In addition to the windows in the exterior walls, clere-story, and dome, lofty lanterns have been provided above the centres of the naves and square halls so as to afford perfect light for the interior.

All the masonry above ground is of red brick of superior quality, built hollow, with air-spaces for outside walls, ornamented and laid in black mortar for the facing of the exterior walls. To neutralize the monotony which would have been the effect of red-brick fronts of such extent, a number of buff and blue enamelled bricks were introduced. A base course of Richmond granite extends around the building. The wrought work of the main entrance, window-sills, inscription plates, copings, etc., are of the Euclid, Ohio, freestone.

The floor-beams, girders, and roofs are of iron; the floors are fire-proofed by brick arches and concrete. There are no less than thirty-seven roofs, laid upon fire-proofed gratings, as suggested by General Meigs. The slates are fastened to iron purlines. The window-sashes have double panes, giving an intermediate air-space.

The floors of the exhibition halls are of marble and tile, and those of the offices and smaller halls are of Florida pine. The interior is plastered in sand finish, washed in tints.

THE ARMY MEDICAL MUSEUM

Is in a large and handsome building at the corner of Seventh and B Streets, S. W. It is two hundred and forty by one hundred and thirty-five feet, with three stories and a basement. It was erected in 1887, from designs by Cluss and Schulze, and cost $200,000.

The Library, on the second floor, is the largest and best collection of medical works in the world, containing over two hundred thousand books and pamphlets. Some of these are exceedingly rare and valuable, and physicians from all parts of the country are constantly making use of this unrivalled collection.

The Museum contains exhibits illustrating the diseases to which soldiers are liable, the various operations of military surgery, and the casualties of the march and battle-field. There is also a large display of surgical instruments, both ancient and modern, and models of ambulances and hospital cars. Models of barracks, with all the modern sanitary improvements to prevent the spread of diseases to which large cantonments of soldiers are so liable, are also shown.

THE CORCORAN GALLERY OF ART,

Including ground, building, its contents, and endowment fund, is the gift of the late Mr. William Wilson Corcoran to the public. In his own words to the Trustees to whom the property was deeded May 10, 1869, "it was designed for the encouragement of the Fine Arts;" and in the deed the object of the institution is stated as "the perpetual establishment and encouragement of Painting, Sculpture, and the Fine Arts generally."

The institution was chartered by Act of Congress May 24, 1870. By that Act the building and its contents were declared exempt from all taxation.

The building was designed by Mr. James Renwick, architect, and begun in 1859, but before its completion the Civil War broke out and caused delays in the construction, so that all was not finished until 1871. In 1873 a Trustee went to Europe empowered to purchase works of art for the Gallery, and Mr. Corcoran's private collection of pictures and statuary was then placed in it.

On April 29, 1874, the Halls of Sculpture and of Bronzes were opened to the public, and in December, 1874, the two side galleries

THE CORCORAN GALLERY OF ART.

of Sculpture adjoining the main hall; so that all the rooms of the institution for exhibition purposes were then opened to the public.

The building stands on the north-east corner of Pennsylvania Avenue and Seventeenth Street, fronting one hundred and six feet on the Avenue and one hundred and twenty-five feet on Seventeenth Street. It is two stories in height, in the Renaissance style, built of brick, with brownstone facings and ornaments, a mansard roof rising ten feet, having a large central pavilion and a smaller one at each corner facing the streets. The front, under the main and corner pavilions, is divided into recesses by pilasters with foliated capitals, and is ornamented with wreaths, with the monogram of the founder, and over the central pavilion is the inscription: "Dedicated to Art."

In the central pediment is a large bronze medallion profile portrait of Mr. Corcoran, with decorations of foliage, and on the tops of the two columns are bronze groups of children holding garlands, and the emblems of Architecture and Music.

On the front of the building are four, and on the side seven, niches with statues seven feet high. The first group contains those of Phidias, Raphael, Michael Angelo, and Albert Dürer; the latter those of Titian, Da Vinci, Rubens, Rembrandt, Murillo, Canova, and Crawford. They were executed by M. Ezekiel, a native artist. The bronze medallion of Mr. Corcoran and the groups of children are also his works.

A pair of colossal bronze Lions, one at either side, rest upon the stone coping of the steps at the entrance to the building. These were cast from moulds made over the famous lions by Canova, at the tomb of Clement XIII., in St. Peter's, Rome.

On each side of the inner stairway a corridor, lighted from the open courts, leads to the vestibule of the main Hall of Sculpture, with which the vestibule communicates through three arched entrances. This hall, ninety-five by twenty-four feet, is lighted by windows on the north side, and opens into two adjoining galleries of Sculpture on the east side of the building and into the room containing the Tayloe Collection. On the west side it opens into the Hall of Bronzes, etc., sixty-two by nineteen feet. This last also communicates with the Trustees' room. The central portion of the ceiling of this hall, panelled and richly decorated, is supported by four Corinthian columns, with gilt capitals. The height of this story is nineteen feet nine inches.

The Picture Galleries are in the second story. The ascent to the main gallery is a notable feature of the building. The stairway leads to an upper landing, with decorated arched ceiling, and Corinthian pilasters dividing the arched recesses over the eight windows, with spaces between.

The main picture gallery is ninety-five by forty-four feet, with a height of twenty-four feet to the cornice of the arched ceiling, and thirty-eight feet to the inner skylight. The ceiling is richly frescoed and gilded. The scroll-work decoration is in the Italian style of the sixteenth century. In the middle of the panel opposite the main entrance is the figure of Minerva, and in the middle of the other panels the muses of Sculpture, Painting, and Architecture, all full length. Between them are medallion portraits of Giulio Romana, Titian, Raphael, Rubens, Van Dyck, Dürer, Michael Angelo, Holbein, Murillo, Cranach, Teniers, and Da Vinci. Between the brackets of the cornice are the names and dates of forty-six painters of different countries, from Cimabue to Fortuny. This decorative work was done by Mr. Vincenzo Stiepevich. All of the picture galleries are lighted from the roof, and supplied with ample electric lights for night exhibitions.

On the east and west sides of the building the main gallery opens into smaller ones, and these again into two corner galleries in the front of the building. Between the corner galleries, and immediately opposite the entrance to the main gallery, is the Octagon Room. It has a skylight, but is chiefly lighted by a south window, suitably screened, and contains a number of marble busts, with the "Greek Slave," by Hiram Powers, as the central ornament.

The Gallery is open every day (Sundays, the Fourth of July, and Christmas day excepted), from 10 A.M. to 4 P.M. from October 1st to May 1st, and from 9 A.M. to 4 P.M. from May 1st to October 1st. On other public holidays, from 10 A.M. to 2 P.M.

On holidays and Tuesdays, Thursdays, and Saturdays the attendance is free.

On Mondays, Wednesdays, and Fridays an admission fee of twenty-five cents is charged.

THE ORDNANCE MUSEUM.

On Seventeenth Street, opposite the State, War, and Navy Building, is the Ordnance Museum, under the control of the War Department. It contains a very large and interesting collection of military articles and many relics of the wars in which the United States have been engaged. Arms of all nations, both ancient and modern, and of all kinds, are exhibited here, the collection of those of America being very complete. Some of the weapons show that many ideas, supposed to be modern, were well understood by ancient artificers.

The Naval Observatory.

Notwithstanding its present high reputation and the great value of its scientific work, the Observatory had for many years a very hard struggle for existence. It had its beginnings as an adjunct of the Coast Survey, and for a long time it was almost impossible to get any appropriations for astronomical instruments. Even so late as 1842, it was known by the humble name of the " Depot," and its chief work lay in the regulation of chronometers for the Navy. The appearance of Encke's comet probably turned the scale in favor of the Observatory. Lieutenant Gilliss, then in charge, had read a paper on the subject before the National Institute. He had previously repeatedly urged upon the Naval Committee of Congress the necessity of appropriations for instruments, but had been unable to influence any of the members. When he made his last intended visit to the Senate Committee, Preston, of South Carolina, asked, "Are you the one who gave us notice of the comet? I will do all I can to help you." As a result, $25,000 was appropriated, though still " for a Depot of Charts and Instruments." The Secretary of the Navy, however, was no longer bound by the name, and the institution became known as the Observatory.

The Observatory is in the south-western part of the city, at Twenty-third and E Streets. The site was chosen by President Tyler, and is fraught with historic interest. It embraces the whole of " Reservation No. 4," made, by the old Commissioners for laying out the City of Washington, for a National University—a favorite idea of General Washington. It was the landing-place of Braddock, April 11, 1755. At a later day it was known as Camp Hill, from its being occupied by the American forces the day before their unfortunate advance and retreat from Bladensburg. The square embraces a little more than nineteen acres in measurement. It is now tastefully laid out and ornamented. Nearly central within it stands the building. It is on the second highest eminence within the city limits, commanding a view of the public buildings and also of Georgetown, Arlington, and Alexandria.

The Observatory is under the control of the Bureau of Navigation and contains many objects of interest. The chief is the great equatorial with its object-glass twenty-six inches in diameter. Its weight, with its mountings, is more than six tons, and it rests on a pier deeply sunk in the earth, in order to avoid all possible vibrations. The object-glass is the work of the famous Clarks, of Boston, and the instrument complete cost $47,000. It was by means of this telescope that Professor Hall, in 1877, discovered the two moons of Mars.

Under a smaller dome is the nine and one-half inch equatorial, used for minor observations. Through the centre of this dome passes the meridian of Washington.

Precisely at noon each day the time-ball is dropped from the flag-staff, giving the time to the city and the shipping on the river. The ball itself is a frame-work of oak ribs of two and a half feet in diameter. It is hoisted by halyards to the top of the flag-staff, the metal eye at the end of the rope passing over a steel spring, which is governed by a magnet. At the instant of noon the pressure on the key by the naval officer in the chronometer-room below breaks the electric circuit, the magnet above releases the metallic eye by the flying back of the spring, and the ball drops.

In the chronometer-room the work of regulating the chronometers of the Navy is done. As many as two hundred of these instruments have been here at one time. From this room *standard time* is furnished daily at noon to the Western Union Telegraph office in Washington for dispatch throughout the United States. The naval officer, standing by the standard mean clock, and having the astronomical correction of that clock also before him, at three minutes before 12 M. calls the telegraph operator at his office, and, at the instant of true noon, taps the electric key, giving the time to the company's office. He also drops the dome ball.

THE SIGNAL OFFICE,

Better known as the Weather Bureau, is in a brick building on G Street, between Seventeenth and Eighteenth, N. W. The numerous queer appliances on the roof show at once that work of some peculiar nature is done inside.

The Bureau is in charge of a Chief Signal Officer, and is a division of the Department of Agriculture. Previous to 1891 it was in charge of the Department of War. Besides the chief officer, there are, a chief clerk, a force of scientific experts, draughtsmen, and others, together with many clerks, copyists, messengers, etc. Throughout the United States there are about four hundred stations, each provided with the best instruments for the "Weather Service"—for observing and accurately recording the constant variations of the weather. From these stations telegraphic reports are sent daily to Washington.

The Signal Office receives reports from the trained observers three times in every twenty-four hours—at 7 A.M., 3 P.M., and at midnight. These reports contain full particulars of the weather in the different districts. Stations in Canada, in Newfoundland, and in other parts of British America, send reports; and, in the seasons of tropical storms, reports by telegraph are daily received from stations in the West Indies. Over three hundred voluntary observers also send reports by mail. The lines of the regular telegraph companies are used, and, besides, various military and sea-coast telegraph lines owned by the Government. The first synchronous weather reports were made on the first of November, 1870, and since then the service has reached a high state of perfection. The display of cautionary signals at American ports was begun in October, 1871.

The weather reports are telegraphed from the signal stations to Washington by means of a secret code, a few figures conveying a large amount of information. A "translator" takes the telegrams in hand and carefully reads them off to eight clerks, each of whom has a special weather map before him, on which he marks the particular readings he has been instructed to take. Afterward these eight maps are combined in one general map, which will fully represent all the phases of the weather in the United States and Canada at the hour the reports were sent. This map is closely studied by the assistant signal officer detailed for the purpose—the assistants alternating in the work, each one serving thirty days at a time—the "storm-centre" is located, the probable course of storms determined, and finally the "weather indications" are made up for the East and West, the North and South, and given to the agent of the Associated Press for transmission to the newspapers of the country.

The completed weather map, which is the finest of the kind issued in the world, is lithographed by the Signal Office, and copies of it are distributed every morning in the sections easily reached from

Washington. In order that the map may have a more extended circulation, certain parties in prominent cities East, West, and South are also charged with its publication by authority of the Agricultural Department, and the "plan of make-up" is telegraphed to them by an efficient system, which enables them to issue an exact copy of the map printed in Washington. Thus it is possible to obtain a weather map hundreds of miles from the Signal Office by noon of the day of its date.

THE GOVERNMENT PRINTING-OFFICE

Occupies the large four-story brick building at the corner of North Capitol and H Streets. It is three hundred by one hundred and seventy-five feet, enclosing a court-yard.

The office is the largest establishment of its kind in the world. The number of employés is nearly three thousand, and the annual expenditure about $3,000,000. It is in charge of an official known as the "Public Printer," who receives a salary of $4500.

All the work required in making a book, from the time the paper is received until the finished volume is issued, is done in this office. The principal employment is in printing the Government documents, such as the bills introduced into Congress and the many reports of the departments and institutions. Some of the special publications have been magnificent specimens of typographical art—issued at a cost of many thousands of dollars. A particularly fine work was "The Medical and Surgical History of the War of the Rebellion." It was printed on very costly paper, and contained a great number of superb illustrations. Requests to be supplied with it came from all the principal libraries of the world.

CHAPTER VI.

MINOR OBJECTS OF INTEREST—FORD'S THEATRE—THE NAVY YARD—THE CONGRESSIONAL CEMETERY—BENEVOLENT AND EDUCATIONAL INSTITUTIONS—THE LOUISE HOME—W. W. CORCORAN—THE COLUMBIA INSTITUTION FOR THE DEAF AND DUMB—THE GOVERNMENT HOSPITAL FOR THE INSANE—HISTORIC HOUSES.

THERE are a large number of objects in Washington that will repay the visitor for the time taken in their examination. Some of these are unique, and all have some particular feature distinguishing them from similar institutions elsewhere. These are scattered all over the city, and the visitor who endeavors to see them all will probably agree with Charles Dickens, that Washington is a city of magnificent distances.

The District Court-House is located in the southern portion of Judiciary Square, and is a building in the Grecian style of architecture. It was designed by George Hadfield, and was begun in 1820. It has never been finished as originally planned, only the southern portion having been completed. The material is brick covered with stucco. It is two stories in height, and has a frontage of two hundred and fifty feet. It was originally intended for the City Hall, and was occupied by the municipal officers until 1871. In 1873 the Government purchased it, and it is now used entirely for court purposes. Many famous trials have been held here, the most notable of recent years having been that of Guiteau, the assassin of President Garfield.

On Tenth, between E and F Streets, N. W., is a plain, unpretentious building that would hardly attract a moment's notice from the passer-by. It was, however, the scene of one of the greatest tragedies in the world's history. It was originally used as a church, but subsequently became known as Ford's Theatre. In this building, on the night of April 14, 1865, President Lincoln was assassinated by John Wilkes Booth. The theatre was at once closed by order of the Government, and, in 1866, was purchased by Congress for $100,000. It was used for storing the collections of the Army Medical Museum before the construction of the new build-

FORD'S THEATRE.

ing in The Mall. The entire interior was remodelled and made thoroughly fire-proof, and no trace of its former use now remains. It is at present used for office work by the Record and Pension Division of the War Department.

On the house opposite, No. 516, is a marble tablet. It was to this house that the wounded President was removed, and here he died, April 15, 1865.

After the burning of the public buildings by the British in 1814, Congress held its first session in Blodgett's "Great Hotel," where the Post-Office building now stands, and subsequently in a large brick building, erected by the citizens of Washington, on land adjacent to the eastern grounds of the Capitol, at the corner of Mary-

THE OLD CAPITOL PRISON. 131

land Avenue and First Street. This building has always been known as the "Old Capitol." John C. Calhoun died here March 31, 1850. During the Civil War it was used as a prison for Confederates. In the yard, Henry Wirz, the keeper of the Andersonville prison, was hanged for causing the death of several Union

THE OLD CAPITOL PRISON IN 1864.

soldiers by cruel and inhuman treatment, November 10, 1865. The building has been considerably reconstructed, and is now used for private purposes.

The Congressional Cemetery is at the foot of E Street, S. E. It was originally called the "Washington Parish Burial Ground," and was laid out in 1807 by residents of the eastern portion of the city. It afterwards came under the control of the vestry of Christ Church, but as Congress made liberal appropriations for its maintenance, it received the name of the "Congressional Cemetery." Many prominent men have been buried here, among the number being Vice-Presidents George Clinton, of New York, and Elbridge Gerry, of Massachusetts; and, also, Tobias Lear, for many years the private secretary and intimate friend of Washington. In the centre of the cemetery are numerous sandstone cenotaphs erected to the memory of deceased Congressmen. The grounds extend along the bank of the Anacostia and comprise an area of about fifty acres.

The Washington Navy Yard is at Eighth and M Streets, S. E. It was formally established by Act of Congress in 1804. It has always been one of the principal yards of the Government, and many of the finest vessels in the old navy were constructed here. Of late years it has been used chiefly for the manufacture of naval supplies. The Gun Foundry is one of the finest plants for making modern high-power guns in the world, and some of the recent productions have proved much superior to the work of foreign shops. In the Museum may be seen many curious objects pertaining to naval warfare, with relics of the wars of the United States, and guns captured from the enemy. Among these are bronze pieces taken from the Tripolitan pirates, a gun used by Cortez in the conquest of Mexico and captured by the United States forces in the Mexican War, and a mortar taken from Lord Cornwallis at Yorktown.

The Marine Barracks occupy the block between Eighth and Ninth and G and I Streets, S. E. The buildings are plain in appearance. Their chief interest is in the fact that they are the headquarters of the famous Marine Band. For many years the Band has made annual trips throughout the country, but most of the time it is at Washington. Concerts are given at the Barracks on certain afternoons, and in seasonable weather on the rear lawn of the White House.

The Naval Hospital is at the corner of Ninth and E Streets, S. E. It is for the benefit of the sick and disabled of the United States Navy and Marine Corps.

At Nineteenth and B Streets, S. E., on Reservation Thirteen, is the United States Jail. It was the place of confinement of Guiteau, the assassin of President Garfield, and here he was executed. The building is a substantial stone structure, erected at a cost of $400,000.

The Washington Barracks occupy a point of land at the junction of the Anacostia with the Potomac, at the southern end of Four and One-Half Street, W. The grounds comprise about seventy acres. There is a very fine Rifle Range where daily practice is carried on. The Guard House is of historic interest as being the place of confinement of Mrs. Surratt and the other conspirators implicated in the assassination of President Lincoln. Those condemned were hanged in front of the building. The body of Booth was brought to the wharf of the Barracks and buried for a time under one of the Guard Houses. The bodies of the other conspirators were also buried here, but all have since been removed.

The building of the United States Fish Commission is at the corner of Sixth and B Streets, S. W. Here, during the proper season, are shown the appliances and processes used in fish-hatching. This is only one of several stations maintained by the Government. The ponds for carp and other fish are in the Reservation lying north and west of the Washington Monument. The carp is one of the most valuable food fishes, and was imported from Europe by the Fish Commission a few years ago. The Commission endeavors to distribute a supply of this fish all over the country, and anyone owning a suitable pond will be supplied with the fish necessary for stocking it. The Commission distribute annually about four hundred thousand fish. Professor S. P. Langley, the Secretary of the Smithsonian Institution, is the Chief Commissioner.

The offices of the United States Coast and Geodetic Survey are in an imposing brick structure on New Jersey Avenue, between B and C Streets, S. E. Although erected for the office, the building is private property.

The object of the Coast Survey is the "survey of the coasts of the United States on tide-water." It was first instituted in 1807, and formally organized in 1833. Its work has been of the greatest importance to mariners, every foot of the difficult coast-line of the country having been carefully measured and represented on charts. As instruments become more perfect, the officials obtain better measurements and are able to correct the inaccuracies of former surveys. The United States standard weights and measures are kept in this building. The Coast Survey is a Bureau of the Treasury Department, but most of its work is done by naval officers, detailed for the duty, and by scientific men particularly qualified for special investigations.

There are numerous benevolent institutions in Washington, for most of which annual appropriations are made by the Government to assist them in their noble work. The City Orphan Asylum is at the corner of Fourteenth and S Streets, N. W. It was founded in 1815. Mrs. Madison was the first Directress and Mrs. Marcia

Van Ness the second. The Children's Hospital, on W Street, between Twelfth and Thirteenth Streets, N. W., was founded in 1871. It is supported mainly by voluntary contributions. St. Ann's Infant Asylum, at the corner of Twenty-fourth and K Streets, N. W., was founded in 1863. It is under the care of the Sisters of Charity. St. Joseph's Male Orphan Asylum, on H Street, between Ninth and Tenth Streets, N. W., was founded in 1855. It is managed by the Sisters of the Holy Cross. St. Vincent's Female Orphan Asylum, at the corner of Tenth and G Streets, N. W., was founded in 1831. It is under the care of the Sisters of Charity. St. John's Hospital for Children, on H Street, between Nineteenth and Twentieth Streets, N. W., is managed by the St. John's Sisterhood of the Protestant Episcopal Church. The National Soldiers' and Sailors' Orphan Home, on G Street, between Seventeenth and Eighteenth, N. W., was founded in 1866. The Garfield Memorial Hospital is at the north end of Tenth Street, N. W. The Freedmen's Hospital, at Fifth and Boundary, was originally intended for colored people, but of late years all classes of patients have been received. The Providence Hospital, at Second and D Streets, S. E., was founded in 1862. The non-resident poor who need medical attendance can receive it here. The Washington Asylum, at the end of C Street, S. E., was erected in 1859, and is for the poor of the District. The Home for the Aged, at Third and H Streets, N. E., is under the care of the Little Sisters of the Poor.

The Young Men's Christian Association occupies a handsome building on New York Avenue west of Fourteenth Street, N. W. A fine library and a free reading-room, well supplied with newspapers and periodicals, form an attractive feature.

The Government Hospital for the Insane, also known as St. Elizabeth's Asylum, is on a hill rising from the eastern bank of the Anacostia, about a mile from the city. It is intended especially for the insane of the Army and Navy, but also receives the insane of the District of Columbia. It is one of the finest hospitals in the world, the greatest care being taken in the selection of its physicians and attendants, and in all its appointments. The building was erected in 1855, at a cost of $1,000,000. The central portion is four stories in height, connecting wings giving a total length of seven hundred and fifty feet, while the width is two hundred feet. There are nearly six hundred rooms, giving accommodation for one thousand patients. The grounds comprise an area of more than

INSANE ASYLUM.

four hundred acres, very tastefully laid out. A magnificent view of the Capitol can be obtained from the western front.

"The Louise Home" is the name given to a noble institution, founded by Mr. William W. Corcoran in memory of his wife and daughter, both of whom bore the name. It is intended for gentlewomen who have met with reverses of fortune that would prevent their living comfortably in their old age. The building is on Massachusetts Avenue, between Fifteenth and Sixteenth Streets, the grounds covering an entire square. It is a handsome brick structure four stories high, with a mansard roof. A large central pavilion with a lofty pyramidal roof gives a fine appearance to the front. The interior is furnished with great taste, and all the appointments are elegant in design and finish. The Home has accommodations for fifty-five inmates, and is managed by a board of nine trustees, all ladies. It has an endowment fund of $250,000, and was erected in 1871 at a cost of $200,000.

Mr. William W. Corcoran was long a notable figure in Washington society, not merely from his great wealth, but on account of the philanthropic use he made of it. He was born at Georgetown, December 27, 1798, and was always a citizen of the District of Columbia. He began his business career as a clerk in a drygoods establishment, but subsequently relinquished this position in order

W. W. CORCORAN.

to enter into the banking business, forming a partnership with George W. Riggs. The firm of Riggs and Corcoran dealt extensively in Government loans during the period of the Mexican War, and became very wealthy.

In 1835, Mr. Corcoran married Miss Louise Morris, the daughter of Commodore Morris. She died in 1840, leaving a son and daughter, but the former did not survive childhood. His daughter, named Louise from her mother, grew to womanhood, and married Hon. George Eustis, a member of Congress from Louisiana. She died at Cannes, France, in 1867, leaving three children.

Mr. Corcoran was always a public-spirited citizen, and he gave freely of his large means to every noble enterprise. His name will be remembered chiefly, however, from connection with the Art Gallery he established and endowed, and the Louise Home.

He died February 24, 1888, in the ninetieth year of his age.

Washington is supplied with some of the finest educational institutions in the country, and will probably, at no distant day, become the literary centre of the United States.

Columbian University is one of the leading institutions of the city. It was incorporated as a college in 1821, and for many years occupied a building on Meridian Hill, a short distance beyond the northern boundary-line of Washington. In 1873 it was incorporated as a University, and, in 1884, it removed to a fine new building on the corner of Fifteenth and H Streets, N. W. This building is four stories high, constructed of fine pressed brick with terra-cotta ornamentation. It has a frontage of one hundred and twenty feet on Fifteenth Street and sixty-five on H Street. The Medical School holds its sessions in a handsome building on H Street, near Fourteenth. This was the gift of Mr. W. W. Corcoran, erected at the cost of $40,000.

Beyond the boundary-line of the city, at the junction of Seventh and M Streets, N. E., on a beautiful tract of about one hundred acres, known as Kendall Green, are the buildings of the Columbia Institution for the Deaf and Dumb. The Institution was incorporated by Congress in 1857, being intended for the education of the deaf-mute children of the District of Columbia. The originator was Amos Kendall, Postmaster-General from 1835 to 1840. Becoming interested in the unfortunate children so shut off from their fellows, he donated some ground and a small wooden building as a school. He secured as a teacher Edward M. Gallaudet, a son of Dr. Thomas H. Gallaudet, of Hartford, Connecticut, the first instructor of the deaf and dumb in America. The support of the institution was mainly provided by Mr. Kendall, and, in 1859, he erected a brick building for its accommodation. The work gradually attracted the attention of the country, scholarships were endowed by prominent citizens, and, in 1864, Congress established a collegiate department, to be called the National Deaf-Mute College, for the benefit of students from all parts of the United States. In 1872, Congress purchased the whole of Kendall Green for $85,000.

The work performed by the institution has given it a very high rank, and its graduates have distinguished themselves in numerous professions. The studies in the collegiate department embrace Latin, French, and German, the higher mathematics, the natural sciences, philology, history, etc.

The buildings form a picturesque and interesting group. The central one, in the pointed Gothic style, was erected in 1871. It is two hundred and sixteen feet long and seventy-six feet wide, constructed of brownstone with occasional courses of white sandstone. The other buildings are artistically constructed and are well adapted to their purposes. The chapel presents a very attractive sight. The grounds are beautifully laid out. The value of the property is about $500,000.

Howard University is located on a hill near the northern boundary-line of Washington, adjacent to the extension of Seventh Street. This famous institution, which was named after its first President, General Oliver O. Howard, was founded in 1867, and was intended to afford to the colored race facilities for acquiring a higher education. It is, however, open to all, without distinction in regard to sex or race. Besides the ordinary school and college courses, there are departments of law, medicine, and theology. Tuition is free, except in the higher departments, where a small fee is charged. There is a fine library of over ten thousand volumes, and an interesting museum. The buildings are large and well adapted to their purpose, and are surrounded by extensive grounds. The total value of the property is $700,000. Congress appropriates annually about $35,000 for the support of the University.

Wayland Seminary, on Meridian Hill, west of Fourteenth Street, was established in 1867. It is for the education of young colored men who design to enter the ministry, and is under the care of the American Baptist Home Mission Society. The building is a handsome structure, costing $35,000, and has accommodations for two hundred students.

An important Catholic educational institution is the Convent of the Visitation, or, as it is sometimes called, the Academy of the Visitation, occupying the entire block on Connecticut Avenue, between L and M Streets, N. W. It is an offshoot from the famous convent in Georgetown, the "mother" community of the order of the Nuns of the Visitation in the United States. The present building was occupied in 1877. It is a large and beautiful structure, surrounded by spacious grounds enclosed by a brick wall. It forms an attractive feature in a beautiful quarter of the city.

Gonzaga College, conducted under the auspices of the fathers of the Society of Jesus, is on I Street, between North Capitol and First Streets, N. W. It was founded in 1848, and incorporated as a university in 1858.

The Masons have been represented in Washington from an early date, a lodge being established shortly after the foundation of the city. A second lodge was formed in 1816, and since that time the growth of the order has been steady and substantial. There are more than twenty lodges, with a membership exceeding three thousand. The various lodges, chapters, and commanderies hold their meetings in the Masonic Temple, a handsome edifice at the corner of Ninth and F Streets, N. W. The building is constructed of granite and Nova Scotia freestone, and was erected in 1863, at a cost of $200,000. The ground-floor is used for stores, the upper stories being reserved for the purposes of the order. On the second floor is a fine hall, often used for holding public balls and receptions. The rooms used by the members are very handsomely furnished, and are decorated with the various mystic insignia of the different lodges and commanderies.

The Odd Fellows own a fine building on Seventh, between D and E Streets, N. W. It is constructed of brick and iron, with a balcony on the front and three domes on the roof, presenting a very pleasing appearance. The rooms on the ground-floor are rented to merchants, while those above are occupied by the lodges and encampments. The membership of the order numbers over two thousand, and is rapidly increasing, and its affairs are in a very prosperous condition.

Some of the houses erected at an early date are still standing. On North Carolina Avenue, southeast of the Capitol, is Duddington Manor-House, built by Daniel Carroll when he thought the sale of his city lots would bring him such vast wealth. It was considered a grand mansion in its day, although it would attract but little attention now. It is surrounded by stately trees, enclosed by a high wall. Carroll's descendants still have possession of the property.

The famous Van Ness Mansion, at the foot of Seventeeth Street, near the Potomac, is fast going to ruin. It was constructed by Latrobe, the architect of the Capitol, and was famous in the first quarter of the century for its grandeur and the magnificent entertainments given within its walls. Its portico gives it something of a resemblance to the White House. The old cabin of David Burns, from which he refused to remove even after he acquired his great wealth, was untouched by his daughter, and is still standing, although in the last stages of decay. Years ago the last acre of the old Burns property had passed out of the hands of the family. There is a legend, devoutly believed in by the negroes, that on each anniversary of the death of Van Ness, his favorite "troop of six white horses," but without their heads, takes a ghostly gallop around the walls of the deserted mansion.

On New York Avenue, at Eighteenth Street, N. W., is the "Octagon House," a noteworthy old mansion, built by Colonel John Tayloe, in 1798. Tayloe was a wealthy Virginia planter, and invested largely in Washington real estate, thereby acquiring an immense fortune. During the reconstruction of the White House, after its destruction by the British in 1814, Presidents Madison and Monroe resided in the Octagon House.

CHAPTER VII.

THE ENVIRONS OF WASHINGTON—BLADENSBURG—THE CATHOLIC UNIVERSITY—
THE SOLDIERS' HOME—ZOÖLOGICAL PARK—THE NEW NAVAL OBSERVATORY—
OAK HILL CEMETERY—GEORGETOWN—THE COLLEGE—RESERVOIRS—CABIN-
JOHN BRIDGE—THE GREAT FALLS OF THE POTOMAC—ANALOSTAN ISLAND—
ARLINGTON AND ITS OWNERS—THE MILITARY CEMETERY—ALEXANDRIA.

NO visit to Washington is complete unless it includes an examination of the environs of the city. Apart from the many objects of historical interest, the trip presents attractions in the great beauty of the scenery, which is so varied that even residents of the city never cease to feel its charms.

About five miles north-east from Washington is the quaint, old-fashioned town of Bladensburg, Maryland, which was founded in 1750, and named after Thomas Bladen, who was Governor of Maryland in 1742. Before the Revolutionary War it had considerable commerce, and many vessels laden with tobacco sailed from its wharves down the Anacostia. For a number of years it was a fashionable summer resort, as it had a mineral spring reputed to be efficacious in the cure of numerous diseases, and throngs of people went to drink of the water. Near the town the British troops defeated the Americans, August 24, 1814, and then invaded Washington. During the first half of the century Bladensburg was noted as a duelling ground, and on its fields many prominent men have fought to satisfy their "honor." The memorable duel between Commodore Decatur and Commodore Barron took place near the ancient cemetery of the town, on March 22, 1820. Decatur was fatally wounded, and died that night at his residence in Washington. For nearly thirty years no duels have been fought in this locality. The old town long since lost its commerce, its thrift, and enterprise. It has a picturesque location, and is one of the most pleasant environs of Washington.

North of the city, on the Rock Creek Road, some three miles from the Capitol, is the Soldiers' Home, a delightful retreat for aged and invalid private soldiers of the regular Army and veterans of the Mexican War. The grounds comprise about five hundred acres of beautiful diversified hill and dale, to which the public has free access at all times. There are more than seven miles of broad, well-made drives, shaded by gigantic oaks with luxuriant foliage. Silvery lakes are interspersed with stretches of meadow, and picturesque arbors on the hills give charming prospects of the landscape for miles around, while pretty villas and statuary add to the beauty of the scene.

The Soldiers' Home was founded in 1851, at the suggestion of General Winfield Scott. Congress appropriated $119,000—the

THE SOLDIERS' HOME.

balance of the indemnity paid by the City of Mexico to ransom the city from pillage for violation of the truce—as a fund towards the establishment and maintenance of the institution. This has been augmented by a tax of twelve cents a month on the pay of privates of the regular Army, and the money received from fines, forfeitures of pay, etc. The fund also receives the unclaimed pay of deceased soldiers, and the total derived from all these sources amounts to nearly $2,000,000. Soldiers of the regular Army who have served faithfully for twenty years, or who have become disabled during service, are entitled to a residence in the Home for the remainder of their lives. The number of inmates is usually about six hundred. They are under a very mild discipline, are generously provided for while well, and tenderly nursed when sick. The greater part of the work about the Home and grounds is done by the more able-bodied of the inmates, liberal compensation being paid for their labor. The Home is in charge of a Superintendent, and is conducted under the supervision of a board of Army officers, at the head of which is the General in command of the Army.

The main building is of white marble, and has a frontage of two hundred feet, with a wing of sixty feet, and a tall central tower. It is three stories in height, and is fashioned after the Norman order of architecture. On the grounds are several elegant marble cottages occupied by the officials, a pretty church of Seneca stone, a capacious hospital building with wide piazzas, from which charming views of Washington and the Potomac can be had, a fine library building, well stocked with books and periodicals, and numerous other structures. On the brow of one of the hills stands a bronze statue of General Scott, by Launt Thompson, erected in 1874, at a cost of $18,000. The entire estate is enclosed by a low stone wall, surmounted by a small iron fence of handsome design. Fifty acres are under cultivation, and fine crops of fruits and vegetables are raised.

Near the main building is a large cottage often used by the Presidents of the United States as a summer residence. It is surrounded by noble trees, and has a very attractive appearance. Pierce was the first President to pass the summer here, and Buchanan, Lincoln, Johnson, Hayes, and Arthur have preferred its quiet comfort to the statelier life in the White House.

South of the Home lie the pretty grounds of Glenwood Cemetery, containing some fine monuments. To the west of the cemetery is the large new reservoir, supplied by mains from the distributing basin at Georgetown.

The Catholic University of America owns a property comprising about sixty-five acres, east of the grounds of the Soldiers' Home, at the junction of Lincoln and Bunker Hill Roads. The building for the Divinity Department was completed in 1889, from designs by E. F. Baldwin, of Baltimore. It is a handsome structure of bluestone, two hundred and seventy feet long, and one hundred and ten feet deep. The central portion is five stories in height, and the rest

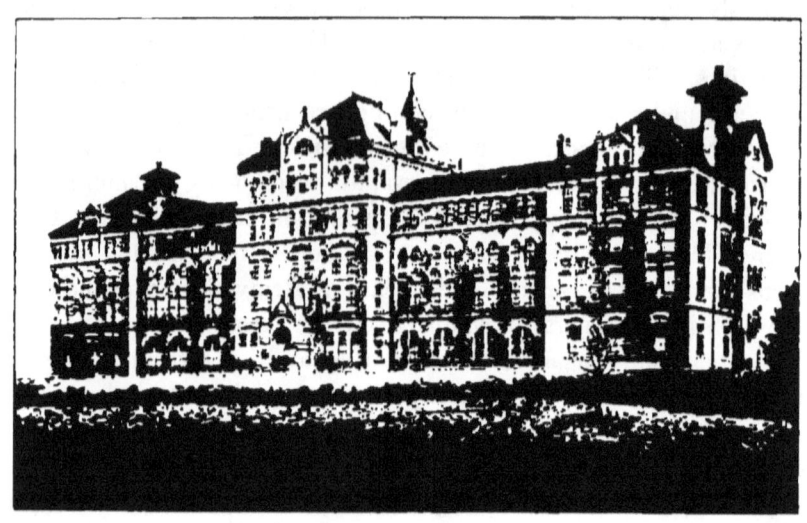

THE CATHOLIC UNIVERSITY.

of the building four stories. There are commodious dormitories and spacious halls for class-rooms and for recreation purposes. There is a beautiful chapel in the rear of the central structure.

North of the Home is the National Military Cemetery, containing the graves of more than five thousand of the soldiers of the Civil War. In the granite Memorial Chapel rest the remains of Major-General John A. Logan.

West of the Cemetery is Rock Creek Cemetery, belonging to St. Paul's Episcopal Church. This is the oldest church in the District, having been erected, in 1719, of bricks imported from England. Although remodelled in 1815, and again in 1868, the original walls are still standing.

The new National Park lies about two miles north-west of the city, and contains nearly two thousand acres. The ground was purchased by the Government, in 1890, for $1,200,000. It is being rapidly improved, and will soon become one of the most beautiful pleasure-grounds in the country. Lying on both sides of picturesque

Rock Creek, its natural features give rare facilities to the landscape gardener to produce varied and beautiful scenes.

South of the Park are the grounds of the new Zoölogical Gardens, containing about one hundred and seventy acres. Congress purchased the property in 1889, at a cost of $175,000. It is proposed to make this the finest establishment of its kind in the country, and suitable buildings are being rapidly erected to contain the valuable collections belonging to the Government.

About one mile west of the Zoölogical Park, on the Georgetown and Rockville Pike, is "Oak View," the charming summer residence purchased by Grover Cleveland, while President of the United States.

A short distance north of Georgetown, near the Rockville Pike, and on the line of the extension of Massachusetts Avenue, are the grounds of the new Naval Observatory. The tract comprises about seventy acres, and affords an extensive view of the city and surrounding country. A better location for a great observatory could hardly be desired. The land was purchased by Congress, in 1881, at a cost of $72,000. The buildings, when completed, will cost nearly $800,000. They are being very carefully constructed from designs by Richard M. Hunt, of New York. The chief material is white marble, from the Tuckahoe quarries on the Hudson. The main building is three hundred and ten feet from east to west, with a depth of seventy feet. At the eastern end is the dome for the great equatorial, having a radius of twenty-three feet.

When it is considered how great was the difficulty in procuring the sanction of the Government for the first establishment of the Observatory, and the long struggle necessary to obtain money for instruments, the liberal appropriations for the new buildings show how well the labors of the astronomers are now appreciated by the people.

Immediately north of Georgetown is Oak Hill Cemetery. The grounds comprise about twenty-five acres, lying along the western bank of Rock Creek, and are beautifully laid out in a series of terraces. Half of the property, together with the sum of $90,000, was given by the generous philanthropist, W. W. Corcoran. There are several fine mausoleums, notable ones being those of the Corcoran and Van Ness families. Many distinguished persons are buried in the cemetery, among them being Chief Justice Chase, Bishop Pinckney, General Eaton, Secretary Stanton, Professor Joseph Henry, and Rear-Admiral John Rogers. Near the chapel rest the mortal remains of John Howard Payne, the author of " Home, Sweet Home." Payne was American Consul at Tunis, and died there, April 9, 1852. Mr. Corcoran bore the expense of having the body brought home, and it was interred here, with suitable ceremonies, June 9, 1883 —the ninety-first anniversary of the poet's birth.

PAYNE MONUMENT.

An Act passed by the Maryland Legislature, in 1751, authorized the laying out of " Georgetown, on the Potomac, above the mouth of Rock Creek," but the town was not incorporated until 1789. Some have thought it was named from George II., the then King of England. Others derive the name from George, the son of Ninian Beall, the original holder of patents for the land on the " Rock of Dumbarton," on which much of the town is built. It is now, however, consolidated with the city, and is called West Washington, although it will probably always be known by its original name.

Georgetown lies on the western border of Rock Creek, and is connected with the city by several bridges. The land rises rapidly as it recedes from the Potomac and Rock Creek. There are several fine old mansions belonging to the early days of Washington, as well as handsome modern dwellings, for the suburb has always been a favorite abode for those doing business in the city. An important institution is the Convent of the Nuns of the Visitation, at Thirty-fifth and P Streets, founded in 1799, the " mother " community of the order in the United States. A daughter of General Scott, a religieuse of the order, was buried in the vault of the Convent.

The most important institution is the College of the Jesuits, or Georgetown College, the oldest Roman Catholic College in the country. It is situated on a hill west of the town, its grounds comprising about one hundred and seventy acres, and possessing many places of beauty. The old building was erected in 1792, but proved so inadequate to the growing needs of the College, that in 1877 the present magnificent structure, on the north side of the quadrangle, one of the finest of its kind in the United States, was erected at a cost of $200,000. The style is known as Rhenish-Romanesque, frequently used by the Jesuits in Europe, and is peculiarly well adapted to educational institutions. Its high stories and lofty towers give it an imposing appearance, greatly enhanced by its commanding situation.

The College was founded by the Rt. Rev. John Carroll, the first Catholic Bishop of Baltimore. It was raised to the dignity of a University in 1815. The library is very valuable, containing many rare and ancient works, some dating from the fifteenth century. The museum contains many articles of great value, among which are a fine collection of coins made by Commodore Decatur, and various personal relics. An article of great interest is the dining-table of Lord Baltimore, around which he and the Council of Maryland frequently sat while discussing the affairs of the Colony.

At the head of Market Street is the High Service Reservoir, having a capacity of one million gallons. It is two hundred and fifteen feet above tide-water, and seventy feet higher than the Distributing Reservoir. It is supplied by a pumping station at the Washington Aqueduct Bridge.

Leading north-west from Georgetown, along the course of the Potomac, is the Conduit Road, so called because following the route of the aqueduct from the Great Falls of the Potomac. About one mile out is the Distributing Reservoir. It has an elevation of one hundred and fifty feet, and an area of nearly thirty-five acres, with a capacity of three hundred million gallons. The mains leading to the various parts of the city begin here. The supply is received through a nine-foot conduit leading from the Great Falls. Two miles further is the Receiving Reservoir, with a capacity of one hundred and sixty million gallons. Three miles beyond this is the famous Cabin-John Bridge, crossing the creek of that name, and carrying the aqueduct. It has the longest single arch of masonry in the world, having a clear span of two hundred and twenty feet, with a rise of fifty-seven feet. The length of the bridge is four hundred feet.

Fifteen miles above Washington are the Great Falls of the Potomac. The river rises in the Alleghany Mountains, and its

CABIN-JOHN BRIDGE.

volume is swelled by several affluents on its course to the sea. At Harper's Ferry it bursts through the barrier of the Blue Mountains, and, rushing on in its impetuous course, about fifty miles below meets another barrier in a great granite wall. Hurling itself over this, it makes a fall of forty feet, and then continues in a series of cascades, falling through a vertical height of eighty feet in a distance of two miles. Six miles above Georgetown are the Little Falls, a series of cascades. Thenceforward its passage is calm and uninterrupted. Three miles below is the Chain Bridge. The original bridge at this place was supported by chains, and although several of different design have since successively taken its place, the name has always been retained.

The Chesapeake and Ohio Canal follows the course of the river in its northern bank. It was constructed for the transport of grain and coal from the West, and was a work of vast magnitude. It extends to Cumberland, Maryland, and has a total length of one hundred and eighty-two miles. The canal was chartered in 1784, and constructed as far as the Great Falls. In 1828, work was resumed, the intention being to continue it to Pittsburg, but Cumberland was finally selected as the terminus. The total cost was $13,000,000.

A fine view of the river scenery can be obtained by driving along the River Road from the Great Falls to Georgetown.

From Georgetown the Aqueduct Bridge crosses the Potomac just above the head of Analostan Island. The Island was the scene of famous hospitality in days gone by. It was the home of John Mason. Commodious grounds were laid out with stately trees and rare and beautiful plants. Among the curiosities was a kind of maize, with beautiful purple flowers, from which was procured a brilliant dye. Some of the seeds were carried to France and presented to the Empress Josephine. She sowed them with her own hand in her garden at Malmaison, where they flourished luxuriantly.

General Mason was noted for his hospitality, and entertained all the distinguished visitors to Washington.

Mr. Mason, the Commissioner of the Confederate States to Europe, who, with Mr. Slidell, was captured by Captain Wilkes, was born on Analostan Island.

About one mile south of the Aqueduct Bridge is the historic estate of Arlington, long famous as the home of the Custis and Lee families, and made sacred as the final resting-place of thousands of brave soldiers who gave to their country "the last full measure of devotion." Besides its past and present associations, Arlington possesses great attractions for the visitor in the rare beauty of its scenery, and thousands of strangers yearly visit the lovely place.

The estate is on the Virginia side of the Potomac, directly opposite the city, and lying south-west of the White House. It comprises about twelve hundred acres. It was purchased for £11,000 by John Custis, the father-in-law of Martha Washington, early in the eighteenth century, and named from his home on the Eastern shore.

John Custis was quite a celebrated character in the Colonial days of the Old Dominion. He belonged to one of the first families of Virginia, and was very wealthy, owning much other property besides Arlington. He was very unfortunate in his marriage, espousing the daughter of Colonel Daniel Parke, celebrated for her beauty, and also for an exceedingly bad temper. His wife soon died, however, and the widower could scarcely restrain his joy at his release. But she left a son and a daughter, who soon made him realize that the joys of bachelorhood had forever departed. The daughter married, against her father's wish, an officer in the English army. The son refused to accept his father's choice of a bride, and insisted on marrying Martha Dandridge, the belle of Williamsburg. Old John Custis was furious, threatening to disinherit his son; but having, at some Colonial assembly, met the young lady, he became so fascinated by her beauty and the grace of her manner, that he vowed that if his son did not marry her, he would—such a treasure should not go out of the family.

Daniel Parke Custis married Martha Dandridge and lived on the White House Farm on the Pamunkey. At his father's death he inherited the Arlington estate. The will directed the son, under severe penalties, to have placed on the father's tomb the following inscription:

"Beneath this Marble Tomb lies ye body
of the Honorable John Custis, Esq.,
of the City of Williamsburg and Parish of Burton,
Formerly of Hungars Parish on the Eastern Shore of
Verginia, and the County of Northampton the
place of his Nativity.
Aged 71 years and yet lived but seven years
Which was the space of time he kept
A Bachelor's House at Arlington
On the Eastern Shore of Verginia."

Daniel Custis lived happily at Arlington until his death, at the age of thirty-five, leaving to the care of his widow two children—a boy and a girl. The boy, John Parke Custis, was to inherit Arlington, while the White House estate went to the girl. His widow received property to the value of $100,000, making her the wealthiest woman in Virginia. After the period of her mourning was over, while visiting some Virginia friends, she met a young officer of the Virginia militia, who had greatly distinguished himself during Braddock's campaign, Colonel George Washington. It seemed a clear case of mutual love at first sight, and so great was Washington's infatuation that it is on record that he forgot the calls of duty, and overstayed his time several hours.

ARLINGTON HOUSE.   151

After their marriage, they resided at Mount Vernon, which Washington had lately inherited from his half-brother. The two Custis children resided with them, their estates being carefully looked after by Colonel Washington.

John Parke Custis married a member of the Calvert family of Maryland. He was present at the siege of Yorktown as aide-de-camp to his step-father, but died shortly after, leaving two children— George Washington Parke Custis and Nelly Custis. They were

ARLINGTON HOUSE.

formally adopted by Washington, but always retained their family name. Nelly Custis grew up to be a most beautiful woman. She married Major Lawrence Lewis, of Virginia. Her brother, on reaching his majority, took possession of Arlington, vastly increased in value through the prudent care of Washington.

He immediately began the erection of the present mansion, desiring a house in keeping with his great estate. It presents a fine appearance, its pillared front looming up grandly from the summit of the hill.

Arlington House consists of a central building sixty feet long, with a portico of eight Ionic columns, modelled after the celebrated temple at Pæstum, near Naples. There are two wings, each forty feet long, giving an entire frontage of one hundred and forty feet. In the rear are the slave quarters, kitchens, stables, etc. It is constructed of brick, covered with stucco.

George Washington Parke Custis married Mary Lee Fitzhugh, whose mother was a Randolph. Of his four children, all girls, but one survived infancy. Custis lived at Mount Vernon until his death, in 1857. As the adopted son of Washington, he was always held in affectionate esteem by his countrymen.

His only surviving child, Mary Randolph Custis, married, in 1832, the playmate of her childish years, Lieutenant Robert Edward Lee, the youngest child of Governor Henry Lee, the intimate friend and eulogist of Washington. The married pair lived an ideally happy life at Arlington until the outbreak of the Civil War. When

THE MILITARY CEMETERY.

Colonel Lee departed from Arlington to take service in the Confederate army, the mansion had a large number of relics of Washington, bequeathed by Mrs. Washington to her grandson Custis, and by him removed from Mount Vernon to Arlington. As the family thought their retirement would be but temporary, these were not removed, but were left in charge of the servants; and when, shortly after, the house was seized by the Federal troops, the relics were all confiscated and are now in the National Museum at Washington. As the estate was entailed on the eldest son of Mrs. Lee, it could not be confiscated, but was sold for arrears of taxes and purchased by the Government for $26,800, in 1864. The sale was subsequently set aside as illegal by the Supreme Court of the United States, and the property was decided to belong to the heir, George Washington Custis Lee. As a military cemetery had been established there since 1864, Mr. Lee proposed a compromise with the Government, and transferred to it all his right and title to the estate for the sum of $150,000.

The portion of Arlington set apart for the Cemetery, comprising about two hundred acres, borders on the Georgetown and Alexandria road. The grounds are surrounded by a low wall. The many magnificent oaks, some of them two hundred years old, and the rich lawns, studded with beds of gleaming flowers, and intersected by the carefully kept paths and drives, present a scene of surpassing beauty.

TOMB OF THE UNKNOWN DEAD.

At the main entrance is a marble arch adorned with lofty columns taken from the old War Department building. On three of them are the names of Scott, Lincoln, and Stanton.

The portion of the Cemetery lying west of the house is devoted to the white soldiers, that on the northern side is allotted to the black soldiers. In front of the house is the tomb of General Philip H. Sheridan.

The thousands of plain white headstones, stretching far away into the distance, form a most impressive sight. Contrary to the usual custom in cemeteries, the ground is perfectly flat, none of the ordinary mounds over the graves being seen.

South of the mansion is a large granite monument, over a vault in which lie the remains of the "Unknown Dead." It is surrounded by cannon and piles of shot, and bears the following inscription:

BENEATH THIS STONE
REPOSE THE BONES OF TWO THOUSAND ONE HUNDRED AND ELEVEN UNKNOWN SOLDIERS
GATHERED AFTER THE WAR
FROM THE FIELDS OF BULL RUN AND THE ROUTE TO THE RAPPAHANNOCK.
THEIR REMAINS COULD NOT BE IDENTIFIED BUT THEIR NAMES AND DEATHS ARE
RECORDED IN THE ARCHIVES OF THEIR COUNTRY, AND ITS GRATEFUL CITIZENS
HONOR THEM AS OF THEIR NOBLE ARMY OF MARTYRS. MAY THEY REST IN PEACE.
SEPTEMBER, A.D. 1866.

The total number of bodies interred in the Cemetery is over sixteen thousand, nearly one thousand more than are at Gettysburg. In the mansion are books in which are kept careful records of the name and description of every soldier who was known, together with the date of his death and the position of his grave.

Large iron frames on the borders of the burial-fields contain selections from the beautiful poem by Colonel Theodore O'Hara, read at the dedication of the Soldiers' Monument at Frankfort, Kentucky. O'Hara fought in both the Mexican and Civil Wars. He was a journalist as well as a poet, and was for some time editor of the *Mobile Register*. He died at Columbus, Georgia, in 1867.

The poem, entitled "The Bivouac of the Dead," is as follows:

"The muffled drum's sad roll has beat
   The soldier's last tattoo!
No more on life's parade shall meet
   That brave and fallen few.
On Fame's eternal camping-ground
   Their silent tents are spread,
And glory guards with solemn round
   The bivouac of the dead.

"No rumor of the foe's advance
   Now swells upon the wind,
Nor troubled thought at midnight haunts
   Of loved ones left behind.
No vision of the morrow's strife
   The warrior's dream alarms,
No braying horn, no screaming fife
   At dawn shall call to arms.

"The neighing troop, the flashing blade,
   The bugle's stirring blast,
The charge, the dreadful cannonade,
   The din and shout are past.
Nor war's wild notes, nor glory's peal
   Shall thrill with fierce delight
Those breasts that never more may feel
   The rapture of the fight.

"Rest on, embalmed and sainted dead!
   Dear is the blood you gave—
No impious footsteps here shall tread
   The herbage of your grave;
Nor shall your glory be forgot
   While Fame her record keeps,
Or Honor points the hallowed spot
   Where Valor proudly sleeps."

In the eastern grounds of the west cemetery are the tombs of George Washington Parke Custis and his wife, bearing their names and the dates of their deaths.

A short distance north-west of Arlington is Fort Myer. It was constructed during the Civil War for the defence of Washington, and is the only one remaining of the great circle of fortifications. It is now used as a cavalry station.

ALEXANDRIA.

The city of Alexandria lies on the Virginia side of the Potomac, about six miles below Washington. It was founded in 1748, under the name of Belhaven, and is especially interesting from its connection with the daily life of the " Father of his Country." Elsewhere the great chief is on horseback, or sits high in some chair of state, lofty and removed from common men; but in Alexandria he is dismounted and afoot—a townsman and neighbor.

The town rapidly became a place of considerable commercial importance, and, at one time, it was expected to out-trip Baltimore as a great port. A semi-weekly newspaper, called the *Columbian Mirror and Alexandria Gazette*, was established in 1792, and was for many years the only newspaper published in this part of the country.

Washington's connection with Belhaven or Alexandria began when he was quite a boy. He had given up his idea of going to sea as a midshipman, and was beginning the study of surveying, being employed to explore the wild lands belonging to Lord Fairfax. He was living at Mount Vernon, the residence of his brother, and tradition says that he came into Alexandria ten times during one week, each time riding a different horse, any one of which would have delighted the soul of a cavalryman. Washington took great interest in training the militia of the town, and many of its people accompanied him on his march against Fort Du Quesne.

After Washington had married and inherited Mount Vernon, he grossly shocked " society " by sending in a market-cart, to dispose of the produce of his estate.

Washington became a trustee of the town in 1766, and devoted much time to its affairs. He was instrumental in having erected the first town-pump—the humble predecessor of a modern city's waterworks. He insisted that grain should be bought and sold by weight, fixing fifty-six pounds to the bushel as the standard of wheat, and compelled the weights and measures of the tradespeople to be compared with standards brought from England, and still used as the market standards of the town.

Washington was a vestryman of Christ Church and a regular attendant while at home. He was also greatly interested in the schools and contributed annually £50 to their support. At his death he left the sum of $4000 toward the support of a free school.

He had been elected an honorary member of the Friendship Fire Company, and while at Philadelphia as delegate to the Continental Congress of 1775 he purchased a small engine for £80 and sent it to

CHRIST CHURCH, ALEXANDRIA.

the company. He always assisted, in his younger days, in extinguishing fires, and in the last year of his life showed his continued interest in the subject. While riding through the town, he saw the Friendship engine proceeding to a fire, but going very slowly from its being insufficiently manned. Calling to a group of well-dressed men standing near, "Why are you idle there, gentlemen? It is your business to lead in these matters," he leaped from his horse and seized the ropes. His action created such enthusiasm that the old engine went to the fire as it never did before or since.

On his return from the war, in 1783, he renewed his interest in the commercial prosperity of the town, and was instrumental in having the locks built around the Great Falls of the Potomac—an enterprise since merged in the Chesapeake and Ohio Canal.

He regularly voted at all the elections, always making it a point to vote early. An anecdote is told of the election in 1799—the last year of his life. The polling-booth was in the second story of the building and the flight of outside steps by which it was reached had become old and shaky. As the General reached the steps he placed his hand on the railing and gave a shake to test the security. Instantly a score of brawny shoulders were placed beneath the steps, and not a man moved until the venerable chief returned to firm ground.

The last scene in the connection of Washington and the town was when the news of his death was brought as the bells were ringing for service on Sunday morning, December 15, 1799. The ringing was at once stopped and immediately they began to toll, never ceasing day nor night until the mortal remains of the hero were deposited in the tomb.

When the last solemn rites were celebrated, the military escort was supplied by Alexandria volunteers, the salute at the grave was fired by Alexandria artillerists, Alexandria Freemasons conducted the ceremonies, and the official mourners were the Mayor and Town Council of Alexandria.

Inserted in the walls of the Washington Monument is a stone with the inscription, " From the people of Alexandria, the descendants of the friends and neighbors of Washington."

The most interesting landmark to-day is old Christ Church, where Washington so long attended divine service. It was erected in 1765, with bricks imported from England. His family pew, No. 59, is still preserved as he left it. There are three seats, two facing each other and the third against the wall. The latter was the one used by the General, who always sat quite erect, facing the congregation. All the others have been modernized. Pew No. 49 was formerly used by the Lee family, who drove here from Arlington.

Some interesting relics are preserved in the house of the Washington Lodge of Free Masons. Among them is the clock taken from his room at Mount Vernon, its hands still pointing to the hour of his death. There are portraits of Washington, Jefferson, Lafayette, and of Thomas, Lord Fairfax, the last being the only known picture of the old Virginia nobleman. There is the apron, worked by the fair hands of the Marquise de Lafayette, and used by Washington at the laying of the corner-stone of the Capitol in 1793, and also one of his field-compasses, and his farm spurs.

INTERIOR OF CHRIST CHURCH.

An interesting landmark is the old Carlyle House, known as Braddock's headquarters. It is a substantial stone building, and was once elegantly fitted up, but it is now sadly dilapidated, and almost hidden by the encompassing walls of an hotel. It was in its panelled drawing-room that the conference took place between Braddock and the Colonial authorities. Five governors were present, Dinwiddie of Virginia, Morris of Pennsylvania, De Lancey of New York, Sharpe of Maryland, and Shirley of Massachusetts. Major Washington was summoned from Mount Vernon to give his views on the proper conduct of the campaign, and vainly endeavored to induce the General to abandon the stilted tactics of Europe in favor of those of border warfare. Notwithstanding his failure, Washington accompanied the expedition, and on the death of Braddock brought back in safety the remainder of his forces. Washington exposed himself fearlessly during the battle, had several horses shot under him and his clothes pierced with bullets, but was unhurt.

CHAPTER VIII.

MOUNT VERNON—THE TRIP DOWN THE POTOMAC—THE MOUNT VERNON LADIES' ASSOCIATION—THE TOMB OF WASHINGTON—THE OLD TOMB—THE MANSION-HOUSE—THE BANQUETING HALL—WASHINGTON'S LIBRARY—LAFAYETTE'S ROOM—THE ROOM OF NELLY CUSTIS—THE ROOM IN WHICH WASHINGTON DIED—MRS. WASHINGTON'S BEDROOM—THE OUT-BUILDINGS—THE GARDEN—THE HISTORY OF MOUNT VERNON—THE ANCESTRY OF WASHINGTON.

MOUNT VERNON, the Home of Washington, is situated on the west bank of the Potomac, sixteen miles below the Capital. The trip to the hallowed spot may be made by either land or water, though the latter is the means usually chosen. A fine steamer, built expressly for the service, and named the "Charles Macalester," in honor of one of the earlier friends of the Mount Vernon Ladies' Association, makes daily trips from the foot of Seventh Street wharf.

The trip down the river is very delightful. Soon after leaving the pier, the grounds of the Arsenal are seen on the left. They present a beautiful appearance—the numerous buildings surrounded by wide stretches of lawn and shaded by stately trees giving one the idea of some peaceful sylvan retreat, were it not for the sight of cannon and piles of shot and shell, picturesque indeed, but grimly suggestive of deadly war.

Just beyond there is a glimpse of the Government Hospital for the Insane, rising from the summit of a hill across the Anacostia, looking like some fine old baronial mansion, with its lofty towers and battlemented stories.

The first stopping-place is Alexandria, some six miles below the city, the quaint spire of old Christ Church coming into view as the boat approaches the landing.

A short distance below, at the mouth of Hunting Creek, is Jones' Point, where there is a light-house, built in 1855.

The second stop is made at Fort Foote, on the Maryland shore. The fortification, now dismantled, is located on a bluff one hundred feet high. It was constructed during the Civil War, and formed one of the numerous works built for the defence of Washington.

The next landing-place is at Fort Washington, about twelve miles below the city. There is a tradition that Washington advised the selection of the site. The original fort was abandoned and blown up by the American forces, in 1814, at the time of the British invasion. The present structure was begun in 1815, and finished in 1824, at a cost of $560,000.

From Fort Washington the visitor gets the first view of Mount Vernon. The breadth of the river at this point is nearly two miles, and the mansion, as viewed across the wide stretch of water, presents a noble appearance. It stands on a hill, about one hundred and fifty feet high. A beautiful lawn, dotted with stately trees, slopes to the water's edge, and in summer the house is nearly hidden by the luxuriant masses of foliage. The view here is more impressive than it becomes on a nearer approach—the broad piazza, with its lofty panelled pillars reaching to the roof, presenting a stately and substantial appearance that is somewhat lessened when the spectator stands immediately before it and finds that it is built of wood.

As the steamer nears the landing-place and passes the Tomb of Washington, the bell is tolled. This beautiful custom is said to owe its origin to Commodore Gordon, of the British Navy, who ordered his ship's bell to be tolled while passing Mount Vernon in 1814.

THE MOUNT VERNON LADIES' ASSOCIATION.

The estate of Mount Vernon comprises, at present, about two hundred acres, and is owned and controlled by the Mount Vernon Ladies' Association. The Association owes its origin to the patriotic efforts of a Southern lady, Miss Ann Pamela Cunningham. When the last proprietor, Mr. John A. Washington, announced his intention of disposing of the property, she conceived the idea of making the sacred place the property of the nation. Obtaining the refusal of the estate she appealed to Congress, but without success. Undismayed by her failure, she appealed to the "Women of America," writing under the *nom-de-plume* of "The Southern Matron." An

Act incorporating the Association was unanimously passed by the Virginia Legislature, March 17, 1856—a condition being made that the estate should never pass out of its hands. The Association was organized with Miss Cunningham as Regent, and a Board of Vice-Regents, selected to represent the different States. By the zealous efforts of these noble ladies, the purchase-money, $200,000, was quickly raised, and the property was saved for the American People. Contributions came from all parts of the country. Edward Everett contributed $68,494.59, the proceeds of his lectures on the "Life and Character of Washington," and of his writings in *The New York Ledger*. A generous gift was made in 1887, when Mr. Jay Gould, of New York, purchased for the Association a tract of land containing thirty-three and one-half acres adjoining the north-eastern boundary, and considered a very valuable addition to the estate.

The Association established the rule to assign to the Vice-Regent of each State some particular portion of the building. This has had a most happy result in stimulating local pride, every visitor taking pleasure in seeing that his own State is suitably represented, and leaving with the desire to do all in his power to support and increase its fair fame.

The landing-place is on the site of the old wharf from which Washington used to ship the produce of his estate. It is provided with a pretty pavilion, giving grateful shelter from either rain or sunshine.

From the wharf the visitor ascends the hill to

The Tomb of Washington.

It is a plain structure, "built of brick," as directed by the terms of Washington's will. There is a wall surrounding it, with double iron gates. Over these is a marble tablet inscribed, "Within this enclosure rest the remains of General George Washington." The marble sarcophagus containing the body is directly in front of the opening. It is eight feet long, three feet wide, and two feet high. On the lid, in high relief, are the arms of the United States, and beneath, the single word, "Washington." To the left is a similar sarcophagus, containing the remains of Mrs. Washington, inscribed,

"Martha, consort of Washington. Died May 21st, 1801, aged 71 years."

These sarcophagi were the gift of John Struthers, of Philadelphia, and were the work of his own hands. Each one is made from a solid block of Pennsylvania marble. They were presented in 1837.

Near the entrance are four marble monuments, erected to the memory of relatives of Washington. These were Bushrod Washington, Associate Justice of the United States Supreme Court; John Augustine Washington, nephew of Bushrod Washington, and the owner of Mount Vernon from 1829 to 1832; Mrs. Eleanor Parke Lewis (Nelly Custis), and Mrs. Conrad, daughter of Mrs. Lewis.

THE TOMB OF GEORGE WASHINGTON.

At the rear of the Tomb is a vault extending into the bank. It is closed by a solid iron door, over which is a marble tablet inscribed: "I am the Resurrection and the Life. He that believeth in Me, though he were dead, yet shall he live." Within are the remains of about thirty of the relatives of Washington, members of the Washington, Custis, Lewis, and Bushrod families.

THE OLD TOMB,

Where the remains of Washington rested from his death until 1831, is on the right of the path, some two hundred yards south of the

THE MOUNT VERNON MANSION-HOUSE.

mansion. It contained the remains of several members of the family, but its location was unsatisfactory to Washington, and by the terms of his will he directed that the new one should be built on its present site, "at the foot of what is commonly called the Vineyard Enclosure." It was to this old tomb that Lafayette came, while visiting this country in 1824–25, to render his loving homage to the remains of his revered commander.

After the removal of the bodies, in 1831, the tomb was for a long time in a state of great neglect, but was restored through the liberality of Mrs. Elizabeth Rathbone, of Michigan.

The old barn on the summit of the hill was built by Lawrence Washington, in 1733. The bricks, like those of all buildings erected at that early date, were imported from England.

THE MOUNT VERNON MANSION-HOUSE

Is constructed of wood, cut and painted in imitation of stone. It is ninety-six feet long and thirty feet wide, and has two stories and an

MOUNT VERNON MANSION-HOUSE.

attic. On the rear, facing the river, is a piazza, fifteen feet wide and twenty-five feet high, paved with tiles brought from the Isle of Wight. Eight panelled pillars support a roof ornamented by a balustrade. Above rises a cupola. The central portion of the building was built by Lawrence Washington in 1743, the north and south wings being added by General Washington after the Revolutionary War. On the western side curved colonnades lead from the corners of the mansion to the kitchens and servants' quarters.

The Hall.

The interior of the house is plain, and most of the rooms rather small. The main hall extends through the building from east to west. It is assigned to Alabama. Of the relics preserved here, the most interesting is the "Key of the Bastile," hanging on the south wall. It was presented to Washington by Lafayette after the destruction of that famous prison. Here also are the agreement made by Lafayette to serve in the American Army, a sword worn by Washington at the time of Braddock's defeat, and some old engravings. There is a mahogany table with a marble top, formerly belonging to Washington. In the corner is the visitors' register, in which are the names of the many thousands who make the pilgrimage to Mount Vernon.

The Music Room,

Assigned to Ohio, has been elegantly furnished. The furniture is not, however, of the time of Washington, but is as near as possible a reproduction. Original articles are the silver-mounted flute of Washington and the harpsichord given by him to his dearly-loved adopted daughter, Nelly Custis. It is sad to see how it has suffered from the ravages of the modern Vandals—the keys stripped of their ivory and the inlaid brass-work from the frame. A cabinet contains several genuine articles, among them being Washington's spectacles, and some glass-ware and porcelain belonging to Mrs. Washington.

The Banqueting Hall,

Assigned to New York, is in the north wing, and is the largest room in the house. The windows in the front of the house are small, with tiny panes; in this room there is a large triple window, with an arched centre, and though the panes are small, the effect is very

THE BANQUETING HALL.

pleasing. The ceiling is adorned with stucco-work, in arabesque patterns. The walls are also finely decorated, and the whole room presents a very attractive appearance. On the south wall is an elaborately carved mantel, of Carrara marble, said to be the work of Canova. The supporting pillars are of Sienna marble. On the mantel is an old French clock, and two porcelain vases, once belonging to Washington, and a portrait of Nelly Custis. The mirror

THE BANQUETING HALL.

over the mantel is hanging in its original place. It is unfortunately broken, but most of the pieces have been restored to their proper places. The gilt frame has on the sides columns supporting a toppiece, on which is an American eagle with outspread wings. Beneath is a panel on which is painted the Washington coat-of-arms. Copies of portraits of Washington by Gilbert Stuart and Colonel Trumbull, made and presented by Lambdin, of Philadelphia, are over the doors. A very interesting article is the reproduction in silk of the head of the Stuart portrait, woven in France, and presented by W. W. Evans, of New York, a grandson of a member of Washington's staff. On the west wall hangs the large equestrian painting of "Washington before Yorktown," by Rembrandt Peale, presented to the Association by the heirs of the artist. The magnificent walnut frame was made from a tree grown on the estate of Robert Morris, of Philadelphia, the famous financier of the Revolution. On the left is a portrait of David Rittenhouse, formerly belonging to Washington. An interesting relic is the foot-rest of the pew occupied by Washington when attending service at Old Trinity Church, New York. A stand of swinging frames contains a number of letters written by Washington, his wife, Nelly Custis, and others. There is a magnificent carved mahogany sideboard, containing some valuable relics, among them being the large porcelain punch-bowl, and various articles for the table-service.

Above the sideboard are three interesting paintings in water-color, representing Sulgrave Manor, the English home of the Washingtons; Great Brington Church, where many members of the family were buried; and the Washington Cottage, in Little Brington, where the family once resided. The model of the Bastile, made from a stone taken from the original building, was presented to Washington by Lafayette.

The West Parlor

Is assigned to Illinois. A curious old painting over the mantel is entitled "Admiral Vernon before Carthagena." It was presented to Lawrence Washington by the Admiral in recognition of his services, in 1741. Among other interesting relics is a white-and-gold chair of the sixteenth century. It is from the Chateau of Chavagniac, Auvergne, where Lafayette was born, and was presented to the Association by the grandson of the gallant Frenchman. Several other chairs were used by the Washington family. On the wall is a fine full-length engraving of Louis XVI., a copy of one sent to Washington by the monarch, with many kind expressions of his great regard. A stand of swinging frames contains a fine collection of portraits of Revolutionary generals.

Mrs. Washington's Sitting Room

Has been assigned to Georgia. There is a fine engraving of "The Washington Family," and a photograph of Miss Pamela Cunningham—"The Southern Matron." Here are also the clock, writing-desk, and spinning-wheel used by Martha Washington.

THE FAMILY DINING ROOM

Is assigned to South Carolina. It is very tastefully furnished in the style of the Washington period. In a cupboard is a set of china which is a reproduction of that presented to Mrs. Washington by officers of the French Navy, in 1792. Portraits of Generals Marion, Moultrie, Pickens, and Sumter, and of Baron de Kalb, are the gift of citizens of South Carolina. There is also a fine portrait of Miss Cunningham, painted by Lambdin, of Philadelphia. The sideboard originally belonged to Washington, but was removed to Arlington by Mr. Custis. It was presented to the Association by his daughter, Mrs. Robert E. Lee.

WASHINGTON'S LIBRARY,

In the south wing, is assigned to Massachusetts. Two large windows lead to a southern portico, a reproduction of the one designed

THE FAMILY DINING ROOM.

by Washington when he remodelled his house. An interesting relic is a painting entitled "The Great Falls of the Potomac," by Beck. The point of view was selected by Washington and the painting originally hung in this room. It was presented by the Hon. Theodore Lyman, of Boston. Many of the books formerly belonging here have been restored to their places, but are carefully kept under lock and key. Around the room, concealed by the wainscoting and the wall panels, are numerous closets, used for the storing of silverware and other valuable articles.

An interesting object, presented by Mr. George W. Childs, of Philadelphia, is a proof of Washington's Farewell Address, a copy of Claypole's *American Daily Advertiser*, for September 19, 1796. It contains the corrections made by Washington's own hand. It is handsomely mounted and set in a beautifully carved swinging frame.

The stairway leading from the central hall to tne upper floors is of severely plain construction. It is in three sections, having two landings, thus resembling greatly some of the latest modern constructions.

On the second floor the chamber known as

LAFAYETTE'S ROOM,

Occupied by the distinguished Frenchman while on his visits to Mount Vernon, is allotted to the care of New Jersey. The bureau was placed here at the time of his visit; the dressing-case was formerly in a room in a house at Elizabethtown, New Jersey, and was used by him while visiting that place. There are engravings of General and Mrs. Washington and of Lafayette.

THE RIVER ROOM,

Used as a guest-chamber, is assigned to the State of Pennsylvania. Much of the antique furniture dates from the time of the Revolution and some of it was used by Washington during his campaigns. The bedstead was used by him while on his way to Valley Forge. A chair, presented by Colonel Etting, of Philadelphia, was formerly in the Executive Mansion in that city during Washington's administration. A fine mahogany chair was once the property of Franklin.

THE ROOM OF NELLY CUSTIS.

The room on the south side of the hall, assigned to Maryland, was formerly occupied by Nelly Custis. The antique washstand and chairs came from the old family seat of Charles Carroll of Carrollton.

THE GREEN ROOM,

Which overlooks the river, is assigned to West Virginia. The old bedstead was once the property of Colonel Bassett, the brother-in-law of Martha Washington. Upon this bed John Custis, the son of Martha Washington, died, in 1781. He was aide-de-camp to General Washington, and greatly beloved by him. Washington immediately adopted the two infant children, Eleanor Parke Custis and George Washington Parke Custis. Two mahogany chairs in this room were once owned by Benjamin Harrison, Governor of Virginia, and "One of the Signers." They were afterwards the property of his son, President William Henry Harrison, "Old Tippecanoe," the grandfather of President Benjamin Harrison. On the wall is a colored crayon view of "Wakefield," in Westmoreland County, Virginia, the birthplace of Washington. There are fine portraits of Lawrence Washington and Mrs. Betty Lewis, his sister, copies of the original portraits.

THE ROOM IN WHICH WASHINGTON DIED.

The most hallowed place in the building is very properly allotted to Virginia, the native State of Washington. It is the Room in which Washington Died. It is a medium-sized apartment, with a large fire-place, a smaller chamber used as a dressing-room opening

THE ROOM IN WHICH WASHINGTON DIED.

off from it. The bed stands now just where it did nearly a century ago, when the great soldier and statesman, the true friend and loving husband, yielded up his soul to his Maker. Every article in the room was formerly used by Washington or his wife. Here is the secretary at which he wrote, the surveyor's tripod he had used, the old hair-covered trunk studded with brass nails, the liquor-case presented to him by his friend Lord Fairfax, the old leathern chair in which he sat. The dressing-case on the bureau was used by Mrs. Washington; the old arm-chair was her favorite seat.

Mrs. Washington's Bedroom.

The room in which Mrs. Washington died, May 21, 1801, is reached by a small stairway, and is assigned to Wisconsin. Many wonder why she withdrew to the attic for the last eighteen months of her life. It was the custom of the family to close a room for two

MRS. WASHINGTON'S BEDROOM.

years after the death of its occupant. Even if Mrs. Washington intended to use her husband's room again, her own death took place before that time had elapsed. The room is very tastefully furnished, but has in it only one piece of original furniture, the mahogany corner-washstand. All the other pieces are, however, faithful reproductions of the original articles.

In the other rooms of the attic, there is little of interest, except to admirers of antique furniture, most of the articles being of the Revolutionary period.

THE OUT-BUILDINGS.

The octagonal cupola, rising from the centre of the mansion, affords a fine view of both shores of the river.

The principal front of the house is toward the west, where a fine lawn spreads out, around which goes the drive leading to the porter's lodge at the entrance to the estate. On the lawn, in front of the main entrance, is a sun-dial, erected by citizens of Rhode Island, standing on the same spot as the original one set up by Washington.

THE OUT-BUILDINGS.

North of the lawn is the "Office," a long, low building, formerly used as the great kitchen, where the state dinners were cooked. The family kitchen, where the ordinary meals of the family were prepared, is on the opposite side. It is now used as a luncheon room for visitors. These out-kitchens were, and to some extent are still, a feature of Southern plantation life. Under the covered colonnades would daily march the troops of little darkies, bearing the savory dishes to be placed on the family board. Just outside the family kitchen is the old well, and close by various other out-buildings, such as the milk-house, wash-house, smokehouse, etc. Next the kitchen is the small house formerly used by the clerk of the estate, and close by is a magnificent magnolia tree, planted by Washington in 1799. It has flourished most luxuriantly, attaining a size rarely seen except in more southern latitudes. Many of the trees on the estate were planted by Washington, and he always showed the greatest interest in their condition.

THE KITCHEN.

THE GARDEN.

To the left of the lawn is the vegetable garden; to the right, the flower garden. At the entrance to the latter are four magnificent trees, planted by Washington. Just beyond are four calycanthus or sweet-shrub bushes, presented to Washington by Thomas Jefferson. They are named after the Presidents who succeeded Washington— Adams, Jefferson, Madison, and Monroe. The garden is remarkable for the magnificent borders of box, now veritable hedges, clipped in old-fashioned style. The plan is exactly as Washington designed it. Near the walk is an hydrangea, brought by Lafayette from the grave of Napoleon at St. Helena, and planted by him while on his visit in 1824. A famous plant is the "Mary Washington Rose," said to have been produced by Washington and named in honor of his mother. At the end of the central walk is the green-house, built on the site of the original one destroyed by fire in 1835. The courteous attendants have for sale slips from the rose-bushes, bulbs, and flowers grown in the garden, making interesting souvenirs for the visitor, the proceeds going to the treasury of the Association.

Mount Vernon is yearly becoming more and more attractive to the visitor, as the furnishing of the mansion is made more complete and the number of valuable historical relics increased. Women are proverbially earnest in whatever they undertake, and the members of the Association are constantly endeavoring to add to the treasures of the sacred place.

The History of Mount Vernon.

The title to the estate afterwards known as Mount Vernon was granted by a patent, issued by Lord Culpepper, in 1670, to John Washington, the founder of the American branch of the family. He came from England and settled in Virginia in 1657. His second son, Lawrence Washington, married Mildred Warner, daughter of Augustine Warner. Augustine, second son of Lawrence, married, first, Jane Butler, by whom he had issue four children; secondly, Mary Ball, by whom he had issue six children, the eldest of whom was George, born February 22, 1732. The eldest son by the first marriage, Lawrence Washington, inherited the estate. He married Anne Fairfax, daughter of Colonel William Fairfax, of Belvoir, Maryland, who had an estate on the opposite side of the river. That his bride might be near her parents, Lawrence Washington built the house at Mount Vernon, choosing the name in honor of Admiral Vernon, of the British Navy, with whom he had served before Carthagena.

Lawrence Washington died in 1752, leaving an infant daughter to the care of his half-brother George, the eldest son by his father's second marriage. The early death of the girl, in 1753, put George Washington in possession of the estate. He was barely twenty-one, but his fine inheritance at once gave him position among the large land-owners of Virginia. The troubles of the French and Indian War gave Washington but little time to attend to his estate, but when, in 1758, he returned, crowned with laurels, and with his fame trumpeted throughout all the Province, he settled down to his life as a planter. On January 17, 1759, he married Martha Dandridge, the widow of Daniel Parke Custis. She was beautiful and accomplished, and was considered the wealthiest woman in Virginia.

For seventeen years Washington enjoyed an ideally happy life upon his plantation. He was surrounded by the dear friends of his childhood, possessed good health and ample means, and was blessed in the companionship of a noble woman to whom he gave boundless esteem and devotion.

In the matter of daily occupation a page from Washington's home-life reads pretty much like that of any other Virginia planter of his day. The industries of the servants' quarter embraced every trade necessary to supply their own wants. Not content with the supervision bestowed by his overseers, Washington rode from field or orchard to mill, to saw-mill, to carpenter's shop, to fishery, to plantation, to stables, etc., extending to each in turn his personal attention. To visit the ailing negroes upon his estate was a duty scrupulously performed; we read in his diary of "Cupid, ill of a pleurisy at Dogue Run quarter," and of "Grig and Lucy nothing better." The greater part of a day is spent in helping Peter, his smith, to make a new plow of his own invention. One Sunday, unable to go to church because the chariot has not returned from Colonel Fairfax's, he is obliged to put to rout a saucy oysterman who "lies at his landing," and "plagues" him by "disorderly behavior." He conditions for a purchase of land from a miserly neighbor; and himself goes into Alexandria to select a keg of butter, "being entirely out of that article." He bottles "thirty-five dozen of cider," and notes a very "great circle around the moon."

When the spring-tides of the Potomac bring herring to their nets, he is with the men, helping to haul in the seine. Whenever the season permits, he hunts with Lord Fairfax, George William Fairfax, Mr. Alexander, and others. Horses, hounds, horns made the Mount Vernon woods resound, and after a day of sport the rough-riding squires put in for dinner at any one of their respective residences which might be most convenient. When the weather is so bad as to keep even the stalwart Washington indoors, he has an opportunity of "posting my books and putting them in good order," or of preparing orders to his agent in London for the semi-yearly invoice of agricultural implements, harness, livery, equipages, wearing apparel, etc , thought suitable for a gentleman of condition in the Provinces. In ordering clothes for himself, he specifies that he is to have neither lace nor embroidery, since "plain clothes with gold or silver buttons" are "all that he desires." There is in one of his letters an implied complaint against "one Charles Lawrence," who has hitherto made his garments. "Whether it be the fault of the tailor or of the measure sent, I cannot say, but certain it is my clothes have never fitted me well." He is also concerned because a recent invoice contained last year's fashions. For Mrs. Washington and her children no stuffs were too rich and substantial, and the description of those old brocades and tabbinets, lustrings, and gold-wrought gauzes, seems to belong to times remote from the simplicity of later Republican days.

Life at Mount Vernon before the Revolution was, in short, happily uneventful. As Washington himself described it, in a letter to a kinsman then in London : " The occurrences of this part of the world are at present scarce worth reciting, for, as we live in a state of peaceful tranquillity ourselves, so we are at very little trouble to inquire after the operations against the Cherokees, who are the only people that disturb the repose of this great continent."*

This tranquil life was rudely disturbed by the outbreak of war between the Colonies and England. Washington went to Philadelphia, in 1775, as a delegate to the Continental Congress, and, in 1776, assumed the command of the American army. For eight years he was little more than a visitor to his old home, the estate being left in charge of a relative, Mr. Lund Washington. In 1781, the agent, alarmed by the threats of the enemy to burn the house, tried to placate them by gifts of the produce of the farms. For this he was sternly rebuked by the General, who gave him peremptory orders " to let the estate be completely devastated rather than give the foe the slightest assistance." Fortunately, the alternative was not again presented.

Peace was proclaimed in 1783, and orders came for the British troops to withdraw, the last boat-load of the foreigners leaving New York November 25, 1783—Evacuation Day.

* From an article by Constance Cary Harrison, entitled, "The Homes and Haunts of Washington," in the Century Magazine, vol. xxxv., No. 1.

Mingled with Washington's joy at the termination of the war, was his sorrow that he must take leave of his officers—his faithful companions in many a trying time. He was about to go to Congress and resign his commission, in order that he might once more enjoy the delights of private life at "beloved Mount Vernon." On the day of his departure from New York, December 4, 1783, he summoned his officers to meet him at Fraunce's Tavern, and there he bade them an affectionate farewell. Colonel Benjamin Tallmadge, in his memoirs, gives an account of the pathetic scene:

We had been assembled but a few moments when his Excellency entered the room. His emotion, too strong to be concealed, seemed to be reciprocated by every officer present. After partaking of a slight refreshment in almost breathless silence, the General filled his glass with wine, and turning to the officers, said: "With a heart full of love and gratitude I now take leave of you. I most devoutly wish that your latter days may be as prosperous and happy as your former ones have been glorious and honorable."
After the officers had taken a glass of wine, the General added: "I cannot come to each of you, but shall feel obliged if each of you will come and take me by the hand." General Knox, being nearest to him, turned to the Commander-in-Chief, who, suffused in tears, was incapable of utterance, but grasped his hand, when they embraced each other in silence. In the same affectionate manner every officer in the room marched up to, kissed, and parted with his General-in-Chief. Such a scene of sorrow and weeping I had never before witnessed, and hope I may never be called upon to witness again. Not a word was uttered to break the solemn silence that prevailed, or to interrupt the tenderness of the interesting scene. The simple thought that we were about to part from the man who had conducted us through a long and bloody war, and under whose conduct the glory and independence of our country had been achieved, and that we should see his face no more in this world, seemed to me utterly insupportable. But the time of separation had come, and waving his hand to his grieving children around him, he left the room, and passing through a corps of light infantry who were paraded to receive him, he walked silently on to Whitehall, where a barge was in waiting. We all followed in mournful silence to the wharf, where a prodigious crowd had assembled to witness the departure of the man who, under God, had been the great agent in establishing the glory and independence of these United States. As soon as he was seated, the barge put off into the river, and when out in the stream, our great and beloved General waved his hat, and bade us a silent adieu.

The memorable scene at Annapolis, when Washington returned to the representatives of the people the great authority with which they had entrusted him, has been admirably depicted by Trumbull in his famous painting in the Rotunda of the Capitol.

Again a plain private citizen, Washington left Annapolis and pushed on to Mount Vernon. He was accompanied by several officers of his staff, and also by Comte de Rochambeau and General Chastellux, and had sent word of his home-coming and of his distinguished visitors.

No one who is unfamiliar with the bounteous magnificence of the old-style methods of Southern hospitality can realize the amount of cheery labor preluding an event like this. In all Virginia country houses, the preparation of ornamental confectionery devolved upon the ladies of the family. For days before the arrival of guests the entire pantry and store-room staff was in a state of pleasing animation. There were eggs to beat, butter to cream, loaf-sugar to crack, jelly to strain, plum-pudding and black cake to mix, festoons of icing, pink and white, to apply through a paper cone, wonderful paper frills to cut for mighty ham-bones. A score of servants were set to work polishing floors and furniture, brass and crystal. Every candlestick in the house must have its sprig of cedar or of holly. The bedrooms, plain but exquisitely neat, were aired and garnished. The beds were made up with linen like that of the inn in Walton's "Angler"—"sheets that look white and smell of lavender"—and decorated, moreover, with white dimity curtains and counterpanes of home-made knotted-work. Every fire-place was piled high with logs, and was haunted by a small dark personage brandishing a turkey wing, ready, as might be needed, to fan a flame or to sweep away the ashes. Tradition tells how noble Martha Washington, although saddened by the loss of her son two years before, and bearing fresh in memory the bitter privations of the American soldiers, nerved herself to do the honors as a good housewife upon the occasion of the happy Christmas of 1783. To her, as she confessed, all the prospects of future worldly happiness were "in the still enjoyments of the fireside of Mount Vernon," and her one prayer was that "the General" might be left to grow old with her in solitude and tranquillity. How heartily these sentiments were echoed by Washington himself, may be seen in his letters of the time. "To move gently down the stream of life until I sleep with my fathers," was the aspiration of his heart.*

For the next five years the old life was as far as possible resumed. During this period, there was a constant series of visitors at Mount Vernon, brought thither by the world-wide fame of its owner, and tributes of esteem and affection came from all quarters of the globe.

* Ibid.

As it became evident that the Constitution would be ratified by the number of States necessary to give it force, Washington was given to understand that another sacrifice was required of him, and that he must once more give up his dearly-loved retirement and devote his energies to the service of the people. The idea was exceedingly distasteful to him. In his letters to friends, there is evidenced the hard struggle between his sense of duty and his desire for personal happiness. In answer to an old comrade, he said he was so wedded to a state of retirement and to rural occupations, that to be drawn again into public life, at his advanced age, would require a sacrifice that would admit of no compensation. He was then in his fifty-seventh year.

Washington was a man of singular modesty, and it must, I think, be admitted that he was, at least at this period of his life, without ambition; for if ambition be that longing for further distinction which leads men to covet posts of honor and responsibility, and to reach the highest attainable position, it is certain that Washington, after he had passed the middle period of life, never did one of the acts which usually indicate the existence and influence of this passion. There is no evidence and no contemporary suggestion that he sought or desired the appointment of Commander-in-Chief at the beginning of the war; and he was closely observed by those who would have noted his efforts to obtain the appointment, and would have caused them to be known to posterity, if he had made any. He himself solemnly assured his wife, in a letter that could have been intended for no eye but hers, that so far from having sought it, he had used every endeavor to avoid it, not only from an unwillingness to part with her and his family, but from the consciousness that the trust was too great for his capacity. To his brother Augustine he made the same declaration.

But although he was unambitious, he was careful of his fame; and when he received from all quarters the offer, so to speak, of the Presidency, his reputation, which filled the civilized world, was rather an impediment than an incentive to new exertions in untried fields of labor. His judgment was so calm that he could distrust his own powers—an exertion of the judgment to which more brilliant and more aspiring men, who have had much success in life, have often been unequal. He felt a strong reluctance to put at hazard the glory that he had gained, by assuming a position and a responsibility so new to him.

In addition to this, he had a real love of private life, of the pursuits of agriculture, and of domestic pleasures. He was fond of the exercise of hospitality, and accustomed to a large indulgence of his social tastes. His personal situation was all that such a man, with such feelings and such a life to look back upon, could desire. His estate was ample, and under his management productive. He was an object of the deepest interest to the enlightened of every nation, and no stranger who could be introduced to him thought of leaving our shores without seeking his house. By his neighbors and friends, by the whole body of his countrymen, in truth, he was revered as no other man has ever been. What he had accomplished, and the reputation which it had gained for him, were enough for any mortal happiness. So calmly, however, so justly, and with such moderated feelings, did he look backward and forward, that he promised himself no higher felicity than to glide smoothly on through an old age of domestic happiness to what might remain for him beyond the grave. Why should such a man covet public station? Why, rather, should Washington have been willing to accept that new, weighty, and hazardous responsibility?

Fond as he was of private life, and careful as he was of his fame, Washington held his personal advantage in all things and at all times constantly subordinate to the public good. We know that he so acted when he consented to take the command for the Revolution, and when he yielded to the earnest desire of his friends and became a member of the Convention which framed the Constitution. On both occasions he put a great deal at risk: he incurred the risk at once, as soon as he saw the duty, but he hesitated until the duty was plain to him. We may trace a similar operation of his mind through that long period of suspended decision, from the time when the Presidency was first suggested to him, in the spring of 1788, to the close of that year and the beginning of the next. There was the same struggle caused by his personal inclinations and his depreciation of himself; and it is abundantly apparent that one of his chief reasons for his extremely cautious replies to those who wrote to him on the subject was that he could not see the necessity for his services in the same light in which others saw it.*

In 1789, Washington was once more called from private life by the unanimous wishes of his fellow-citizens, who insisted that he alone was worthy to become the First President of the United States.

In their life at Philadelphia, where the Capital was temporarily located, the President and his wife found but little to compensate them for the joys of Mount Vernon.

Mrs. Washington gave receptions of a very simple nature, though party feeling then ran so high that they were reproached as "introductory to the pageantry of courts." At the evening receptions Mrs. Washington offered her guests tea and coffee with plum-cake; at nine o'clock she warned her visitors that the General kept early hours, and after such an announcement they had no choice but to

---

* George Ticknor Curtis, in *Harper's Magazine*, vol. lxiv., No. 382.

do the same. The President was frequently present, but was considered merely a guest, retiring with the others.

The receptions of the President were very formal affairs, and for invited guests only. According to a description written by a contemporary, he stood before the fire-place, dressed in black velvet, and his hair powdered. He wore gloves and silver buckles, and at his side was a plain sword. When a gentleman was presented after the announcement of his name, the President bowed but did not shake hands. The doors were closed at half-past three, and the guests then formed in a circle, while the President proceeded to address a few words to each in turn. They then bowed profoundly and retired. Not so pleasant, surely, as the joyous reunions of friends at Mount Vernon.

During the later years of his administration, Washington was the object of much personal abuse. Party feeling ran riot in those days, and even Washington could not escape. The Federalists, towards whom the President undoubtedly leaned, were accused of monarchical tendencies, and their opponents, the Democrats, found no epithet too violent to be hurled at them. One coarse woodcut represents Washington on a guillotine alongside the French King. The most furious attacks came from the pen of Philip Freneau, and were published in the *National Gazette.* Notwithstanding all his self-control, Washington must have been irritated by these persistently malicious attacks, especially as the editor always took care to send him several marked copies.

He published his Farewell Address in September, 1796, and addressed Congress for the last time on December 7. On the last day of his term of office he wrote to General Knox, comparing himself to "the weary traveller who sees a resting-place, and is bending his body to lean thereon. To be suffered to do this in peace," he added, "is too much to be endured by some."

From these disquieting scenes and these bitter personal attacks, Washington finally retired, March 4, 1797. Once more returning to his home, he spent the last two years of his life in putting his household in order, seeming to have a premonition of his approaching end.

A ride about the estate on a snowy December day was the immediate cause of the illness that brought his life to a close. The exposure resulted in an acute attack of laryngitis from which he was unable to rally, and, after a two days' struggle, he died, December 14, 1799.

The following account of the sad scenes of those last two days was written by Mr. Tobias Lear, for many years his intimate friend and private secretary. Under date of December 14, 1799, Mr. Lear writes:

On Thursday, December 12th, the General rode out to his farms about ten o'clock, and did not return home till past three. Soon after he went out the weather became very bad, rain, hail, snow falling alternately, with a cold wind. When he came in I carried some letters to him to frank, intending to send them to the post-office in the evening. He franked the letters, but said the weather was too bad to send a servant to the office that evening. I observed to him that I was afraid he had got wet. He said No; his greatcoat had kept him dry. But his neck appeared to be wet, and the snow was hanging upon his hair. He came to dinner (which had been waiting for him) without changing his dress. In the evening he appeared as well as usual.

A heavy fall of snow took place on Friday, which prevented the General from riding out as usual. He had taken cold, undoubtedly, from being so much exposed the day before, and complained of a sore throat. He, however, went out in the afternoon into the ground between the house and the river to mark some trees which were to be cut down in the improvement of that spot. He had a hoarseness, which increased in the evening, but he made light of it.

In the evening the papers were brought from the post-office, and he sat in the parlor with Mrs. Washington and myself reading them till about nine o'clock, when Mrs. Washington went up into Mrs. Lewis's room, who was confined, and left the General and myself reading the papers. He was very cheerful, and when he met with anything interesting or entertaining he read it aloud, as well as his hoarseness would permit. He requested me to read to him the debates of the Virginia Assembly on the election of a Senator and Governor, and, on hearing of Mr. Madison's observations respecting Mr. Monroe, he appeared much affected, and spoke with some degree of asperity on the subject, which I endeavored to moderate, as I always did on such occasions. On his retiring I observed to him that he had better take something to remove his cold. He answered, "No; you know I never take anything for a cold. Let it go as it came."

Between two and three o'clock on Saturday morning he awoke Mrs. Washington, and told her that he was very unwell, and had had an ague. She observed that he could scarcely speak, and breathed with difficulty, and would have got up to call a servant, but he would not permit her, lest she should take a cold. As soon as the day appeared the woman (Caroline) went into the room to make a fire, and Mrs. Washington sent her immediately to call me. I got up, put on my clothes as quickly as possible, and went to his chamber. Mrs. Washington was then up, and related to me his being ill, as before stated. I found the General breathing with difficulty, and hardly able to utter a word intelligibly. He desired Mr. Rawlins (one of the overseers) might be sent for to bleed him before the doctor could arrive. I despatched a servant immediately for Rawlins, and another for Dr. Craik, and returned again to the General's chamber, where I found him in the same situation as I had left him.

A mixture of molasses, vinegar, and butter was prepared to try its effects in the throat, but he could not swallow a drop. Whenever he attempted it he appeared to be distressed, convulsed, and almost suffocated. Rawlins came in soon after sunrise, and prepared to bleed him. When the arm was ready the General, observing that Rawlins appeared to be agitated, said, as well as he could speak, "Don't be afraid." And when the incision was made he observed, "The orifice is not large enough." However, the blood ran pretty freely. Mrs. Washington, not knowing whether bleeding was proper or not in the General's situation, begged that much might not be taken from him, lest it should be injurious, and desired me to stop it; but when I was about to untie the string the General put up his hand to prevent it, and, as soon as he could speak, he said, "More, more." Mrs. Washington being still very uneasy lest too much blood should be taken, it was stopped after taking about half a pint. Finding that no relief was obtained from bleeding, and that nothing would go down the throat, I proposed bathing it externally with *sal volatile*, which was done; and in the operation, which was with the hand, and in the gentlest manner, he observed, "It is very sore." A piece of flannel dipped in *sal volatile* was put around his neck, and his feet bathed in warm water, but without affording any relief.

In the meantime, before Dr. Craik arrived, Mrs. Washington desired me to send for Dr. Brown, of Port Tobacco, whom Dr. Craik had recommended to be called, if any case should ever occur that was seriously alarming. I despatched a messenger for Dr. Brown between eight and nine o'clock. Dr. Craik came in soon after, and, upon examining the General, he put a blister of cantharides on the throat, took some more blood from him, and had a gargle of vinegar and sage tea prepared; and ordered some vinegar and hot water for him to inhale the steam of it, which he did; but in attempting to use the gargle he was almost suffocated. When the gargle came from the throat some phlegm followed, and he attempted to cough, which the doctor encouraged him to do as much as possible; but he could only attempt it. About eleven o'clock Dr. Craik requested that Dr. Dick might be sent for, as he feared Dr. Brown would not come in time. A messenger was accordingly despatched for him. About this time the General was bled again. No effect, however, was produced by it, and he remained in the same state, unable to swallow anything.

Dr. Dick came about three o'clock, and Dr. Brown arrived soon after.

Upon Dr. Dick's seeing the General, and consulting a few minutes with Dr. Craik, he was bled again. The blood came very slow, was thick, and did not produce any symptoms of fainting. Dr. Brown came into the chamber soon after, and, upon feeling the General's pulse, the physicians went out together. Dr. Craik returned soon after. The General could now swallow a little. Calomel and tartar emetic were administered, but without any effect.

About four o'clock he desired me to call Mrs. Washington to his bedside, when he requested her to go down into his room and take from his desk two wills which she would find there and bring them to him, which she did. Upon looking at them, he gave her one, which he observed was useless, as being superseded by the other, and desired her to burn it, which she did, and took the other and put it into her closet.

After this was done I returned to his bedside and took his hand. He said to me, "I find I am going. My breath cannot last long. I believed from the first that the disorder would prove fatal. Do you arrange and record all my late military letters and papers. Arrange my accounts and settle my books, as you know more about them than any one else, and let Mr. Rawlins finish recording my other letters which he has begun." I told him this should be done. He then asked if I recollected anything which it was essential for him to do, as he had but a very short time to continue with us. I told him that I could recollect nothing, but that I hoped he was not so near his end. He observed, smiling, that he certainly was, and that, as it was the debt which we must all pay, he looked to the event with perfect resignation.

In the course of the afternoon he appeared to be in great pain and distress from the difficulty of breathing, and frequently changed his posture in the bed. On these occasions I lay upon the bed and endeavored to raise him, and turn him with as much ease as possible. He appeared penetrated with gratitude for my attentions, and often said, "I am afraid I shall fatigue you too much;" and upon my assuring him that I could feel nothing but a wish to give him ease, he replied, "Well, it is a debt we must pay to each other, and I hope when you want help of this kind you will find it."

He asked when Mr. Lewis and Washington Custis would return (they were then in New Kent). I told him about the 20th of the month.

About five o'clock Dr. Craik came again into the room, and, upon going to the bedside, the General said to him, "Doctor, I die hard, but I am not afraid to go. I believed from my first attack that I should not survive it. My breath cannot last long." The doctor pressed his hand, but could not utter a word. He retired from the bedside, and sat by the fire absorbed in grief.

Between five and six o'clock Dr. Dick and Dr. Brown came into the room, and with Dr. Craik went to the bed, when Dr. Craik asked him if he could sit up in the bed. He held out his hand, and I raised him up. He then said to the physicians, "I feel myself going; I thank you for your attentions, but I pray you take no more trouble about me. Let me go off quietly. I cannot last long." They found that all which had been done was without effect. He lay down again, and all retired except Dr. Craik. He continued in the same situation—uneasy and restless—but without complaining, frequently asking what hour it was. When I helped him to move at this time he did not speak, but looked at me with strong expressions of gratitude.

About eight o'clock the physicians came again into the room and applied blisters and cataplasms of wheat bran to his legs and feet, after which they went out, except Dr. Craik, without a ray of hope. I went out about this time and wrote a line to Mr. Law and Mr. Peter, requesting them to come with their wives (Mrs. Washington's granddaughters) as soon as possible to Mount Vernon.

About ten o'clock he made several attempts to speak to me before he could effect it. At length he said, "I am just going. Have me decently buried, and do not let my body be put into the vault in less than three days after I am dead." I bowed assent, for I could not speak. He then looked at me again and said, "Do you understand me?" I replied, "Yes." "'Tis well," said he.

About ten minutes before he expired (which was between ten and eleven o'clock) his breathing became easier. He lay quietly; he withdrew his hand from mine and felt his own pulse. I saw his countenance change. I spoke to Dr. Craik, who sat by the fire. He came to the bedside. The General's hand fell from his wrist. I took it in mine and pressed it to my bosom. Dr. Craik put his hands over his eyes, and he expired without a struggle or a sigh.

While we were fixed in silent grief, Mrs. Washington, who was sitting at the foot of the bed, asked with a firm and collected voice, "Is he gone?" I could not speak, but held up my hand as a signal that he was no more. "'Tis well," said she, in the same voice; "all is now over; I shall soon follow him; I have no more trials to pass through."

At the time of his decease Dr. Craik and myself were in the situation above mentioned. Mrs. Washington was sitting near the foot of the bed. Christopher was standing near the bedside. Caroline, Molly, and Charlotte were in the room, standing near the door.

As soon as Dr. Craik could speak after the distressing scene was closed, he desired one of the servants to ask the gentlemen below to come up-stairs. When they came to the bedside I kissed the cold hand which I had held to my bosom, laid it down, and went to the other end of the room, where I was for some time lost in profound grief, until aroused by Christopher desiring me to take care of the General's keys, and other things which were taken out of his pockets, and which Mrs. Washington directed him to give to me. I wrapped them in the General's handkerchief, and took them to my room. About twelve o'clock the corpse was brought down-stairs and laid out in the large room.

During his whole illness he spoke but seldom, and with great difficulty and distress, and in so low and broken a voice as at times hardly to be understood. His patience, fortitude, and resignation never forsook him for a moment. In all his distress he uttered not a sigh nor a complaint, always endeavoring, from a sense of duty as it appeared, to take what was offered him, and to do as he was desired by the physicians.

Mr. Lear gives the following account of the funeral ceremony, which took place at Mount Vernon on Wednesday, December 18th:

About eleven o'clock numbers of people began to assemble to attend the funeral, which was intended to have been at twelve o'clock; but as a great part of the troops expected could not get down in time, it did not take place till three. Eleven pieces of artillery were brought from Alexandria, and a schooner, belonging to Mr. Robert Hamilton, came down and lay off Mount Vernon to fire minute-guns while the body was being carried to the grave. About three o'clock the procession began to move. The pall-bearers were Colonels Little, Simms, Payne, Gilpin, Ramsey, and Marsteler. Colonel Blackburn preceded the corpse. The procession moved out through the gate at the left wing of the house, and proceeded round in front of the lawn and down to the vault on the right wing of the house. The procession was as follows:

The Troops, horse and foot.
The Clergy, namely, the Reverend Messrs. Davis, Muir, Moffatt, and Addison.
The General's horse, with his saddle, holsters, and pistols, led by two grooms, Cyrus and Wilson, in black.
The Body, borne by the Freemasons and Officers.
Principal Mourners, namely, Mrs. Stuart and Mrs. Law. Misses Nancy and Sally Stuart. Miss Fairfax and Miss Dennison. Mr. Law and Mr. Peter. Mr. Lear and Dr. Craik. Lord Fairfax and Fernando Fairfax. Lodge No. 22. Corporation of Alexandria.
All other persons, preceded by Mr. Anderson and the Overseers.

When the body arrived at the vault the Rev. Mr. Davis read the service, and pronounced a short address. The Masons performed their ceremonies, and the body was deposited in the vault.

The *Alexandria Times and Advertiser* of Friday, December 20, 1799, thus announced Washington's death and funeral:

The effect of the sudden news of his death upon the inhabitants of Alexandria can better be conceived than expressed. At first a general disorder, wildness, and consternation pervaded the town. The tale appeared as an illusory dream, as the raving of a sickly imagination. But these impressions soon gave place to sensations of the most poignant sorrow and extreme regret. On Monday and Wednesday the stores were all closed and all business suspended, as if each family had lost its father. From the time of his death to the time of his interment the bells continued to toll, the shipping in the harbor wore their colors half-mast high, and every public expression of grief was observed. On Wednesday the inhabitants of the town, of the county, and the adjacent parts of Maryland proceeded to Mount Vernon to perform the last offices to the body of their illustrious neighbor. All the military within a considerable distance and three Masonic lodges were present. The concourse of people was immense. Till the time of interment the corpse was placed on the portico fronting the river, that every citizen might have an opportunity of taking a lasting farewell of the departed benefactor.

At the time of Washington's death Congress was in session at Philadelphia. When the news was received both Houses immediately adjourned.

The next morning, as soon as the House of Representatives had convened, Mr. Marshall, afterwards Chief Justice, rose in his place and addressed the Speaker in an eloquent and pathetic speech, briefly recounting the public acts of Washington. He then offered three resolutions, previously prepared by General Henry Lee, which were accepted. By these it was proposed that the House should in a body wait on the President to express their condolence; that the Speaker's chair should be shrouded in black, and the members and officers of the House be dressed in black during the session; and that a committee in conjunction with a committee from the Senate should be appointed to consider the most suitable manner of paying honor to the memory of Washington. The Senate had similar proceedings. A joint committee of the two Houses was appointed, who reported resolutions recommending that a marble monument should be erected to commemorate the great events in the military and political life of Washington; that an oration suited to the occasion should be pronounced in the presence of both Houses of Congress; that the people of the United States should wear crape on the left arm thirty days as a badge of mourning; and that the President, in the name of Congress, should be requested to write a letter of condolence to Mrs. Washington. These resolutions were unanimously adopted. The funeral ceremonies were appropriate and solemn. A procession consisting of the members of the two Houses, public officers, and a large assemblage of citizens moved from the hall of Congress to the German Lutheran Church, where a discourse was delivered by General Henry Lee, then a Representative in Congress.

The funeral ceremonies took place December 26, 1799. In General Lee's oration were these words :

First in war, first in peace, and first in the hearts of his countrymen, he was second to none in the humble and endearing scenes of private life; uniform, dignified, and commanding, his example was as edifying to all around him as were the effects of that example lasting. To his equals he was condescending; to his inferiors, kind; and to the dear object of his affections, exemplarily tender; correct throughout, vice shuddered in his presence, and virtue always felt his fostering hand; the purity of his private character gave effulgence to his public virtues. His last scene comported with the whole tenor of his life. Although in extreme pain, not a sigh, not a groan escaped him; and with undisturbed serenity he closed his well-spent life. Such was the man America has lost; such was the man for whom our nation mourns.

Washington left property valued, according to his own estimate, at $530,000. Besides his Mount Vernon estate, he had 13,000 acres of land in other parts of Virginia, over 1000 acres in Maryland, about 1200 in New York and Pennsylvania, and great tracts, amounting to over 8000 acres, in Kentucky and what was then called the "northwest territory" on the Little Miami River. He had lots in the cities of Washington, Alexandria, and Winchester. He possessed $25,000 worth of shares in the Bank of Columbia and Bank of Alexandria in Alexandria, and the Potomac Company and James River Company. His live stock at Mount Vernon was valued at $35,000. No estimate was made of his slaves, as he proposed to free them.

By his will Washington directed that the entire estate should be given to Mrs. Washington for life. At her death the mansion, together with a considerable portion of the property, should revert to his nephew, Bushrod Washington, and his heirs.

Justice Bushrod Washington died in 1829, and Mount Vernon was inherited by his nephew, John Augustine Washington. At his death, in 1832, it passed to his widow, Jane Washington, and in 1855 to her son, John A. Washington. His means were insufficient for keeping it in a suitable condition, and in 1860 he sold it, for $200,000, to the Mount Vernon Ladies' Association.

THE ANCESTRY OF WASHINGTON.

Great interest has always attached to Washington's ancestry, and for a long time it was a puzzle to genealogists. The descent from John, the Virginia emigrant, was easily traced, but the connection with the English family was obscure. Washingtons were to be found in a score of English counties, and it seemed impossible to determine from which branch the Americans descended. Washington himself thought his family came from Yorkshire or some other northern county, and therein was not far wrong, as it is almost certain that the early home was in Durham.*

Researches made toward the close of the last century seemed to give Northamptonshire as the proper county, but still the connection was obscure and absolutely unproved. Even the surmises were incorrect, as the Lawrence Washington who emigrated to Virginia was long supposed to be the father, instead of the younger brother of John Washington, who was himself confused with his uncle, Sir John.

It was reserved to Mr. Henry F. Waters to finally unravel the tangled skein and to trace the ancestry of the President for nearly four centuries. It is owing to his genius in genealogical research, backed by untiring industry, that the long list of the ancestors of the great patriot can now be given unbroken.†

The earliest English Washingtons of whom there is any certain knowledge lived in the County of Durham, where the main line became extinct about the beginning of the fifteenth century. An offshoot of this stock settled in Lancashire, where they seem to have been people of property and position, as their arms are found in the parish church of Warton. Of this branch was John Washington, of Whitfield, Lancashire. Of his eldest son, John, nothing is known. His second son, Robert, who removed to Warton, was three times married. By his first wife, a lady of Westfield, he had issue two sons, John and Thomas, and a daughter, Ella. The eldest son, John, of Warton, married Margaret, daughter of Robert Kitson, and sister of Sir Thomas Kitson, Kt., an Alderman of London.

A son of this marriage, Lawrence, was an enterprising and suc-

* A very curious contribution to genealogical lore was made by the publication, in New York, in 1879, of the "*Pedigree and History of the Washington Family, Derived from Odin, the Founder of Scandinavia,* B. C. 70. By Albert Welles, President of the American College for Genealogical Registry and Heraldry." It has been suggested that President Welles showed lack of zeal in not carrying the pedigree back to Adam.

† See a very interesting article entitled "Genealogical Gleanings in England," by Henry F. Waters, published in the *New England Genealogical Register* for October, 1890.

cessful man. He was a member of the Society of Gray's Inn, but seems to have relinquished his profession in order to engage in the wool trade. His uncle, Sir Thomas Kitson, was a wool merchant, and was connected by marriage with the famous Spencers, of Althorp, Northamptonshire, a family which has produced many men of note. The Spencers were great wool-growers, and it was doubtless this connection that induced Lawrence to settle in their county. That he was a man of wealth and position is evidenced by the fact that he became Mayor of Northampton in 1532, and again in 1546.

When Henry VIII. ordered the dissolution of the monasteries, in 1538, Lawrence must have had influence at Court, for, in 1539, he was granted the Manor of Sulgrave, formerly belonging to the Priory of St. Andrew.

By his second wife, Anne (or Aimee), daughter of Robert Pargiter, of Gretworth, he had issue four sons and seven daughters. He died in 1584, and his tomb can still be seen in Sulgrave church. On it are his shield, much defaced, and portions of four brass plates bearing effigies of himself, his wife, his four sons, and his seven daughters, showing the quaint costumes of the time.

His son and heir, Robert, was twice married, and had sixteen children. The eldest son by his first wife, Elizabeth, daughter of Robert Lighte, of Radway, Warwickshire, was Lawrence. Doubtless on account of his large family, Robert became embarrassed, and united with his heir, Lawrence, in cutting off the entail of his property. Between 1606 and 1610 he removed to Little Brington, where he built the small cottage known as the Washington House. It was, in its day, a house of some pretension, for there are stone mouldings over the windows and door, and above the latter a slab with the inscription:

    The Lord giveth, the Lord taketh away;
     Blessed be the name of the Lord.
      Constrvcta 1606.

The inscription probably refers to the fallen state of the family fortunes. Robert died March 11, 1622 or 1623.

Robert's son and heir, Lawrence, married, in 1588, Margaret, the daughter of William Butler, of Tighes, Sussex. By her he had issue eight sons and nine daughters. He died in 1616, and his tomb can be seen in the church at Brington. Upon it is a shield, bearing his arms impaled with those of his wife.

Though in reduced circumstances, Lawrence was able to give his children a good education, and several of them rose to distinction. The eldest son was Sir William Washington, of Packington, Leicestershire, knighted in 1622. He married Anne, daughter of Sir George Villiers, and half-sister to George Villiers, the famous Duke of Buckingham, favorite of James I. and of his son Charles I. A son of this marriage, Henry, was a colonel in the Royalist army, and Governor of Worcester. Sir John, of Thrapston, Northants, knighted in 1623, was also an officer in the Royal army. The sixth son, Thomas, was a page to Prince Charles, and accompanied him on the romantic expedition to Madrid, and died there.

Interest chiefly centres in Lawrence, the fifth son. He entered Brasenose College, Oxford, in 1619, matriculated in 1621, became a Fellow in 1624, and Lector in 1627, and in 1631 was appointed Proctor of the University. His career at Oxford shows that he was a man of learning, and also had interest at Court, doubtless through his brothers. In 1632, he was appointed Rector of Purleigh, Essex. He married Amphillis, daughter of John Roades, the bailiff or steward of Sir Edmund Verney.

Purleigh was a rich living, and Lawrence lived there in comfort until 1643, when he was removed by the Parliamentary Commissioners on account of his Royalist sympathies. An interesting relic of Lawrence was a seal ring which had belonged to his brother Robert, and which was bequeathed to him by the latter's widow. This ring was afterwards taken to Virginia and impressed the seal on the title to President Washington's birthplace, in Westmoreland County. After his removal from Purleigh, Lawrence seems to have obtained some poor living, probably in the neighborhood of Tring, Hertfordshire, where his wife had relatives. There is no record of his death, but from documents relating to the family it seems to have occurred 1654 or 1655.

His eldest son, John, was born in 1634 or 1635, and his second son, Lawrence, in 1635. These two were the Virginia emigrants. There were doubtless many causes leading them to this step. Their father had been in straitened circumstances, and what little property he left was needed for his widow and younger children. The Commonwealth seemed firmly established and there was but little chance of advancement for members of a family renowned for its devotion to the King. Virginia, "The Old Dominion," had proclaimed Charles II., and was full of Cavaliers exiled or emigrated from England. For whatever reason it may have been, John Washington emigrated, probably about 1656. There is a patent, granting him three hundred acres of land in Westmoreland County, bearing date of 1657. Lawrence was married in England, but his wife having died shortly after the birth of a daughter, he emigrated to Virginia, about 1660, leaving his daughter, Mary, to the care of her mother's family. Lawrence again married in Virginia, and was the ancestor of a numerous progeny.

John Washington was twice married, the second wife being Ann Pope, a Virginia lady. By her he had issue two sons, John and Lawrence, and a daughter, Anne, who married Major Francis Wright.

The second son, Lawrence, married Mildred, daughter of Colonel Augustine Warner. By her he had issue two sons, John and Augustine, and a daughter, Mildred. John married Catherine Whiting, and had five children, two sons and three daughters.

Augustine Washington, the second son of John, married, first, Jane, the daughter of Caleb Butler. By her he had issue three sons: Butler, who died young; Lawrence, who built Mount Vernon; and Augustine; and a daughter, Jane, who died young. His second wife was Mary Ball. By her he had issue four sons: George, Samuel, John Augustine, and Charles; and two daughters, Betty and Mildred. Mildred died young, but her sister, Betty, became the wife of Fielding Lewis, and mother of Lawrence Lewis, who married Nelly Custis.

The eldest son of Augustine Washington by his second wife, Mary Ball, was GEORGE WASHINGTON (born February 22, 1732;* died December 14, 1799), the First President of the United States. He married, in 1759, Martha Dandridge, daughter of John Dan-

---

* Washington was born February 11, 1732, Old Style. When England adopted the Gregorian calendar, in 1752, the error arising from the Julian calendar amounted to eleven days. This error was corrected by calling the day after September 2d September 14th, and then regularly continuing. February 22d is, therefore, the correct date of the anniversary of Washington's birth.

dridge, of Williamsburg, and widow of Daniel Parke Custis, of Arlington. He had no children.

WASHINGTON'S COAT-OF-ARMS.

Description: *Argent, two bars gules in chief, three mullets of the second. Crest—Out of a ducal coronet or, a raven with wings disclosed proper.* That is, a white shield crossed by two red bars and having in the upper portion three red spur-rowels or stars. The crest: A raven, natural color, with open wings rising from a golden ducal coronet. The ducal, as an ancient form of coronet, has no reference to rank, and is used simply as a convenient base.

That there is probably no connection between this coat-of-arms and the American flag becomes obvious by considering the colors. The banner has white stars on a blue field, while the coat has red stars on a white field. The flag displayed by Washington at Cambridge was the regulation British ensign with cotton stripes sewed on the field, the union remaining intact. When first seen by the British they thought it indicated a surrender.

OUR NATION'S CAPITAL.

WASHINGTON'S PEDIGREE.

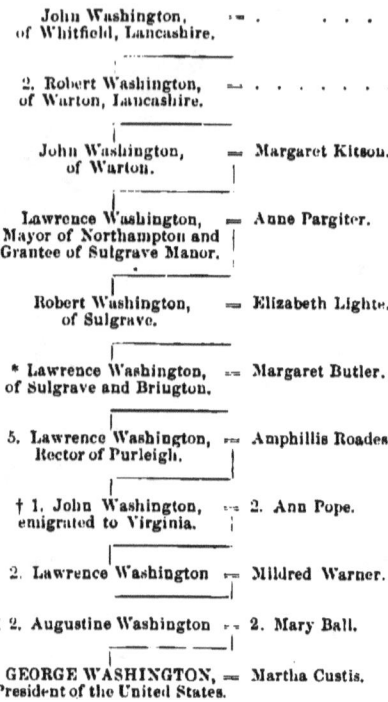

John Washington,
of Whitfield, Lancashire.

2. Robert Washington,
of Warton, Lancashire.

John Washington, = Margaret Kitson.
of Warton.

Lawrence Washington, = Anne Pargiter.
Mayor of Northampton and
Grantee of Sulgrave Manor.

Robert Washington, = Elizabeth Lighte.
of Sulgrave.

* Lawrence Washington, = Margaret Butler.
of Sulgrave and Briugton.

5. Lawrence Washington, = Amphillis Roades.
Rector of Purleigh.

† 1. John Washington, = 2. Ann Pope.
emigrated to Virginia.

2. Lawrence Washington = Mildred Warner.

‡ 2. Augustine Washington = 2. Mary Ball.

GEORGE WASHINGTON, = Martha Custis.
President of the United States.

---

* Noted children of Lawrence Washington and Margaret Butler:
    1. Sir William Washington, = Anne Villiers.
       of Packington.
       Col. Henry Washington.
    2. Sir John Washington, of Thrapston.
    6. Thomas Washington, died at Madrid.

† 2. Lawrence Washington, brother of John, emigrated to Virginia about 1660.

‡ 2. Augustine Washington = 1. Jane Butler.

        Butler,   Lawrence,   Augustine.   John,
        died young. of Mt. Vernon.   died young.
    "   "   - 2. Mary Ball.

D. P. Custis   Martha Custis = GEORGE. Betty=Fielding Lewis. Sam'l. John Aug. Chas. Mildred.
    J. P. Custis - Nelly Calvert.
       Nelly Custis.   =   Lawrence Lewis.   Bushrod Washington.

NOTE.—A numeral in front of a man's name indicates which son; in front of a woman's, which wife.

APPENDIX.

FAMOUS STATE PAPERS, SPEECHES, ETC.
    THE DECLARATION OF INDEPENDENCE.
    THE CONSTITUTION OF THE UNITED STATES.
    WASHINGTON'S FAREWELL ADDRESS.
    THE EMANCIPATION PROCLAMATION.
    LINCOLN'S SPEECH AT GETTYSBURG.
    LINCOLN'S SECOND INAUGURAL ADDRESS.
    LINCOLN'S FAVORITE POEMS.

A SHORT HISTORY OF THE CITY OF WASHINGTON.

LISTS OF THE PRESIDENTS, VICE-PRESIDENTS, JUSTICES OF THE SUPREME COURT, AND CABINET OFFICERS OF THE UNITED STATES, FROM 1789, AND THE DATES OF ADMISSION OF THE STATES.

DIRECTORY OF THE CITY, AND GENERAL INFORMATION FOR VISITORS.

DECLARATION OF INDEPENDENCE.

HE Declaration of Independence was adopted about midday, July 4, 1776, by a Congress of Representatives of the Thirteen Colonies, assembled in the State House, Philadelphia. It was sent forth with the signature of President John Hancock only, but was afterward written on parchment, and on August 2, 1776, the names of all but two of the Signers were affixed. These two were added afterward. Charles Carroll, the last survivor of the Signers, died in 1832.

When, in the course of human events, it becomes necessary for one people to dissolve the political bands which have connected them with another, and to assume, among the powers of the earth, the separate and equal station to which the laws of nature and of nature's God entitle them, a decent respect to the opinions of mankind requires that they should declare the causes which impel them to the separation.

We hold these truths to be self-evident, that all men are created equal; that they are endowed by their Creator with certain unalienable rights; that among these, are life, liberty, and the pursuit of happiness. That, to secure these rights, governments are instituted among men, deriving their just powers from the consent of the governed; that, whenever any form of government becomes destructive of these ends, it is the right of the people to alter or to abolish it, and to institute a new government, laying its foundation on such principles, and organizing its powers in such form, as to them shall seem most likely to effect their safety and happiness. Prudence, indeed, will dictate that governments long established, should not be changed for light and transient causes; and, accordingly, all experience hath shown, that mankind are more disposed to suffer, while evils are sufferable, than to right themselves by abolishing the forms to which they are accustomed. But, when a long train of abuses and usurpations, pursuing invariably the same object, evinces a design to reduce them under absolute despotism, it is their right, it is their duty, to throw off such government, and to provide new guards for their future security. Such has been the patient sufferance of these colonies, and such is now the necessity which constrains them to alter their former systems of government. The history of the present king of Great Britain is a history of repeated injuries and usurpations, all having, in direct object, the establishment of an absolute tyranny over these States. To prove this, let facts be submitted to a candid world:

He has refused his assent to laws the most wholesome and necessary for the public good.

He has forbidden his governors to pass laws of immediate and pressing importance, unless suspended in their operation till his assent should be obtained; and, when so suspended, he has utterly neglected to attend to them.

He has refused to pass other laws for the accommodation of large districts of people, unless those people would relinquish the right of representation in the legislature; a right inestimable to them, and formidable to tyrants only.

He has called together legislative bodies at places unusual, uncomfortable, and distant from the depository of their public records, for the sole purpose of fatiguing them into compliance with his measures.

He has dissolved representative houses repeatedly, for opposing, with manly firmness, his invasions on the rights of the people.

He has refused, for a long time after such dissolutions, to cause others to be elected: whereby the legislative powers, incapable of annihilation, have returned to the people at large for their exercise; the State remaining, in the meantime, exposed to all the danger of invasion from without, and convulsions within.

He has endeavored to prevent the population of these States; for that purpose, obstructing the laws for naturalization of foreigners; refusing to pass others to encourage their migration hither, and raising the conditions of new appropriations of lands.

He has obstructed the administration of justice, by refusing his assent to laws for establishing judiciary powers.

He has made judges dependent on his will alone, for the tenure of their offices, and the amount and payment of their salaries.

He has erected a multitude of new offices, and sent hither swarms of officers to harass our people, and eat out their substance.

He has kept among us, in times of peace, standing armies, without the consent of our legislature.

He has affected to render the military independent of, and superior to, the civil power.

He has combined, with others, to subject us to a jurisdiction foreign to our constitution, and unacknowledged by our laws: giving his assent to their acts of pretended legislation:

For quartering large bodies of armed troops among us:

For protecting them, by a mock trial, from punishment, for any murders which they should commit on the inhabitants of these States:

For cutting off our trade with all parts of the world:

For imposing taxes on us without our consent:

For depriving us, in many cases, of the benefits of trial by jury:

For transporting us beyond seas to be tried for pretended offences:

For abolishing the free system of English laws in a neighboring province, establishing therein an arbitrary government, and enlarging its boundaries, so as to render it at once an example and fit instrument for introducing the same absolute rule into these colonies:

For taking away our charters, abolishing our most valuable laws, and altering, fundamentally, the powers of our governments:

For suspending our own legislatures, and declaring themselves invested with power to legislate for us in all cases whatsoever.

He has abdicated government here, by declaring us out of his protection, and waging war against us.

He has plundered our seas, ravaged our coasts, burnt our towns, and destroyed the lives of our people.

He is, at this time, transporting large armies of foreign mercenaries to complete the works of death, desolation, and tyranny, already begun, with circumstances of cruelty and perfidy scarcely paralleled in the most barbarous ages, and totally unworthy the head of a civilized nation.

He has constrained our fellow-citizens, taken captive on the high seas, to bear arms against their country, to become the executioners of their friends and brethren, or to fall themselves by their hands.

He has excited domestic insurrections amongst us, and has endeavored to bring on the inhabitants of our frontiers, the merciless Indian savages, whose known rule of warfare is an undistinguished destruction, of all ages, sexes, and conditions.

In every stage of these oppressions, we have petitioned for redress, in the most humble terms; our repeated petitions have been answered only by repeated injury. A prince, whose character is thus marked by every act which may define a tyrant, is unfit to be the ruler of a free people.

Nor have we been wanting in attention to our British brethren.

We have warned them, from time to time, of attempts made by their legislature to extend an unwarrantable jurisdiction over us. We have reminded them of the circumstances of our emigration and settlement here. We have appealed to their native justice and magnanimity, and we have conjured them, by the ties of our common kindred, to disavow these usurpations, which would inevitably interrupt our connections and correspondence. They, too, have been deaf to the *voice of justice and consanguinity. We must, therefore, acquiesce in the necessity which denounces our separation, and hold them as we hold the rest of mankind, enemies in war, in peace, friends.*

We, therefore, the representatives of the UNITED STATES OF AMERICA, in GENERAL CONGRESS assembled, appealing to the Supreme Judge of the world for the rectitude of our intentions, do, in the name, and by the authority of the good people of these colonies, solemnly publish and declare, That these United Colonies are, and of right ought to be, FREE AND INDEPENDENT STATES; that they are absolved from all allegiance to the British crown, and that all political connection between them and the state of Great Britain, is, and ought to be, totally dissolved; and that, as FREE AND INDEPENDENT STATES, they have full power to levy war, conclude peace, contract alliances, establish commerce, and to do all other acts and things which INDEPENDENT STATES may of right do. And, for the support of this Declaration, with a firm reliance on the protection of DIVINE PROVIDENCE, we mutually pledge to each other, our lives, our fortunes, and our sacred honor.

[On the opposite page are fac-similes, reduced, of the signatures to the Declaration of Independence.]

Signatures of the signers of the Declaration of Independence.

CONSTITUTION OF THE UNITED STATES OF AMERICA.

THE Constitution of the United States was adopted September 17, 1787, by a convention of delegates from the Thirteen Original States, which began its sessions in the State House, in Philadelphia, in May of the same year. The Constitution was ratified by the States as follows: Delaware, December 7, 1787; Pennsylvania, December 12, 1787; New Jersey, December 18, 1787; Georgia, January 2, 1788; Connecticut, January 9, 1788; Massachusetts, February 6, 1788; Maryland, April 28, 1788; South Carolina, May 23, 1788; New Hampshire, June 21, 1788; Virginia, June 26, 1788; New York, July 26, 1788; North Carolina, November 21, 1789; Rhode Island, May 29, 1790.

PREAMBLE.

WE, the people of the United States, in order to form a more perfect Union, establish justice, insure domestic tranquillity, provide for the common defence, promote the general welfare, and secure the blessings of liberty to ourselves and our posterity, do ordain and establish this Constitution for the United States of America.

ARTICLE I.

SECTION 1.—All legislative powers herein granted shall be vested in a Congress of the United States, which shall consist of a Senate and House of Representatives.

SEC. 2.—1. The House of Representatives shall be composed of members chosen every second year by the people of the several States, and the electors in each State shall have the qualifications requisite for electors of the most numerous branch of the State Legislature.

2. No person shall be a Representative who shall not have attained to the age of twenty-five years, and been seven years a citizen of the United States, and who shall not, when elected, be an inhabitant of that State in which he shall be chosen.

3. Representatives and direct taxes shall be apportioned among the several States which may be included within this Union, according to their respective numbers, which shall be determined by adding to the whole number of free persons, including those bound to service for a term of years, and excluding Indians not taxed, three-fifths of all other persons. The actual enumeration shall be made within three years after the first meeting of the Congress of the United States, and within every subsequent term of ten years, in such manner as they shall by law direct. The number of Representatives shall not exceed one for every thirty thousand, but each State shall have at least one Representative; and, until such enumeration shall be made, the State of New Hampshire shall be entitled to choose three, Massachusetts eight, Rhode Island and Providence Plantations one, Connecticut five, New York six, New Jersey four, Pennsylvania eight, Delaware one, Maryland six, Virginia ten, North Carolina five, South Carolina five, and Georgia three.

4. When vacancies happen in the representation from any State, the executive authority thereof shall issue writs of election to fill such vacancies.

5. The House of Representatives shall choose their Speaker and other officers; and shall have the sole power of impeachment.

SEC. 3.—1. The Senate of the United States shall be composed of two Senators from each State, chosen by the Legislature thereof, for six years; and each Senator shall have one vote.

2. Immediately after they shall be assembled in consequence of the first election, they shall be divided, as equally as may be, into three classes. The seats of the Senators of the first class shall be vacated at the expiration of the second year; of the second class, at the expiration of the fourth year; and of the third class, at the expiration of the sixth year; so that one-third may be chosen every second year; and if vacancies happen by resignation, or otherwise, during the recess of the Legislature of any State, the executive thereof may make temporary appointments until the next meeting of the Legislature, which shall then fill such vacancies.

3. No person shall be a Senator who shall not have attained to the age of thirty years, and been nine years a citizen of the United States, and who shall not, when elected, be an inhabitant of that State for which he shall be chosen.

4. The Vice-President of the United States shall be President of the Senate, but shall have no vote, unless they be equally divided.

5. The Senate shall choose their other officers, and also a President *pro tempore*, in the absence of the Vice-President, or when he shall exercise the office of President of the United States.

6. The Senate shall have the sole power to try all impeachments. When sitting for that purpose, they shall be on oath or affirmation. When the President of the United States is tried, the Chief Justice shall preside; and no person shall be convicted without the concurrence of two-thirds of the members present.

7. Judgment in cases of impeachment shall not extend further than to removal from office, and disqualification to hold and enjoy any office of honor, trust, or profit, under the United States; but the party convicted shall, nevertheless, be liable and subject to indictment, trial, judgment, and punishment, according to law.

SEC. 4.—1. The times, places, and manner, of holding elections for Senators and Representatives, shall be prescribed in each State by the Legislature thereof; but the Congress may at any time, by law, make or alter such regulations, except as to the places of choosing Senators.

2. The Congress shall assemble at least once in every year, and such meeting shall be on the first Monday in December, unless they shall by law appoint a different day.

SEC. 5.—1. Each House shall be the judge of the elections, returns, and qualifications of its own members, and a majority of each shall constitute a quorum to do business; but a smaller number may adjourn from day to day, and may be authorized to compel the attendance of absent members, in such manner, and under such penalties, as each House may provide.

2. Each House may determine the rules of its proceedings, punish its members for disorderly behavior, and, with the concurrence of two-thirds, expel a member.

3. Each House shall keep a journal of its proceedings, and, from time to time, publish the same, excepting such parts as may, in their judgment, require secrecy; and the yeas and nays of the members of either House, on any question, shall, at the desire of one-fifth of those present, be entered on the journal.

4. Neither House, during the session of Congress, shall, without the consent of the other, adjourn for more than three days, nor to any other place than that in which the two Houses shall be sitting.

SEC. 6.—1. The Senators and Representatives shall receive a compensation for their services, to be ascertained by law, and paid out of the treasury of the United States. They shall, in all cases, except treason, felony, and breach of the peace, be privileged from arrest during their attendance at the session of their respective Houses, and in going to, and returning from, the same; and for any speech or debate in either House, they shall not be questioned in any other place.

2. No Senator or Representative shall, during the time for which he was elected, be appointed to any civil office under the authority of the United States, which shall have been created, or the emoluments whereof shall have been increased during such time; and no person, holding any office under the United States, shall be a member of either House during his continuance in office.

SEC. 7.—1. All bills for raising revenue shall originate in the House of Representatives; but the Senate may propose or concur with amendments as on other bills.

2. Every bill, which shall have passed the House of Representatives and the Senate, shall, before it become a law, be presented to the President of

the United States; if he approve, he shall sign it, but if not, he shall return it, with his objections, to that House in which it shall have originated, who shall enter the objections at large on their journal, and proceed to reconsider it. If, after such reconsideration, two-thirds of that House shall agree to pass the bill, it shall be sent, together with the objections, to the other House, by which it shall likewise be reconsidered, and, if approved by two-thirds of that House, it shall become a law. But in all such cases the votes of both Houses shall be determined by yeas and nays, and the names of the persons voting for and against the bill shall be entered on the journal of each House respectively. If any bill shall not be returned by the President within ten days (Sundays excepted) after it shall have been presented to him, the same shall be a law, in like manner as if he had signed it, unless the Congress, by their adjournment, prevent its return, in which case it shall not be a law.

3. Every order, resolution, or vote, to which the concurrence of the Senate and the House of Representatives may be necessary (except on a question of adjournment), shall be presented to the President of the United States; and before the same shall take effect, shall be approved by him, or, being disapproved by him, shall be repassed by two-thirds of the Senate and House of Representatives, according to the rules and limitations prescribed in the case of a bill.

SEC. 8.—The Congress shall have power

1. To lay and collect taxes, duties, imposts, and excises, to pay the debts, and provide for the common defence and general welfare, of the United States; but all duties, imposts, and excises, shall be uniform throughout the United States:

2. To borrow money on the credit of the United States:

3. To regulate commerce with foreign nations, and among the several States, and with the Indian tribes:

4. To establish a uniform rule of naturalization, and uniform laws on the subject of bankruptcies, throughout the United States:

5. To coin money, regulate the value thereof, and of foreign coin, and fix the standard of weights and measures:

6. To provide for the punishment of counterfeiting the securities and current coin of the United States:

7. To establish post-offices and post-roads:

8. To promote the progress of science and useful arts, by securing, for limited times, to authors and inventors, the exclusive right to their respective writings and discoveries:

9. To constitute tribunals inferior to the Supreme Court:

10. To define and punish piracies and felonies, committed on the high seas, and offences against the law of nations:

11. To declare war, grant letters of marque and reprisal, and make rules concerning captures on land and water:

12. To raise and support armies; but no appropriation of money to that use shall be for a longer term than two years:

13. To provide and maintain a navy:

14. To make rules for the government and regulation of the land and naval forces:

15. To provide for calling forth the militia to execute the laws of the Union, suppress insurrections, and repel invasions:

16. To provide for organizing, arming, and disciplining the militia, and for governing such part of them as may be employed in the service of the United States, reserving to the States respectively the appoinment of the officers, and the authority of training the militia, according to the discipline prescribed by Congress:

17. To exercise exclusive legislation in all cases whatsoever, over such district (not exceeding ten miles square) as may, by cession of particular States, and the acceptance of Congress, become the seat of the government of the United States, and to exercise like authority over all places, purchased by the consent of the Legislature of the State in which the same shall be, for the erection of forts, magazines, arsenals, dock-yards, and other needful buildings:—And

18. To make all laws which shall be necessary and proper for carrying into execution the foregoing powers, and all other powers vested by this Constitution in the Government of the United States, or in any department or officer thereof.

SEC. 9.—1. The migration or importation of such persons, as any of the States, now existing, shall think proper to admit, shall not be prohibited by the Congress prior to the year one thousand eight hundred and eight; but a tax or duty may be imposed on such importation, not exceeding ten dollars for each person.

2. The privilege of the writ of *habeas corpus* shall not be suspended, unless when, in cases of rebellion or invasion, the public safety may require it.

3. No bill of attainder, or *ex post facto* law, shall be passed.

4. No capitation, or other direct tax, shall be laid, unless in proportion to the census or enumeration hereinbefore directed to be taken.

5. No tax or duty shall be laid on articles exported from any State. No preference shall be given by any regulation of commerce or revenue to the ports of one State over those of another; nor shall vessels bound to, or from, one State, be obliged to enter, clear, or pay duties, in another.

6. No money shall be drawn from the treasury, but in consequence of appropriations made by law; and a regular statement and account of the receipts and expenditures of all public money shall be published from time to time.

7. No title of nobility shall be granted by the United States; and no person, holding any office of profit or trust under them, shall, without the consent of the Congress, accept of any present, emolument, office, or title, of any kind whatever, from any king, prince, or foreign State.

SEC. 10.—1. No State shall enter into any treaty, alliance, or confederation; grant letters of marque and reprisal; coin money; emit bills of credit; make anything but gold and silver coin a tender in payment of debts; pass any bill of attainder, *ex post facto* law, or law impairing the obligation of contracts, or grant any title of nobility.

2. No State shall, without the consent of the Congress, lay any imposts or duties on imports or exports, except what may be absolutely necessary for executing its inspection laws; and the net produce of all duties and imposts, laid by any State on imports or exports, shall be for the use of the treasury of the United States; and all such laws shall be subject to the revision and control of the Congress. No State shall, without the consent of Congress, lay any duty of tonnage, keep troops, or ships of war, in time of peace, enter into any agreement or compact with another State, or with a foreign power, or engage in war, unless actually invaded, or in such imminent danger as will not admit of delay.

ARTICLE II.

SECTION 1.—1. The Executive power shall be vested in a President of the United States of America. He shall hold his office during the term of four years, and together with the Vice-President, chosen for the same term, be elected as follows:

2. Each State shall appoint, in such manner as the Legislature thereof may direct, a number of Electors, equal to the whole number of Senators and Representatives, to which the State may be entitled in the Congress; but no Senator or Representative, or person holding an office of trust or profit, under the United States, shall be appointed an Elector.

3. The Electors shall meet in their respective States, and vote by ballot for two persons, of whom one, at least, shall not be an inhabitant of the same State with themselves. And they shall make a list of all the persons voted for, and of the number of votes for each; which list they shall sign and certify, and transmit, sealed, to the seat of the Government of the United States, directed to the President of the Senate. The President of the Senate shall, in the presence of the Senate and House of Representatives, open all the certificates, and the votes shall then be counted. The person having the greatest number of votes shall be the President, if such number be a majority of the whole number of Electors appointed; and if there be more than one, who have such majority, and have an equal number of votes, then the House of Representatives shall immediately choose, by ballot, one of them for President; and if no person have a majority, then, from the five highest on the list, the said House shall, in like manner, choose the President. But in choosing the President, the votes shall be taken by States, the representation from each State having one vote; a quorum for this purpose shall consist of a member or members from two-thirds of the States, and a majority of all the States shall be necessary to a choice. In every case, after the choice of the President, the person having the greatest number of votes of the Electors shall be the Vice-President. But if there should remain two or more who have equal votes, the Senate shall choose from them, by ballot, the Vice-President.

4. The Congress may determine the time of choosing the Electors, and the day on which they shall give their votes; which day shall be the same throughout the United States.

5. No person, except a natural-born citizen, or a citizen of the United States at the time of the adoption of this Constitution, shall be eligible to the office of President; neither shall any person be eligible to that office, who shall not have attained to the age of thirty-five years, and been fourteen years a resident within the United States.

6. In case of the removal of the President from office, or of his death, resignation, or inability to discharge the powers and duties of the said office, the same shall devolve on the Vice-President, and the Congress may by law provide for the case of removal, death, resignation, or inability, both of the President and Vice President, declaring what officer shall then act as President, and such officer shall act accordingly, until the disability be removed, or a President shall be elected.

7. The President shall, at stated times, receive for his services, a compensation, which shall neither be increased nor diminished during the period for which he shall have been elected, and he shall not receive, within that period, any other emolument from the United States, or any of them.

8. Before he enter on the execution of his office, he shall take the following oath or affirmation:

9. "I do solemnly swear (or affirm), that I will faithfully execute the office of President of the United States, and will, to the best of my ability, preserve, protect, and defend the Constitution of the United States."

SEC. 2.—1. The President shall be Commander-in-Chief of the army and navy of the United States, and of the militia of the several States, when called into the actual service of the United States; he may require the opinion, in writing, of the principal officer in each of the executive departments upon any subject relating to the duties of their respective offices, and he shall have power to grant reprieves and pardons for offences against the United States, except in cases of impeachment.

2. He shall have power, by and with the advice and consent of the Senate, to make treaties, provided two-thirds of the Senators present concur; and he shall nominate, and, by and with the advice and consent of the Senate, shall appoint ambassadors, other public ministers, and consuls, judges of the Supreme Court, and all other officers of the United States whose appointments are not herein otherwise provided for, and which shall be established by law; but the Congress may by law vest the appointment of such inferior officers, as they think proper, in the President alone, in the courts of law, or in the heads of departments.

3. The President shall have power to fill up all vacancies that may happen during the recess of the Senate, by granting commissions which shall expire at the end of their next session.

SEC. 3.—He shall, from time to time, give to the Congress information of the state of the Union, and recommend to their consideration such measures as he shall judge necessary and expedient; he may, on extraordinary occasions, convene both Houses, or either of them, and in case of disagreement between them with respect to the time of adjournment, he may adjourn them to such time as he shall think proper; he shall receive ambassadors and other public ministers; he shall take care that the laws be faithfully executed, and shall commission all the officers of the United States.

SEC. 4.—The President, Vice-President, and all civil officers of the United States, shall be removed from office on impeachment for, and conviction of, treason, bribery, or other high crimes and misdemeanors

ARTICLE III.

SECTION 1.—The judicial power of the United States shall be vested in one Supreme Court, and in such inferior courts as the Congress may, from time to time, ordain and establish. The judges, both of the Supreme and inferior courts, shall hold their offices during good behavior, and shall, at stated times, receive for their services a compensation which shall not be diminished during their continuance in office.

SEC. 2.—1. The judicial power shall extend to all cases, in law and equity, arising under this Constitution, the laws of the United States, and treaties made, or which shall be made, under their authority; to all cases affecting ambassadors, other public ministers, and consuls; to all cases of admiralty and maritime jurisdiction; to controversies to which the United States shall be a party; to controversies between two or more States, between a State and citizens of another State, between citizens of different States, between citizens of the same State claiming lands under grants of different States, and between a State, or the citizens thereof, and foreign States, citizens, or subjects.

2. In all cases affecting ambassadors, other public ministers and consuls, and those in which a State shall be a party, the Supreme Court shall have original jurisdiction. In all the other cases before mentioned, the Supreme Court shall have appellate jurisdiction, both as to law and fact, with such exceptions and under such regulations as the Congress shall make.

3. The trial of all crimes, except in cases of impeachment, shall be by jury; and such trial shall be held in the State where the said crimes shall have been committed; but when not committed within any State the trial shall be at such place or places as the Congress may by law have directed.

SEC. 3.—1. Treason against the United States shall consist only in levying war against them, or in adhering to their enemies, giving them aid and comfort. No person shall be convicted of treason unless on the testimony of two witnesses to the same overt act, or on confession in open court.

2. The Congress shall have power to declare the punishment of treason, but no attainder of treason shall work corruption of blood or forfeiture, except during the life of the person attainted.

ARTICLE IV.

SECTION 1.—Full faith and credit shall be given in each State to the public acts, records, and judicial proceedings of every other State. And the Congress may, by general laws, prescribe the manner in which such acts, records, and proceedings shall be proved, and the effect thereof.

SEC. 2.—1. The citizens of each State shall be entitled to all privileges and immunities of citizens in the several States.

2. A person charged in any State with treason, felony, or other crime, who shall flee from justice, and be found in another State, shall, on demand of the executive authority of the State from which he fled, be delivered up, to be removed to the State having jurisdiction of the crime.

3. No person held to service or labor in one State, under the laws thereof, escaping into another, shall, in consequence of any law or regulation therein, be discharged from such service or labor, but shall be delivered up on claim of the party to whom such service or labor may be due.

SEC. 3.—1. New States may be admitted by the Congress into this Union; but no new State shall be formed or erected within the jurisdiction of any other State; nor any State be formed by the junction of two or more States, or parts of States, without the consent of the Legislatures of the States concerned as well as of the Congress.

2. The Congress shall have power to dispose of and make all needful rules and regulations respecting the territory or other property belonging to the United States; and nothing in this Constitution shall be so construed as to prejudice any claims of the United States, or of any particular State.

SEC. 4.—The United States shall guarantee to every State in this Union a republican form of government, and shall protect each of them against invasion; and on application of the Legislature, or of the executive (when the Legislature cannot be convened), against domestic violence.

ARTICLE V.

The Congress, whenever two-thirds of both Houses shall deem it necessary, shall propose amendments to this Constitution, or, on the application of the Legislatures of two-thirds of the several States, shall call a convention for proposing amendments, which, in either case, shall be valid, to all intents and purposes, as part of this Constitution, when ratified by the Legislatures of three-fourths of the several States, or by conventions in three-fourths thereof, as the one or the other mode of ratification may be proposed by the Congress: provided that no amendment which may be made prior to the year one thousand eight hundred and eight, shall, in any manner, affect the first and fourth clauses in the ninth section of the first Article; and that no State, without its consent, shall be deprived of its equal suffrage in the Senate.

ARTICLE VI.

SECTION 1.—All debts contracted and engagements entered into, before the adoption of this Constitution, shall be as valid against the United States under this Constitution as under the Confederation.

SEC. 2.—This Constitution, and the laws of the United States which shall be made in pursuance thereof, and all treaties made, or which shall be made, under the authority of the United States, shall be the supreme law of the land; and the judges in every State shall be bound thereby, anything in the constitution or laws of any State to the contrary notwithstanding.

SEC. 3.—The Senators and Representatives before mentioned, and the members of the several State Legislatures, and all executive and judicial officers, both of the United States and of the several States, shall be bound, by oath or affirmation, to support this Constitution; but no religious test shall ever be required as a qualification to any office or public trust under the United States.

ARTICLE VII.

The ratification of the conventions of nine States shall be sufficient for the establishment of this Constitution between the States so ratifying the same.

AMENDMENTS.

ARTICLE I.

Congress shall make no law respecting an establishment of religion, or prohibiting the free exercise thereof; or abridging the freedom of speech, or of the press; or the right of the people peaceably to assemble and to petition the Government for a redress of grievances.

ARTICLE II.

A well-regulated militia being necessary to the security of a free State, the right of the people to keep and bear arms shall not be infringed.

ARTICLE III.

No soldier shall, in time of peace, be quartered in any house, without the consent of the owner; nor in time of war, but in a manner to be prescribed by law.

ARTICLE IV.

The right of the people to be secure in their persons, houses, papers, and effects, against unreasonable searches and seizures, shall not be violated; and no warrants shall issue, but upon probable cause, supported by oath or affirmation, and particularly describing the place to be searched, and the persons or things to be seized.

ARTICLE V.

No person shall be held to answer for a capital, or otherwise infamous, crime, unless on a presentment or indictment of a grand jury, except in cases arising in the land or naval forces, or in the militia, when in actual service, in time of war, or public danger; nor shall any person be subject, for the same offence, to be twice put in jeopardy of life or limb; nor shall be compelled, in any criminal case, to be a witness against himself, nor be deprived of life, liberty, or property, without due process of law; nor shall private property be taken for public use, without just compensation.

ARTICLE VI.

In all criminal prosecutions, the accused shall enjoy the right to a speedy and public trial, by an impartial jury of the State and district wherein the crime shall have been committed, which district shall have been previously ascertained by law; and to be informed of the nature and cause of the accusation; to be confronted with the witnesses against him; to have compulsory process for obtaining witnesses in his favor; and to have the assistance of counsel for his defence.

ARTICLE VII.

In suits at common law, where the value in controversy shall exceed twenty dollars, the right of trial by jury shall be preserved; and no fact, tried by a jury, shall be otherwise re-examined in any court of the United States than according to the rules of the common law.

ARTICLE VIII.

Excessive bail shall not be required, nor excessive fines imposed, nor cruel and unusual punishments inflicted.

ARTICLE IX.

The enumeration in the Constitution of certain rights shall not be construed to deny or disparage others retained by the people.

ARTICLE X.

The powers not delegated to the United States by the Constitution, nor prohibited by it to the States, are reserved to the States respectively, or to the people.

At the first session of the first Congress under the Constitution, begun in New York City, March 4, 1789, many amendments to the National Constitution were offered. The preceding ten, submitted to the Legislatures of the several States, had been ratified by the Constitutional number by the middle of December, 1789.

ARTICLE XI.

The judicial power of the United States shall not be construed to extend to any suit in law or equity, commenced or prosecuted against one of the United States by citizens of another State, or by citizens or subjects of any foreign State.
Proposed March 5, 1794; ratified in 1798.

ARTICLE XII.

1. The Electors shall meet in their respective States, and vote by ballot for President and Vice-President, one of whom, at least, shall not be an inhabitant of the same State with themselves; they shall name in their ballots the person voted for as President, and in distinct ballots the person voted for as Vice-President; and they shall make distinct lists of all persons voted for as President, and of all persons voted for as Vice-President, and of the number of votes for each, which lists they shall sign, and certify, and transmit, sealed, to the seat of the Government of the United States, directed to the President of the Senate; the President of the Senate shall, in the presence of the Senate and House of Representatives, open all the certificates, and the votes shall then be counted; the person having the greatest number of votes for President shall be the President, if such number be a majority of the whole number of Electors appointed; and if no person have such a majority, then, from the persons having the highest numbers, not exceeding three, on the list of those voted for as President, the House of Representatives shall choose, immediately, by ballot, the President. But in choosing the President, the votes shall be taken by States, the representation from each State having one vote; a quorum for this purpose shall consist of a member or members from two-thirds of the States, and a majority of all the States shall be necessary to a choice. And if the House of Representatives shall not choose a President, whenever the right of choice shall devolve upon them, before the fourth day of March next following, then the

Vice-President shall act as President, as in case of the death, or other constitutional disability, of the President.

2. The person having the greatest number of votes as Vice-President shall be the Vice-President, if such number be a majority of the whole number of Electors appointed; and if no person have a majority, then, from the two highest numbers on the list, the Senate shall choose the Vice-President; a quorum for the purpose shall consist of two-thirds of the whole number of Senators; a majority of the whole number shall be necessary to a choice.

3. But no person constitutionally ineligible to the office of President, shall be eligible to that of Vice-President of the United States.

Proposed December 12, 1803; *ratified in* 1804.

A thirteenth amendment, proposed by Congress, May 1, 1810, was never ratified by the States. It was to prohibit citizens of the United States claiming, receiving, or retaining any title of nobility or honor, or any present, pension, office, or emolument of any kind whatever, from any " person, king, prince, or foreign power," without the consent of Congress, under penalty of disfranchisement, or ceasing to be a citizen of the United States.

ARTICLE XIII.

SECTION 1.—Neither slavery nor involuntary servitude, except as a punishment for crime, whereof the party shall have been duly convicted, shall exist within the United States, or any place subject to their jurisdiction.

SEC. 2.—Congress shall have power to enforce this article by appropriate legislation.

Proposed January 31, 1865; *ratified December* 18, 1865.

ARTICLE XIV.

SECTION 1.—All persons born or naturalized in the United States, and subject to the jurisdiction thereof, are citizens of the United States and of the State wherein they reside. No State shall make or enforce any law which shall abridge the privileges or immunities of the citizens of the United States; nor shall any State deprive any person of life, liberty, or property, without due process of law, nor deny to any person within its jurisdiction the equal protection of the laws.

SEC. 2.—Representatives shall be apportioned among the several States according to their respective numbers, counting the whole number of persons in each State, excluding Indians not taxed. But when the right to vote at any election for the choice of Electors for President and Vice-President of the United States, Representatives in Congress, the executive and judicial officers of a State, or the members of the Legislature thereof, is denied to any of the male inhabitants of such State, being twenty-one years of age, and citizens of the United States, or in any way abridged, except for participation in rebellion or other crime, the basis of representation therein shall be reduced in the proportion which the number of such male citizens shall bear to the whole number of male citizens twenty-one years of age in such State.

SEC. 3.—No person shall be a Senator or Representative in Congress, or Elector of President and Vice-President, or hold any office, civil or military, under the United States, or under any State, who, having previously taken an oath, as a member of Congress, or as an officer of the United States, or as a member of any State Legislature, or as an executive or judicial officer of any State, to support the Constitution of the United States, shall have engaged in insurrection or rebellion against the same, or given aid or comfort to the enemies thereof. But Congress may, by a vote of two-thirds of each House, remove such disability.

SEC. 4.—The validity of the public debt of the United States, authorized by law, including debts incurred for payment of pensions and bounties for services in suppressing insurrection or rebellion, shall not be questioned. But neither the United States nor any State shall assume or pay any debt or obligation incurred in aid of insurrection or rebellion against the United States, or any claim for the loss or emancipation of any slave; but all such debts, obligations, and claims shall be held illegal and void.

SEC. 5.—The Congress shall have power to enforce, by appropriate legislation, the provisions of this article.

Proposed June 13, 1866; ratified July 20, 1868.

ARTICLE XV.

SECTION 1.—The right of citizens of the United States to vote shall not be denied or abridged by the United States or by any State on account of race, color, or previous condition of servitude.

SEC. 2.—The Congress shall have power to enforce this article by appropriate legislation.

Proposed February 26, 1869; ratified March 30, 1870.

WASHINGTON'S FAREWELL ADDRESS.

EARLY in 1796 it became generally well known that Washington had decided not to serve a third term, but in spite of this he was strongly urged to do so. He soon put an end to all doubt on this question. Consulting with Hamilton, as before with Madison, he wrote out his "Farewell Address," and had it published in the Philadelphia *Daily Advertiser*, in September, 1796, while all parties were getting ready for a heated canvass. The torrent of abuse which had poured upon him subsided in a manner which sufficiently explained its real nature. Several State Legislatures ordered the Address to be entered in full upon their journals, and when Congress came together it was evident that it contained but a small drop of personal bitterness against the retiring statesman. (*Stoddard's Life of Washington.*)

FRIENDS AND FELLOW-CITIZENS:

The period for a new election of a Citizen to administer the Executive Government of the United States, being not far distant, and the time actually arrived when your thoughts must be employed in designating the person who is to be clothed with that important trust, it appears to me proper, especially as it may conduce to a more distinct expression of the public voice, that I should now apprize you of the resolution I have formed, to decline being considered among the number of those out of whom a choice is to be made.

I beg you at the same time, to do me the justice to be assured, that this resolution has not been taken without a strict regard to all the considerations appertaining to the relation which binds a dutiful citizen to his country—and that, in withdrawing the tender of service which silence in my situation might imply, I am influenced by no diminution of zeal for your future interest, no deficiency of grateful respect for your past kindness; but am supported by a full conviction that the step is compatible with both.

The acceptance of, and continuance hitherto in, the office to which your suffrages have twice called me, have been a uniform sacrifice of inclination to the opinion of duty, and to a deference for what appeared to be your desire. I constantly hoped that it would have been much earlier in my power, consistently with motives which I was not at liberty to disregard, to return to that retirement from which I had been reluctantly drawn. The strength of my inclination to do this, previous to the last election, had even led to the preparation of an address to declare it to you; but mature reflection on the then perplexed and critical posture of our affairs with foreign nations, and the unanimous advice of persons entitled to my confidence, impelled me to abandon the idea.

I rejoice that the state of your concerns, external as well as internal, no longer renders the pursuit of inclination incompatible with the sentiment of duty or propriety; and am persuaded whatever partiality may be retained for my services, that in the present circumstances of our country you will not disapprove my determination to retire.

The impressions with which I first undertook the arduous trust were explained on the proper occasion. In the discharge of this trust, I will only say, that I have, with good intentions, contributed towards the organization and administration of the Government the best exertions of which a very fallible judgment was capable. Not unconscious, in the outset, of the inferiority of my qualifications, experience in my own eyes, perhaps still more in the eyes of others, has strengthened the motives to diffidence of myself; and every day the increasing weight of years admonishes me more and more that the shade of retirement is as necessary to me as it will be welcome. Satisfied that if any circumstances have given peculiar value to my services, they were temporary, I have the consolation to believe, that while choice and prudence invite me to quit the political scene, patriotism does not forbid it.

In looking forward to the moment which is intended to terminate the career of my public life, my feelings do not permit me to suspend the deep acknowledgment of that debt of gratitude which I owe to my beloved country—for the many honors it has conferred upon me; still more for the steadfast confidence with which it has supported me; and for the opportunities I have thence enjoyed of manifesting my inviolable attachment, by services faithful and persevering, though in usefulness unequal to my zeal. If benefits have resulted to our country from these services, let it always be remembered to your praise, and as an instructive example in our annals, that, under circumstances in which the Passions agitated in every direction were liable to mislead, amidst appearances sometimes dubious—vicissitudes of fortune often discouraging—in situations in which not unfrequently want of success has countenanced the spirit of criticism, the constancy of your support was the essential prop of the efforts and a guarantee of the plans by which they were effected. Profoundly penetrated with this idea, I shall carry it with me to the grave, as a strong incitement to unceasing vows that Heaven may continue to you the choicest tokens of its beneficence—that your union and brotherly affection may be perpetual—that the free Constitution, which is the work of your hands, may be sacredly maintained—that its administration in every department may be stamped with wisdom and virtue

—that, in fine, the happiness of the people of these States, under the auspices of liberty, may be made complete, by so careful a preservation and so prudent a use of this blessing as will acquire to them the glory of recommending it to the applause, the affection, and adoption of every nation which is yet a stranger to it.

Here, perhaps, I ought to stop. But a solicitude for your welfare which cannot end but with my life, and the apprehension of danger, natural to that solicitude, urge me on an occasion like the present to offer to your solemn contemplation, and to recommend to your frequent review, some sentiments which are the result of much reflection, of no inconsiderable observation, and which appear to me all-important to the permanency of your felicity as a people. These will be offered to you with the more freedom as you can only see in them the disinterested warnings of a departing friend, who can possibly have no personal motive to bias his counsels. Nor can I forget, as an encouragement to it, your indulgent reception of my sentiments on a former and not dissimilar occasion.

Interwoven as is the love of liberty with every ligament of your hearts, no recommendation of mine is necessary to fortify or confirm the attachment.

The Unity of Government which constitutes you one people is also now dear to you. It is justly so; for it is a main Pillar in the Edifice of your real independence; the support of your tranquillity at home; your peace abroad; of your safety; of your prosperity; of that very Liberty which you so highly prize. But as it is easy to foresee that, from different causes and from different quarters, much pains will be taken, many artifices employed, to weaken in your minds the conviction of this truth; as this is the point in your political fortress against which the batteries of internal and external enemies will be most constantly and actively (though often covertly and insidiously) directed, it is of infinite moment that you should properly estimate the immense value of your national Union to your collective and individual happiness; that you should cherish a cordial, habitual, and immovable attachment to it, accustoming yourselves to think and speak of it as of the Palladium of your political safety and prosperity; watching for its preservation with jealous anxiety; discountenancing whatever may suggest even a suspicion that it can in any event be abandoned, and indignantly frowning upon the first dawning of every attempt to alienate any portion of our Country from the rest, or to enfeeble the sacred ties which now link together the various parts.

For this you have every inducement of sympathy and interest. Citizens by birth or choice of a common country, that country has a right to concentrate your affections. The name of AMERICAN, which belongs to you in your national capacity, must always exalt the just pride of Patriotism more than any appellation derived from local discriminations. With slight shades of difference, you have the same Religion, Manners, Habits, and political Principles. You have in a common cause fought and triumphed together. The Independence and Liberty you possess are the work of joint councils, and joint efforts—of common dangers, sufferings, and successes.

But these considerations, however powerfully they address themselves to your sensibility, are greatly outweighed by those which apply more immediately to your Interest. Here every portion of our country finds the most commanding motives for carefully guarding and preserving the Union of the whole.

The *North* in an unrestrained intercourse with the *South*, protected by the equal laws of a common government, finds in the productions of the latter great additional resources of maritime and commercial enterprise—and precious materials of manufacturing industry. The *South* in the same intercourse, benefiting by the agency of the *North*, sees its agriculture grow and its commerce expand. Turning partly into its own channels the seamen of the *North*, it finds its particular navigation invigorated; and while it contributes, in different ways, to nourish and increase the general mass of the national navigation, it looks forward to the protection of a maritime strength to which itself is unequally adapted. The *East*, in a like intercourse with the *West*, already finds, and in the progressive improvement of interior communications by land and water will more and more find, a valuable vent for the commodities which it brings from abroad, or manufactures at home. The *West* derives from the *East* supplies requisite to its growth and comfort, and what is perhaps of still greater consequence, it must of necessity owe the *secure* enjoyment of indispensable *outlets* for its own productions to the weight, influence, and the future maritime strength of the Atlantic side of the Union, directed by an indissoluble community of interest, as *one Nation*. Any other tenure by which the *West* can hold this essential advantage, whether derived from its own separate strength or from an apostate and unnatural connection with any foreign Power, must be intrinsically precarious.

While, then, every part of our Country thus feels an immediate and particular interest in Union, all the parts combined cannot fail to find in the united mass of means and efforts greater strength, greater resource, proportionably greater security from external danger, a less frequent interruption of their peace by foreign Nations; and, what is of inestimable value! they must derive from Union an exemption from those broils and wars between themselves, which so frequently afflict neighboring countries not tied together by the same government; which their own rivalships alone would be sufficient to produce, but which opposite foreign alliances, attachments, and intrigues would stimulate and embitter. Hence, likewise, they will avoid the necessity of those overgrown Military establishments, which under any form of Government are inauspicious to liberty, and which are to be regarded as particularly hostile to Republican Liberty. In this sense it is that your Union ought to be considered as a main prop of your liberty, and that the love of the one ought to endear to you the preservation of the other.

These considerations speak a persuasive language to every reflecting and virtuous mind, and exhibit the continuance of the UNION as a primary object of Patriotic desire. Is there a doubt whether a common government can embrace so large a sphere? Let experience solve it. To listen to mere speculation in such a case were criminal. We are authorized to hope that a proper organization of the whole, with the auxiliary agency of governments for the respective subdivisions, will afford a happy issue to the experiment. 'Tis well worth a fair and full experiment. With such powerful and obvious motives to Union, affecting all parts of our country, while experience shall not have demonstrated its impracticability, there will always be reason to distrust the patriotism of those who in any quarter may endeavor to weaken its bands.

In contemplating the causes which may disturb our Union, it occurs as matter of serious concern that any ground should have been furnished for characterizing parties by *Geographical* discriminations—*Northern* and *Southern*, *Atlantic* and *Western*, whence designing men may endeavor to excite a belief that there is a real difference of local interests and views. One of the expedients of Party to acquire influence, within particular districts, is to misrepresent the opinions and aims of other districts. You cannot shield yourselves too much against the jealousies and heart-burnings which spring from these misrepresentations; they tend to render alien to each other those who ought to be bound together by fraternal affection. The inhabitants of our Western country have lately had a useful lesson on this head. They have seen, in the negotiation by the Executive, and in the unanimous ratification by the Senate, of the Treaty with Spain, and in the universal satisfaction at that event throughout the United States, a decisive proof how unfounded were the suspicions propagated among them of a policy in the General Government and in the Atlantic States unfriendly to their interests in regard to the MISSISSIPPI. They have been witnesses to the formation of two Treaties, that with Great Britain and that with Spain, which secure to them everything they could desire in respect to our foreign relations toward confirming their prosperity. Will it not be their wisdom to rely for the preservation of these advantages on the UNION by which they were procured? Will they not henceforth be deaf to those advisers, if such there are, who would sever them from their Brethren and connect them with Aliens?

To the efficacy and permanency of your Union, a Government for the whole is indispensable. No alliances, however strict between the parts, can be an adequate substitute. They must inevitably experience the infractions and interruptions which all alliances in all times have experienced. Sensible of this momentous truth, you have improved upon your first essay, by the adoption of a Constitution of Government, better calculated than your former for an intimate Union and for the efficacious management of your common concerns. This Government, the offspring of our own choice, uninfluenced and unawed, adopted upon full investigation and mature deliberation, completely free in its principles, in the distribution of its powers, uniting security with energy, and containing within itself a provision for its own amendment, has a just claim to your confidence and your support. Respect for its authority, compliance with its Laws, acquiescence in its measures, are duties enjoined by the fundamental maxims of true

Liberty. The basis of our political systems is the right of the people to make and to alter their Constitutions of Government. But the Constitution which at any time exists, till changed by an explicit and authentic act of the whole People, is sacredly obligatory upon all. The very idea of the power and the right of the People to establish Government presupposes the duty of every individual to obey the established Government.

All obstructions to the execution of the Laws, all combinations and associations, under whatever plausible character, with the real design to direct, control, counteract, or awe the regular deliberation and action of the constituted authorities, are destructive of this fundamental principle, and of fatal tendency. They serve to organize faction, to give it an artificial and extraordinary force—to put, in the place of the delegated will of the Nation, the will of a party—often a small but artful and enterprising minority of the community; and, according to the alternate triumphs of different parties, to make the public administration the mirror of the ill-concerted and incongruous projects of faction, rather than the organ of consistent and wholesome plans digested by common councils and modified by mutual interests. However combinations or associations of the above description may now and then answer popular ends, they are likely, in the course of time and things, to become potent engines by which cunning, ambitious, and unprincipled men will be enabled to subvert the Power of the People and to usurp for themselves the reins of Government; destroying afterwards the very engines which have lifted them to unjust dominion.

Toward the preservation of your Government and the permanency of your present happy state, it is requisite not only that you steadily discountenance irregular oppositions to its acknowledged authority, but also that you resist with care the spirit of innovation upon its principles, however specious the pretexts. One method of assault may be to effect, in the forms of the Constitution, alterations which will impair the energy of the system, and thus to undermine what cannot be directly overthrown. In all the changes to which you may be invited, remember that time and habit are at least as necessary to fix the true character of Governments as of other human institutions; that experience is the surest standard by which to test the real tendency of the existing Constitution of a Country; that facility in changes upon the credit of mere hypothesis and opinion exposes to perpetual change from the endless variety of hypothesis and opinion; and remember, especially, that for the efficient management of your common interests, in a country so extensive as ours, a Government of as much vigor as is consistent with the perfect security of Liberty is indispensable—Liberty itself will find in such a Government, with powers properly distributed and adjusted, its surest Guardian. It is, indeed, little else than a name, where the Government is too feeble to withstand the enterprises of faction, to confine each member of the Society within the limits prescribed by the laws, and to maintain all in the secure and tranquil enjoyment of the rights of person and property.

I have already intimated to you the danger of Parties in the State, with particular reference to the founding of them on Geographical discriminations.

Let me now take a more comprehensive view, and warn you in the most solemn manner against the baneful effects of the Spirit of Party, generally.

This Spirit, unfortunately, is inseparable from our nature, having its root in the strongest passions of the human mind. It exists under different shapes in all Governments, more or less stifled, controlled or repressed; but in those of the popular form it is seen in it greatest rankness, and is truly their worst enemy.

The alternate domination of one faction over another, sharpened by the spirit of revenge natural to party dissension, which in different ages and countries has perpetrated the most horrid enormities, is itself a frightful despotism. But this leads at length to a more formal and permanent despotism. The disorders and miseries which result gradually incline the minds of men to seek security and repose in the absolute power of an Individual; and sooner or later the chief of some prevailing faction, more able or more fortunate than his competitors, turns this disposition to the purposes of his own elevation, on the ruins of Public Liberty.

Without looking forward to an extremity of this kind (which nevertheless ought not to be entirely out of sight), the common and continual mischiefs of the spirit of Party are sufficient to make it the interest and the duty of a wise People to discourage and restrain it.

It serves always to distract the Public Councils and enfeeble the Public Administration. It agitates the community with ill-founded jealousies and false alarms, kindles the animosity of one part against another, foments occasionally riot and insurrection. It opens the door to foreign influence and corruption, which find a facilitated access to the Government itself through the channels of party passions. Thus, the policy and the will of one country are subjected to the policy and will of another.

There is an opinion that parties in free countries are useful checks upon the Administration of the Government, and serve to keep alive the Spirit of Liberty. This within certain limits is probably true—and in Governments of a Monarchical cast, Patriotism may look with indulgence, if not with favor, upon the spirit of party. But in those of the popular character, in Governments purely elective, it is a spirit not to be encouraged. From their natural tendency, it is certain there will always be enough of that spirit for every salutary purpose—and there being constant danger of excess, the effort ought to be, by force of public opinion, to mitigate and assuage it. A fire not to be quenched, it demands a uniform vigilance to prevent its bursting into a flame, lest, instead of warming it should consume.

It is important, likewise, that the habits of thinking in a free country should inspire caution in those entrusted with its administration, to confine themselves within their respective constitutional spheres; avoiding in the exercise of the powers of one department to encroach upon another. The spirit of encroachment tends to consolidate the powers of all the departments in one, and thus to create, whatever the form of government, a real despotism. A just estimate of that love of power, and proneness to abuse it, which predominates in the human heart, is sufficient to satisfy us of the truth of this position.

The necessity of reciprocal checks in the exercise of political power, by dividing and distributing it into different depositories, and constituting each the Guardian of the Public Weal against invasions by the others, has been evinced by experiments ancient and modern; some of them in our country and under our own eyes. To preserve them must be as necessary as to institute them. If in the opinion of the People, the distribution or modification of the Constitutional powers be in any particular wrong, let it be corrected by an amendment in the way which the Constitution designates. But let there be no change by usurpation; for though this, in one instance, may be the instrument of good, it is the customary weapon by which free governments are destroyed. The precedent must always greatly overbalance in permanent evil any partial or transient benefit which the use can at any time yield.

Of all the dispositions and habits which lead to political prosperity, Religion and Morality are indispensable supports. In vain would that man claim the tribute of Patriotism, who should labor to subvert these great Pillars of human happiness, these firmest props of the duties of Men and Citizens. The mere Politician, equally with the pious man, ought to respect and to cherish them. A volume could not trace all their connections with private and public felicity. Let it simply be asked where is the security for property, for reputation, for life, if the sense of religious obligation *desert* the oaths, which are the instruments of investigation in Courts of Justice? And let us with caution indulge the supposition, that morality can be maintained without religion. Whatever may be conceded to the influence of refined education on minds of peculiar structure, reason and experience both forbid us to expect that national morality can prevail in exclusion of religious principle.

'Tis substantially true that virtue or morality is a necessary spring of popular government. The rule indeed extends with more or less force to every species of Free Government. Who that is a sincere friend to it can look with indifference upon attempts to shake the foundation of the fabric?

Promote then as an object of primary importance institutions for the general diffusion of knowledge. In proportion as the structure of a government gives force to public opinion, it is essential that public opinion should be enlightened.

As a very important source of strength and security, cherish public credit. One method of preserving it is to use it as sparingly as possible: avoiding occasions of expense by cultivating peace, but remembering also that timely disbursements to prepare for danger frequently prevent much greater disbursements to repel it; avoiding likewise the accumulation of debt, not only by shunning occasions of expense, but by vigorous exertions in time of Peace to discharge the debts which unavoidable wars may have occasioned, not ungenerously throwing upon posterity the burthen which we ourselves ought to bear. The execution of these maxims belongs to your Representatives, but it is necessary that public opinion should co-operate. To facilitate to them the performance of their duty, it is essential that you should practically bear in mind, that toward the payment of debts there must be Revenue; that to have Revenue there must be taxes; that no taxes can be devised which are not more or less inconvenient and unpleasant; that the intrinsic embarrassment inseparable from the selection of the proper objects (which is always a choice of difficulties) ought to be a decisive motive for a candid construction of the conduct of the Government in making it, and for a spirit of acquiescence in the measures for obtaining Revenue which the public exigencies may at any time dictate.

Observe good faith and justice towards all Nations. Cultivate peace and harmony with all. Religion and morality enjoin this conduct; and can it be that good policy does not equally enjoin it? It will be worthy of a free, enlightened, and, at no distant period, a great nation, to give to mankind the magnanimous and too novel example of a People always guided by an exalted justice and benevolence. Who can doubt that in the course of time and things the fruits of such a plan would richly repay any temporary advantages which might be lost by a steady adherence to it? Can it be that Providence has not connected the permanent felicity of a Nation with its virtue? The experiment, at least, is recommended by every sentiment which ennobles human nature. Alas! is it rendered impossible by its vices?

In the execution of such a plan nothing is more essential than that permanent, inveterate antipathies against particular nations and passionate attachments for others should be excluded; and that in place of them just and amicable feelings towards all should be cultivated. The Nation which indulges towards another an habitual hatred or an habitual fondness is in some degree a slave. It is a slave to its animosity or to its affection, either of which is sufficient to lead it astray from its duty and its interests. Antipathy in one Nation against another disposes each more readily to offer insult and injury, to lay hold of slight causes of umbrage, and to be haughty and intractable when accidental or trifling occasions of dispute occur. Hence frequent collisions, obstinate, envenomed, and bloody contests. The Nation prompted by ill-will and resentment sometimes impels to War the Government, contrary to the best calculations of policy. The Government sometimes participates in the national propensity, and adopts through passion what reason would reject; at other times, it makes the animosity of the Nation subservient to projects of hostility instigated by pride, ambition, and other sinister and pernicious motives. The peace often, sometimes perhaps the Liberty, of Nations has been the victim.

So likewise a passionate attachment of one Nation for another produces a variety of evils. Sympathy for the favorite Nation, facilitating the illusion of an imaginary common interest in cases where no real common interest exists, and infusing into one the enmities of the other, betrays the former into a participation in the quarrels and wars of the latter, without adequate inducement or justification. It leads also to concessions to the favorite Nation of privileges denied to others, which is apt doubly to injure the Nation making the concessions, by unnecessarily parting with what ought to have been retained, and by exciting jealousy, ill-will, and a disposition to retaliate in the parties from whom equal privileges are withheld; and it gives to ambitious, corrupted, or deluded citizens (who devote themselves to the favorite Nation) facility to betray, or sacrifice the interests of their own country without odium, sometimes even with popularity—gilding with the appearances of a virtuous sense of obligation, a commendable deference for public opinion, or a laudable zeal for public good, the base or foolish compliances of ambition, corruption, or infatuation.

As avenues to foreign influence in innumerable ways, such attachments are particularly alarming to the truly enlightened and independent patriot. How many opportunities do they afford to tamper with domestic factions, to practise the arts of seduction, to mislead public opinion, to influence or awe the public councils! Such an attachment of a small or weak, toward a great and powerful Nation, dooms the former to be the satellite of the latter.

Against the insidious wiles of foreign influence I conjure you to believe me, fellow-citizens, the jealousy of a free people ought to be constantly awake, since history and experience prove that foreign influence is one of the most baneful foes of Republican Government. But that jealousy to be useful must be impartial; else it becomes the instrument of the very influence to be avoided, instead of a defence against it. Excessive partiality for one foreign Nation and excessive dislike of another, cause those whom they actuate to see danger only on one side, and serve to veil and even second the arts of influence on the other. Real Patriots, who may resist the intrigues of the favorite, are liable to become suspected and odious; while its tools and dupes usurp the applause and confidence of the people to surrender their interests.

The great rule of conduct for us, in regard to foreign Nations is, in extending our commercial relations, to have with them as little *Political* connection as possible. So far as we have already formed engagements let them be fulfilled with perfect good faith. Here let us stop.

Europe has a set of primary interests, which to us have none, or a very remote relation. Hence she must be engaged in frequent controversies, the causes of which are essentially foreign to our concerns. Hence, therefore, it must be unwise in us to implicate ourselves by artificial ties in the ordinary vicissitudes of her politics, or the ordinary combinations and collisions of her friendships or enmities.

Our detached and distant situation invites and enables us to pursue a different course. If we remain one People, under an efficient government, the period is not far off when we may defy material injury from external annoyance; when we may take such an attitude as will cause the neutrality we may at any time resolve upon to be scrupulously respected; when belligerent Nations, under the impossibility of making acquisitions upon us, will not lightly hazard the giving us provocation; when we may choose peace or war, as our interests guided by justice shall counsel.

Why forego the advantages of so peculiar a situation? Why quit our own to stand upon foreign ground? Why, by interweaving our destiny with that of any part of Europe, entangle our peace and prosperity in the toils of European ambition, rivalship, interest, humor, or caprice.

'Tis our true policy to steer clear of permanent alliances with any portion of the foreign world—so far, I mean, as we are now at liberty to do it—for let me not be understood as capable of patronizing infidelity to existing engagements (I hold the maxim no less applicable to public than to private affairs, that honesty is always the best policy). I repeat it therefore, let those engagements be observed in their genuine sense. But in my opinion it is unnecessary and would be unwise to extend them.

Taking care always to keep ourselves, by suitable establishments, on a respectably defensive posture, we may safely trust to temporary alliances for extraordinary emergencies.

Harmony, liberal intercourse with all Nations, are recommended by policy, humanity, and interest. But even our commercial policy should hold an equal and impartial hand—neither seeking nor granting exclusive favors or preferences; consulting the natural course of things; diffusing and diversifying by gentle means the streams of commerce, but forcing nothing; establishing with Powers so disposed—in order to give to trade a stable course, to define the rights of our merchants and to enable the Government to support them—conventional rules of intercourse, the best that present circumstances and mutual opinion will permit; but temporary, and liable to be from time to time abandoned or varied, as experience and circumstances shall dictate; constantly keeping in view that 'tis folly in one Nation to look for disinterested favors from another; that it must pay with a portion of its independence for whatever it may accept under that character; that by such acceptance it may place itself in the condition of having given equivalents for nominal favors and yet of being reproached with ingratitude for not giving more. There can be no greater error than to expect or calculate upon real favors from Nation to Nation. 'Tis an illusion which experience must cure, which a just pride ought to discard.

In offering to you, my Countrymen, these counsels of an old and affectionate friend, I dare not hope they will make the strong and lasting impression, I could wish—that they will control the usual current of the passions or prevent our Nation from running the course which has hitherto marked the destiny of Nations. But if I may even flatter myself that they may be productive of some partial benefit, some occasional good; that they may now and then recur to moderate the fury of party spirit, to warn against the mischiefs of foreign intrigue, to guard against the impostures of pretended patriotism—this hope will be a full recompense for the solicitude for your welfare, by which they have been dictated.

How far in the discharge of my official duties I have been guided by the principles which have been delineated, the public records and other evidences of my conduct must witness to you and to the world. To myself, the assurance of my own conscience is, that I have at least believed myself to be guided by them.

In relation to the still subsisting war in Europe, my Proclamation of the 22d of April, 1793, is the index to my plan. Sanctioned by your approving voice and by that of your Representatives in both Houses of Congress, the spirit of that measure has continually governed me—uninfluenced by any attempts to deter or divert me from it.

After deliberate examination, with the aid of the best lights I could obtain, I was well satisfied that our country, under all the circumstances of the case, had a right to take, and was bound in duty and interest to take, a neutral position. Having taken it, I determined, as far as should depend upon me, to maintain it, with moderation, perseverance, and firmness.

The considerations which respect the right to hold this conduct it is not necessary on this occasion to detail. I will only observe, that according to my understanding of the matter, that right, so far from being denied by any of the belligerent Powers, has been virtually admitted by all.

The duty of holding a neutral conduct may be inferred, without anything more, from the obligation which justice and humanity impose on every Nation, in cases in which it is free to act, to maintain inviolate the relations of peace and amity towards other Nations.

The inducements of interest for observing that conduct will best be referred to your own reflections and experience. With me, a predominant motive has been to endeavor to gain time to our country to settle and mature its yet recent institutions, and to progress without interruption to that degree of strength and consistency which is necessary to give it, humanly speaking, the command of its own fortunes.

Though in reviewing the incidents of my Administration, I am unconscious of intentional error—I am, nevertheless, too sensible of my defects not to think it probable that I may have committed many errors. Whatever they may be I fervently beseech the Almighty to avert or mitigate the evils to which they may tend. I shall also carry with me the hope that my country will never cease to view them with indulgence; and that after forty-five years of my life dedicated to its service, with an upright zeal, the faults of incompetent abilities will be consigned to oblivion, as myself must soon be to the mansions of rest.

Relying on its kindness in this as in other things, and actuated by that fervent love toward it which is so natural to a man who views in it the native soil of himself and his progenitors for several generations, I anticipate with pleasing expectation that retreat in which I promise myself to realize, without alloy, the sweet enjoyment of partaking, in the midst of my fellow-citizens, the benign influence of good Laws under a free Government, the ever favorite object of my heart, and the happy reward, as I trust, of our mutual cares, labors, and dangers.

UNITED STATES, 19th September, 1796. GEORGE WASHINGTON.

THE EMANCIPATION PROCLAMATION,

JANUARY 1, 1863.

AT a Cabinet meeting, September 22, 1862, the date of the preliminary Proclamation, the President, after referring to previous discussions and postponements, said: "When the rebel army was at Frederick, I determined, as soon as it should be driven out of Maryland, to issue a proclamation, such as I thought most likely to be useful. I said nothing to anyone; but I made the promise to myself, and [hesitating a little] to my Maker. The rebel army is now driven out, and I am going to fulfil that promise. I do not wish to hear your advice about the main matter, for that I have determined for myself." (*From the Diary of Secretary Chase.*)

No. 1404

To all to whom these presents shall come, Greeting:

I Certify That the document hereunto annexed is a true copy from the original on file in this Department.

In testimony whereof I James G. Blaine Secretary of State of the United States have hereunto subscribed my name and caused the seal of the Department of State to be affixed.

Done at the City of Washington this 29th day of December A.D. 1891 and of the Independence of the United States of America the one hundred and sixteenth.

James G. Blaine

By the President of the United States of America:

A Proclamation.

Whereas, on the twenty-second day of September, in the year of our Lord one thousand eight hundred and sixty-two, a proclamation was issued by the President of the United States, containing, among other things, the following, to-wit:

"That on the first day of January, in the year of "our Lord one thousand eight hundred and sixty-three, "all persons held as slaves within any State or desig-"nated part of a State, the people whereof shall then "be in rebellion against the United States, shall be "then, thenceforward, and forever free; and the Executive "Government of the United States, including the "military and naval authority thereof, will recognize "and maintain the freedom of such persons, and will "do no act or acts to repress such persons, or any of "them, in any efforts they may make for their actual "freedom.

"That the Executive will, on the first day of Janu-"ary aforesaid, by proclamation, designate the States "and parts of States, if any, in which the people "thereof, respectively, shall then be in rebellion against "the United States; and the fact that any State, or the people thereof, shall on that day, be, in good faith, represented in the Congress of the United States by members chosen thereto at elections wherein a majority of the qualified voters of such State shall have participated, shall, in the absence of strong countervailing testimony, be deemed conclusive evidence that such State and the people thereof, are not then in rebellion against the United States."

Now, therefore, I, Abraham Lincoln, President of the United States, by virtue of the power in me vested as Commander-in-Chief, of the Army and Navy of the United States in time of actual armed rebellion against the authority and government of the United States, and as a fit and necessary war measure for suppressing said rebellion, do, on this first day of January, in the year of our Lord one thousand eight hundred and sixty-three, and in accordance with my purpose so to do publicly proclaimed for the full period of one hundred days, from the day first above mentioned, order and designate as the States and parts of States wherein the people thereof respectively, are this day in rebellion against the United States, the following, to wit:

Arkansas, Texas, Louisiana, (except the Parishes of St. Bernard, Plaquemines, Jefferson, St. John, St. Charles, St. James, Ascension, Assumption, Terrebonne, Lafourche, St. Mary, St. Martin, and Orleans, including the City of New Orleans,) Mississippi, Alabama, Florida, Georgia, South Carolina,

North Carolina, and Virginia (except the forty-eight counties designated as West Virginia, and also the counties of Berkley, Accomac, Northampton, Elizabeth City, York, Princess Ann, and Norfolk, including the cities of Norfolk and Portsmouth, and which excepted parts are, for the present, left precisely as if this proclamation were not issued).

And by virtue of the power, and for the purpose aforesaid, I do order and declare that all persons held as slaves within said designated States, and parts of States, are, and henceforward shall be, free; and that the Executive government of the United States, including the military and naval authorities thereof, will recognize and maintain the freedom of said persons.

And I hereby enjoin upon the people so declared to be free to abstain from all violence, unless in necessary self-defence; and I recommend to them that, in all cases when allowed, they labor faithfully for reasonable wages.

And I further declare and make known, that such persons of suitable condition, will be received into the armed service of the United States to garrison forts, positions, stations, and other places, and to man vessels of all sorts in said service.

And upon this act, sincerely believed to be an act of justice, warranted by the Constitution, upon military necessity, I invoke the considerate judgment of mankind, and the gracious favor of Almighty God.

In witness whereof, I have hereunto set my hand and caused the seal of the United States to be affixed.

Done at the city of Washington, this first day of January, in the year of our Lord

one thousand eight hundred and sixty three, and of the Independence of the United States the eighty-seventh.

Abraham Lincoln

By the President:
William H. Seward,
Secretary of State.

LINCOLN'S SPEECH AT GETTYSBURG.

IN the autumn of 1863 the ground adjoining the village cemetery of Gettysburg was purchased and prepared for consecration as a National Burying Ground for the gallant soldiers who fell in that conflict. There, on the 19th of October, with solemn, touching, and most impressive ceremonies, the ground was consecrated to its pious purpose. The President, his Cabinet, the officials of the State of Pennsylvania, governors of States, foreign ministers, officers of the Army and Navy, soldiers and citizens, gathered in great numbers to witness the proceedings. Edward Everett, late Secretary of State, and Senator from Massachusetts, an orator and scholar whose renown had extended over the world, was selected to pronounce the oration. He was a polished and graceful speaker, and worthy of the theme and the occasion. President Lincoln, while in the cars on his way from the White House to the battle-field, was notified that he would be expected to make some remarks also. Asking for some paper, a rough sheet of foolscap was handed to him, and, retiring to a seat by himself, with a pencil he wrote the address which has become so celebrated—an address which for appropriateness and eloquence, for pathos and beauty, for sublimity in sentiment and expression, has hardly its equal in English or American literature. Everett's oration was a polished specimen of consummate oratorical skill. It was memorized and recited without recurring to a single note. It was perhaps too artistic; so much so, that the audience sometimes during its delivery forgot the heroic dead to admire the skill of the speaker before them. When at length the New England orator closed, and the cheers in his honor had subsided, an earnest call for Lincoln was heard through the vast crowd in attendance. Slowly, and very deliberately, the tall, homely form of the President rose—simple, rude, his careworn face now lighted and glowing with intense feeling. All unconscious of himself, absorbed with recollections of the heroic dead, he adjusted his spectacles, and read with the most profound feeling the following address:

Fourscore and seven years ago our fathers brought forth upon this continent a new nation, conceived in liberty, and dedicated to the proposition that all men are created equal.

Now we are engaged in a great civil war, testing whether that nation, or any nation so conceived and so dedicated, can long endure. We are met on a great battle-field of that war. We are met to dedicate a portion of it as the final resting-place of those who here gave their lives that that nation might live. It is altogether fitting and proper that we should do this.

But, in a larger sense, we cannot dedicate—we cannot consecrate—we cannot hallow this ground. The brave men, living and dead, who struggled here, have consecrated it far above our power to add or detract. The world will little note, nor long remember, what we *say* here, but it can never forget what they *did* here. It is for us, the living, rather to be dedicated here to the unfinished work that they have thus far so nobly carried on. It is rather for us to be here dedicated to the great task remaining before us, that from these honored dead we take increased devotion to the cause for which they here gave the last full measure of devotion, that we here highly resolve that the dead shall not have died in vain ; that the nation shall, under God, have a new birth of freedom ; and that government of the people, by the people, and for the people shall not perish from the earth.

Before the first sentence was completed, a thrill of feeling, like an electric shock, pervaded the crowd. That mysterious influence called magnetism, which sometimes so affects a popular assembly, spread to every heart. The vast audience was instantly hushed, and hung upon his every word and syllable When he uttered the sentence, "The world will little *note*, nor long remember, what we *say* here, but it can never forget what they *did* here," everyone felt that it was not the "honored dead" only, but the living actor and speaker, that the world for all time to come would note and remember, and that he, the speaker, in the thrilling words he was uttering, was linking his name forever with the glory of the dead. He seemed so absorbed in honoring the "heroic sacrifices" of the soldiers as utterly to forget himself; but all his hearers realized that the great actor in the drama stood before them, and that the words he was speaking would live as long as the language; that they were words which would be recalled in all future ages, among all peoples ; as often as men should be called upon to die for liberty and country. (*Arnold's Life of Abraham Lincoln.*)

LINCOLN'S SECOND INAUGURAL ADDRESS,

MARCH 4, 1865.

THE scene of Lincoln's re-inauguration was a striking one. The morning had been inclement, storming so violently that it was supposed that the Inaugural Address would have to be delivered in the Senate Chamber. But the people had gathered in immense numbers before the Capitol, in spite of the storm, and just before noon the rain ceased and the clouds broke away, and, as the President took the oath of office, the blue sky appeared above, a small white cloud, like a hovering bird, seemed to hang above his head, and the sunlight broke through the clouds and fell upon him like a glory, afterwards felt to have been an emblem of the martyr's crown so soon to rest upon his head. (From *The Life and Public Services of Abraham Lincoln.* By HENRY J. RAYMOND.)

FELLOW-COUNTRYMEN: At this second appearing to take the oath of the Presidential office, there is less occasion for an extended address than there was at the first. Then, a statement, somewhat in detail, of a course to be pursued, seemed fitting and proper. Now, at the expiration of four years, during which public declarations have been constantly called forth on every point and phase of the great contest which still absorbs the attention and engrosses the energies of the nation, little that is new could be presented. The progress of our arms, upon which all else chiefly depends, is as well known to the public as to myself; and it is, I trust, reasonably satisfactory and encouraging to all. With high hope for the future, no prediction in regard to it is ventured.

On the occasion corresponding to this four years ago, all thoughts were anxiously directed to an impending civil war. All dreaded it—all sought to avert it. While the inaugural address was being delivered from this place, devoted altogether to saving the Union without war, insurgent agents were in the city seeking to destroy it without war—seeking to dissolve the Union, and divide effects, by negotiation. Both parties deprecated war; but one of them would make war rather than let the nation survive; and the other would accept war rather than let it perish. And the war came.

One-eighth of the whole population were colored slaves, not distributed generally over the Union, but localized in the Southern part of it. These slaves constituted a peculiar and powerful interest. All knew that this interest, was, somehow, the cause of the war. To strengthen, perpetuate, and extend this interest was the object for which the insurgents would rend the Union, even by war; while the Government claimed no right to do more than to restrict the territorial enlargement of it. Neither party expected for the war the magnitude or the duration which it has already attained. Neither anticipated that the cause of the conflict might cease with, or even before, the conflict itself should cease. Each looked for an easier triumph, and a result less fundamental and astounding. Both read the same Bible, and pray to the same God; and each invokes his aid against the other. It may seem strange that any men should dare to ask a just God's assistance in wringing their bread from the sweat of other men's faces; but let us judge not, that we be not judged. The prayers of both could not be answered—that of neither has been answered fully. The Almighty has his own purposes. " Woe unto the world because of offences, for it must needs be that offences come; but woe to that man by whom the offence cometh." If we shall suppose that American slavery is one of these offences which, in the providence of God, must needs come, but which, having continued through his appointed time, he now wills to remove, and that he gives to both North and South this terrible war, as the woe due to those by whom the offence came, shall we discern therein any departure from those divine attributes which the believers in a living God always ascribe to him? Fondly do we hope—fervently do we pray—that this mighty scourge of war may speedily pass away. Yet, if God wills that it continue until all the wealth piled by the bondman's two hundred and fifty years of unrequited toil shall be sunk, and until every drop of blood drawn with the lash shall be paid by another drawn with the sword, as was said three thousand years ago, so still it must be said, " The judgments of the Lord are true and righteous altogether."

With malice toward none; with charity for all; with firmness in the right, as God gives us to see the right, let us strive on to finish the work we are in; to bind up the nation's wounds; to care for him who shall have borne the battle, and for his widow, and his orphan—to do all which may achieve and cherish a just and lasting peace among ourselves, and with all nations.

An interesting criticism of the Address was made by Mr. Lincoln himself, in a letter to Mr. Thurlow Weed. He writes:

DEAR MR. WEED: Everyone likes a compliment. Thank you for yours on my little notification speech and on the recent Inaugural Address. I expect the latter to wear as well as, perhaps better than, anything I have produced; but I believe it is not immediately popular. Men are not flattered by being shown that there has been a difference of purpose between the Almighty and them. To deny it, however, in this case, is to deny that there is a God governing the world. It is a truth which I thought needed to be told, and, as whatever of humiliation there is in it falls most directly on myself, I thought others might afford for me to tell it. (From *Abraham Lincoln: A History.* By JOHN G. NICOLAY and JOHN HAY.)

FAVORITE POEMS OF PRESIDENT LINCOLN.

OH! WHY SHOULD THE SPIRIT OF MORTAL BE PROUD?

OH! why should the spirit of mortal be proud?
Like a swift-fleeting meteor, a fast-flying cloud,
A flash of the lightning, a break of the wave,
Man passeth from life to his rest in the grave.

The leaves of the oak and the willow shall fade,
Be scattered around, and together be laid;
And the young and the old, and the low and the high
Shall moulder to dust and together shall lie.

The infant a mother attended and loved;
The mother that infant's affection who proved;
The husband that mother and infant who blessed—
Each, all, are away to their dwellings of rest.

The maid on whose cheek, on whose brow, in whose eye,
Shone beauty and pleasure—her triumphs are by;
And the memory of those who loved her and praised
Are alike from the minds of the living erased.

The hand of the king that the sceptre hath borne;
The brow of the priest that the mitre hath worn;
The eye of the sage, and the heart of the brave,
Are hidden and lost in the depth of the grave.

The peasant whose lot was to sow and to reap;
The herdsman who climbed with his goats up the steep;
The beggar who wandered in search of his bread,
Have faded away like the grass that we tread.

The saint who enjoyed the communion of heaven;
The sinner who dared to remain unforgiven ;
The wise and the foolish, the guilty and just,
Have quietly mingled their bones in the dust.

So the multitude goes, like the flowers or the weed
That withers away to let others succeed ;
So the multitude comes, even those we behold,
To repeat every tale that has often been told.

For we are the same our fathers have been ;
We see the same sights our fathers have seen ;
We drink the same stream, and view the same sun,
And run the same course our fathers have run.

The thoughts we are thinking our fathers would think;
From the death we are shrinking our fathers would shrink ;
To the life we are clinging they also would cling ;
But it speeds for us all, like a bird on the wing.

They loved, but the story we cannot unfold ;
They scorned, but the heart of the haughty is cold ;
They grieved, but no wail from their slumbers will come ;
They joyed, but the tongue of their gladness is dumb.

They died, aye! they died ; and we things that are now,
Who walk on the turf that lies over their brow,
Who make in their dwelling a transient abode,
Meet the things that they met on their pilgrimage road.

Yea! hope and despondency, pleasure and pain,
We mingle together in sunshine and rain;
And the smiles and the tears, the song and the dirge,
Still follow each other, like surge upon surge.

'Tis the wink of an eye, 'tis the draught of a breath,
From the blossom of health to the paleness of death,
From the gilded saloon to the bier and the shroud—
Oh! why should the spirit of mortal be proud?

— *William Knox.*

THE AMERICAN FLAG.

When Freedom from her mountain height
  Unfurled her standard to the air,
She tore the azure robe of night,
  And set the stars of glory there!
She mingled with its gorgeous dyes
The milky baldric of the skies,
And striped its pure celestial white
With streakings of the morning light,
Then, from his mansion in the sun,
She called her eagle bearer down,
And gave into his mighty hand
The symbol of her chosen land!

Majestic monarch of the cloud!
  Who rear'st aloft thy regal form,
To hear the tempest-trumpings loud,
And see the lightning lances driven,
  When strive the warriors of the storm,
And rolls the thunder-drum of heaven—
Child of the sun! to thee 'tis given
  To guard the banner of the free,
To hover in the sulphur smoke,
To ward away the battle stroke,
And bid its blendings shine afar,
Like rainbows on the cloud of war,
  The harbingers of victory!

Flag of the brave! thy fold shall fly,
The sign of hope and triumph high!
When speaks the signal-trumpet tone,
And the long line comes gleaming on,
Ere yet the life-blood, warm and wet,
Has dimmed the glistening bayonet.
Each soldier's eye shall brightly turn
To where thy sky-born glories burn,
And as his springing steps advance,
Catch war and vengeance from the glance.
And when the cannon-mouthings loud
Heave in wild wreaths the battle shroud,

And gory sabres rise and fall
Like shoots of flame on midnight's pall,
Then shall thy meteor glances glow,
   And cowering foes shall shrink beneath
Each gallant arm that strikes below
   That lovely messenger of death.

Flag of the seas! on ocean wave
Thy stars shall glitter o'er the brave;
When death, careering on the gale,
Sweeps darkly round the bellied sail,
And frighted waves rush wildly back
Before the broadside's reeling rack,
Each dying wanderer of the sea
Shall look at once to heaven and thee,
And smile to see thy splendors fly
In triumph o'er his closing eye.

Flag of the free heart's hope and home,
   By angel hands to Valor given,
Thy stars have lit the welkin dome,
   And all thy hues were born in heaven!
Forever float that standard sheet,
   Where breathes the foe but falls before us,
With Freedom's soil beneath our feet,
   And Freedom's banner streaming o'er us!

—Joseph Rodman Drake.

A SHORT HISTORY OF THE CITY OF WASHINGTON.

THE LOCATION OF THE CAPITAL.

DURING the Revolutionary War the Congress of the Confederation held its sessions generally at Philadelphia, then the most important city in the country. The exigencies of war sometimes forced it to withdraw to other places, but as soon as the danger had passed it returned. At the close of the War the question of a permanent Seat of Government at once arose. The discussion of the subject was carried on with considerable acrimony, and the conflicting claims of the various sections of the country seemed irreconcilable. Now one place, now another, was chosen, only to be set aside at a subsequent meeting, and the final determination seemed as far off as ever. New York, Philadelphia, Baltimore, Harrisburg, Trenton, Georgetown, the banks of the Delaware above Philadelphia—all were more or less favored at one time or another.

Meantime, the Congress of the Confederation was going from bad to worse. From the nature of its constitution it was an unwieldy body, besides having no power to enforce its decrees or requisitions. The close of the War released the States from the fear of a common enemy, and gave full play to mutual jealousy and dislike of any superior power. The attendance at Congress fell off, there being often difficulty in obtaining a quorum. No respect was paid to its deliberations; in fact, it was once compelled to withdraw from Philadelphia on account of its sessions having been interrupted by a mob which the city authorities made no attempt to suppress.

It was evident that something must be done to check the growing tendency toward the dismemberment of the Confederation. A convention of delegates from the several States met at Philadelphia in 1787, "in order to form a more perfect union," and there formulated and submitted to the people the draft of the Constitution of the United States. As the question of the National Capital was still unsettled, it was left to the determination of the first Congress under the new Government, power being given "to exercise exclusive legislation in all cases whatsoever, over such district (not exceeding ten miles square) as may, by cession of particular States, and the acceptance of Congress, become the Seat of the Government of the United States."*

The First Congress of the United States met at New York, March 4, 1789, but on account of the non-arrival of some of its members, it was not ready

---

* Constitution of the United States. Art. I., Sec. 8.

for business until a month later. The struggle over the site for the Capital was at once renewed. The claims of many places, among them New York, Philadelphia, Baltimore, Trenton, Carlisle, Harrisburg, Germantown, Lancaster, Alexandria, Georgetown, and others, were put forward and urged with the greatest zeal by different members. Sectional jealousy had much to do with the dispute. The Eastern members would not agree to a site in the South, preferring New York to any other place, while the Southern members declared the Potomac site was the most suitable in every respect. It seemed impossible for Congress to arrive at any decision, notwithstanding that several States had made liberal offers. New York had provided fine accommodations for Congress and the Executive; Maryland had passed an Act offering to cede any district that Congress might desire; Virginia had passed a similar Act.

The conflict seemed at one time likely to end in the selection of a Pennsylvania site, at Germantown. The Senate passed an Act authorizing that location. This was agreed to by the House, but with the proviso that the Pennsylvania laws should, for a time, continue in force. This brought the bill again before the Senate, and, as there remained but forty-eight hours of the session, the whole matter was postponed until the next session.

The second session of the First Congress began January 4, 1790. Necessary public business took up much of the time, and the Capital question was not considered until May. No mention of the Pennsylvania site was made, but a bill was introduced into the Senate and favorably reported by the Committee locating the Capital on the Potomac. President Washington was known to be strongly in its favor. As a young surveyor he had noticed a spot on the eastern bank, some six miles above Alexandria, which was peculiarly well adapted to the needs of a great city, and he used all his influence in urging its selection. The Southern members were unanimously in its favor, but those of the Middle and Eastern States were opposed.

When the bill came before the Senate, June 28, 1790, locating the Seat of Government "on the River Potomac, at some space between the mouths of the Eastern Branch and the Conococheague," all the Southern members voted for it, and they had the support of the two Senators from Pennsylvania, and of one from New Hampshire, the vote standing sixteen yeas to nine nays.

The bill came before the House July 9, 1790, and although a strong attempt was made to substitute Baltimore, it was passed as it came from the Senate. The Southern members had the assistance of the votes of some Pennsylvania and New Jersey members, the vote standing thirty-two yeas to twenty-nine nays. The Act located the Capital at Philadelphia until 1800, when the permanent Capital should be established on the Potomac.

Thomas Jefferson has given what may be called the "inside history" of the passage of the bill, and it reveals a delicate piece of legislative strategy, not to say "log-rolling." At the same time that the bill was before Congress, Alexander Hamilton, Secretary of the Treasury, was trying to pass his famous funding bill. It provided for the assumption by the Federal Government of the war debts of the various States. Most of the claims affected were held by constituents of the Eastern members, who gave it strong support, while the Southern members were vehemently opposed to it. On the two bills, therefore, the positions and interests of the members from the two sections were exactly interchanged. A compromise was effected, and both bills passed.

Jefferson gives an account of how this was done. In his diary he writes: "I proposed to Hamilton to dine with me, and I would invite another friend or two and bring them into conference together, and I thought it impossible that reasonable men consulting together coolly could fail, by some mutual sacrifices of opinion, to form a compromise which was to save the Union. The discussion took place. It was finally agreed that, whatever importance had been attached to the rejection of the funding proposition, the preservation of the Union and of concord among the States was more important, and that therefore it would be better that the vote of rejection should be rescinded, to effect which some members should change their votes. But it was observed that this pill would be peculiarly bitter to the Southern States, and that some concomitant measure should be adopted to sweeten it a little to them. There had been before propositions to fix the Seat of Government either at Philadelphia or at Georgetown on the Potomac; and it was thought by giving it to Philadelphia for ten years, and to Georgetown permanently afterwards, this might act as an anodyne, and calm in some measure the ferment which might be excited by the other measure alone. So two of the Potomac members agreed to change their votes, and Hamilton undertook to carry the other point. In doing this the influence he had established over the Eastern members effected his side of the engagement, and so the Assumption was passed."

Jefferson is generally believed to have been the originator of this scheme, and it is owing to his sagacity that the two bills, which were causing so much trouble, were passed, and a threatened dissolution of the new-made Union prevented.

The "Act for establishing the temporary and permanent Seat of the Government of the United States" was passed by Congress July 9, 1790, and is as follows:

"SECTION 1. *Be it enacted by the Senate and House of Representatives of the United States of America in Congress assembled,* That a district of territory not exceeding ten miles square, to be located as hereafter directed, on the River Potomac, at some space between the mouths of the Eastern Branch and Conococheague, be, and the same is hereby accepted for the permanent Seat of the Government of the United States: *Provided, nevertheless,* that the operation of the laws of the State within such district shall not be affected by this acceptance until the time fixed for the removal of the Government thereto, and until Congress shall otherwise by law provide.

"SEC. 2. *And be it further enacted,* That the President of the United States be authorized to appoint, and, by supplying vacancies happening from refusals to act or other causes, to keep in appointment as long as may be necessary, three Commissioners, who, or any two of whom, shall, under the direction of the President, survey, and by proper metes and bounds define and limit a district of territory under the limitations above mentioned; and the district so defined, limited and located shall be deemed the district accepted by this Act for the permanent Seat of the Government of the United States.

"SEC. 3. *And be it enacted*, That the said Commissioners, or any two of them, shall have power to purchase or accept such quantity of land on the eastern side of the said river within the said district as the President shall deem proper for the use of the United States, and according to such plans as the President shall approve said Commissioners, or any two of them, shall prior to the first Monday in December, in the year one thousand eight hundred, provide suitable buildings for the accommodation of Congress, and of the President, and for the public offices of the Government of the United States.

"SEC. 4. *And be it enacted*, That for defraying the expense of such purchases and buildings, the President of the United States be authorized and requested to accept grants of money.

"SEC. 5. *And be it enacted*, That prior to the first Monday in December next, all offices attached to the Seat of Government of the United States shall be removed to, and until the first Monday in December, in the year one thousand eight hundred, shall remain at the city of Philadelphia, in the State of Pennsylvania, at which place the session of Congress next ensuing the present shall be held.

"SEC. 6. *And be it enacted*, That on the said first Monday in December, in the year one thousand eight hundred, the Seat of the Government of the United States shall by virtue of this Act be transferred to the district and place aforesaid, and all offices attached to the said Seat of Government shall accordingly be removed thereto by their respective holders, and shall, after the said day, cease to be exercised elsewhere; and that the necessary expense of such removal shall be defrayed out of the duties on impost and tonnage, of which a sufficient sum is hereby appropriated.

"July 16, 1790. (Approved.)

"GEORGE WASHINGTON,

"*President of the United States.*"

THE OWNERS AND THE COMMISSIONERS.

The earliest mention of territory of which the District of Columbia forms a part, was made in the writings of Captain John Smith, who made some explorations along the "Patawomeke," as he calls it. Subsequent explorers became quite enthusiastic over the great beauty and rare advantages of the country, and in 1663 a party of Scotch and Irish immigrants founded a settle-

HISTORY OF THE CITY OF WASHINGTON.   53

ment in what is now the District. There is an old deed, bearing date of June 5, 1663, giving the boundaries of what is now Capitol Hill, a tract owned by Francis Pope, and called Rome. A small stream on the west was called the Tiber.

The settlement was small, and so far away from the towns on the seacoast, that it was but little known. The first town of any size was Belvoir, afterwards Alexandria, founded in 1748. It grew very rapidly, and, at one time, was thought likely to rival Baltimore in commercial importance. An unsuccessful effort was made to have Congress choose it as the site of the Capital, and the failure seems to have put a stop to further progress. It is now a quiet, sleepy old place with about fourteen thousand inhabitants.

Georgetown, in the western part of the District, was founded in 1751, although not incorporated until 1789. It was practically the site chosen, although the great public buildings were to be placed to the eastward.

By the Act of Congress, President Washington was directed to select the site within the prescribed limits and to appoint Commissioners to attend to all the details of the business. At his request, Congress amended the Act of July 16, 1790, so as to include the country around Alexandria. By the Act of July 9, 1846, this portion of the District, containing about thirty-six square miles, was retroceded to Virginia.

The proclamation, defining the site, was issued March 30, 1791, and was as follows:

"Beginning at Jones' Point, being the upper cape of Hunting Creek, in Virginia, and at an angle of forty-five degrees west of the north, and running in a direct line ten miles for the first line; then beginning again at the same Jones' Point and running another direct line at a right angle with the first; then from the terminations of the said first and second line, running two other direct lines of ten miles each, the one crossing the Eastern Branch and the other the Potomac, and meeting each other in a point."

The territory, therefore, formed a square containing one hundred square miles.

The Commissioners appointed by the President were General Thomas Johnson, Governor of Virginia; Hon. Daniel Carroll, one of the famous Maryland family; and Dr. David Stuart, of Virginia. All were well known. General Johnson had served through the Revolutionary War; Carroll was a member of Congress and a large landowner; Stuart was the best-known physician in Virginia, and was connected with the Washingtons through his marriage with the widow of John Parke Custis, the son of Mrs. Washington by her first husband.

The first boundary-stone was laid at Jones' Point April 15, 1791, with impressive Masonic ceremonies, naming the district the "Territory of Columbia," and giving to the Capital the name of "The City of Washington."

An admirable engineer and surveyor was found in Major Pierre Charles L'Enfant, a Frenchman, who came to the country in 1777 under Count D'Estaing. He afterwards held a commission in the American army for the remainder of the War, and at its close continued the practice of his profession in America. He prepared the Halls of Congress in New York and Philadelphia, and built for Robert Morris a fine mansion, having the first mansard roof in America. The badge of the Society of the Cincinnati was also his design. L'Enfant was directed to prepare the plan for the city, and although it was not strictly followed out, its more important features were retained, and have given the country the best-planned city in the world. L'Enfant's plan, damaged by usage and yellow with age, is still preserved in the office of the Architect of the Capitol.

L'Enfant had as an assistant Andrew Ellicott, a young man from Pennsylvania, and, for a time, they worked in great harmony with each other and with the Commissioners.

The Commissioners soon found that the troubles in regard to the Capital had by no means ended with the passage of the Act defining the site. Most vexatious delays arose on account of the avarice and obstinacy of the proprietors of the ground. They were, with one or two exceptions, of a very grasping nature, and determined to get as much and give as little as possible. The most exaggerated ideas were afloat in regard to the future greatness of the city. Many expected that in a few years it would rival New York and Philadelphia in size and importance, while some believed a population of a million to be a near possibility. Inflamed by the visions of vast wealth, the owners for a long time refused to part with their land except on the most extravagant terms. Washington was accustomed to ride over from Mount Vernon and meet the Commissioners at a famous tavern at Georgetown, known as Suter's, where the negotiations were carried on. Many a bitter wrangle took place within its walls. One of the proprietors was a crusty, vulgar old Scotchman, who had little reverence for any person on earth. He greatly offended Washington by remarking one day: "I suppose, Mr. Washington, you think people are going to take every grist from you as pure grain, but what would you have been if you hadn't married the rich widow Custis?"

After great trouble and delay, the proprietors and the Commissioners arrived at an agreement, and the work of laying-out the city began.

The agreement gave the Government all the land needed for highways free, and all used for public buildings and reservations at the rate of twenty-five pounds (Maryland money, or sixty-six and two-thirds dollars) per acre. The rest was to be laid off in lots, and one-half of the amount realized at their sale was to be given to the proprietors.

There were quite a number of landowners, some of whom possessed quite extensive tracts. Of the large proprietors, Daniel Carroll, by reason of his wealth and position, was the most prominent. His career was a strange one. He was the largest owner and possessed a large amount of ready money. As one of the Commissioners he succeeded in having the Capitol located on his ground. Much of the land to the east was his, and he expected to become very wealthy by its sale. He built a fine mansion, known as Duddington Manor-House, and lived in a very extravagant style. He refused to sell his lots except at a most exorbitant price, believing that he would eventually obtain several millions for them. The high prices asked drove people to other sections of the city, and the development of the east has been slow. His taxes were high and he soon became financially embarrassed. He managed to save his home for his family, but the rest of the property passed out of his hands, and he died a poor man.

Another famous owner was David Burns. His property stretched from the Potomac, where the Monument now stands, to New York Avenue, and contained the ground now occupied by the Treasury and White House. By the sale of his lots he became a very wealthy man, but made no change in his humble way of living. He had a miserable little log hut, a story and a half high, with scanty accommodations, but would never leave it. He was very fond of liquor, though his hard head probably allowed it little effect, and it was in this habit that the only change was observable—"he took his bottle to Georgetown oftener."

Burns had a daughter, Marcia, a beautiful girl, of agreeable manners and good education. She had been brought up in Baltimore, but returned to live with her father in his little cabin. As she was her father's heiress she soon had a number of suitors. Burns himself was very fond of her, and is reported to have said on his death-bed: "Marcia, you have been a good daughter, and now you will be the richest girl in America."

From her many admirers, Marcia Burns chose General John P. Van Ness, son of Peter Van Ness, a Hollander, who had settled at Kinderhook, New York, and who was quite wealthy. General Van Ness was a member of Congress and afterwards Mayor of Washington. When his wife got possession of her property, they built a magnificent mansion close by Burns's old cabin, but Marcia would never allow the latter to be removed. She seemed to take pleasure in her former home and frequently showed her distinguished visitors through its small, narrow rooms. Mrs. Van Ness was much esteemed for her many amiable qualities and her charity. She was one of the founders of the Washington Orphan Asylum, and was its second president. She died in 1832, her husband surviving until 1851. As they had no children, the property passed to distant heirs, and now the only mementos of their life in Washington are the old mansion and the mausoleum at Oak Hill Cemetery.

Notley Young, a retired sea-captain, was another owner with whom the Commissioners had considerable trouble. He was not so crabbed and grasping as Burns, but desired to determine for himself what to sell and also what to hold. His property lay in the North-West, and the dispute arose concerning what is now Lafayette Square. Young wanted to retain it, well knowing that when divided into building lots, its location, opposite the President's House, would make it very valuable, and the Commissioners had a hard time in getting him to give it up for park purposes.

The Commissioners had further trouble with L'Enfant. He insisted on having everything his own way, and refused to disclose the details of his plan, alleging that if he did so speculators would pick out the most desirable lots. The Government desired a copy of the map but could not obtain it. One of the Commissioners, Daniel Carroll, began the erection of his house across the line of New Jersey Avenue. L'Enfant pulled it down. The angry Commissioner complained to Washington, who ordered it rebuilt, though not in the same place. The disagreements finally became so aggravating and L'Enfant's behavior so arrogant that Washington was compelled to dismiss him from the Government service, March 1, 1792.

While dissatisfied with L'Enfant's conduct, the Government wished to testify its high appreciation of the work he had done, and offered him five hundred guineas (about $2500) and a lot in the city as compensation for his services. He declined to receive anything, doubtless from pique at his removal. Little was heard of him for twenty years. President Madison offered him the position of professor of engineering at West Point, but he returned the commission, writing, "Not accepted, but not refused." James Monroe, while Secretary of War, in 1812, appointed him to construct Fort Washington, on the Potomac. He made the plans, and, for a time, superintended the work, but soon had a disagreement with the War Department, and resigned.

The remainder of his life was passed without employment. Much of his time he lived in the manor-houses of the Digges family, of Maryland, a pensioner on their bounty. He died June 4, 1824, at the home of Dudley Digges, near Bladensburg, and was buried on the estate. It was a sad ending to the career of a talented man. No stone marks his resting-place, nor has any monument been erected to the memory of the man who made possible the beautiful city of to-day.

Although L'Enfant had refused to disclose his plan to the Commissioners, either before or after his removal from office, its general nature was known, and his assistant, Andrew Ellicott, was enabled, by means of notes he had taken under L'Enfant's orders, to design a new plan very similar to the old one. The details have not been carried out exactly as originally intended, but the changes have been slight and unimportant. It was this planning entirely in advance of construction that made Washington what it is, and gave it such vast possibilities for the future. Most large cities have grown out of small hamlets, and the streets are narrow and ill-arranged. In Washington the highways form part of a well-devised system.

THE BUILDING OF THE CITY.

The corner-stone of the President's House was laid October 13, 1792, and that of the Capitol September 18, 1793. The work on these important buildings was carried on as rapidly as the meagre appropriations of Congress would allow. Had it not been for gifts and loans made by Maryland and Virginia, it is doubtful if they would have been ready for occupancy at the appointed time, 1800. However, the White House was so far finished that the President's family could live in it, though Mrs. Adams has left a graphic description of some of its discomforts. Of the Capitol, only the north, or

Senate, wing was finished, and that was so badly constructed that it was afterwards torn down.

A very good description of Washington, as it appeared in 1800, was written by John Cotton Smith, member of Congress from Connecticut. He wrote: "Our approach to the city was accompanied with sensations not easily described. One wing of the Capitol only had been erected, which, with the President's House, a mile distant from it, both constructed with white sandstone, were shining objects in dismal contrast with the scene around them. Instead of recognizing the avenues and streets portrayed on the plan of the city, not one was visible, unless we except a road, with two buildings on each side of it, called the New Jersey avenue. The Pennsylvania avenue, leading, as laid down on paper, from the Capitol to the Presidential mansion, was nearly the whole distance a deep morass covered with elder bushes, which were cut through to the President's House; and near Georgetown a block of houses had been erected which bore the name of the 'six buildings.' There were also two other blocks consisting of two or three dwelling-houses in different directions, and now and then an insulated wooden habitation; the intervening spaces, and, indeed, the surface of the city generally, being covered with scrub-oak bushes on the higher grounds, and on the marshy soil either trees or some sort of shrubbery. The desolate aspect of the place was not a little augmented by a number of unfinished edifices at Greenleaf's Point, and on an eminence a short distance from it, commenced by an individual whose name they bore, but the state of whose funds compelled him to abandon them. There appeared to be but two really comfortable habitations in all respects within the bounds of the city, one of which belonged to Daniel Carroll and the other to Notley Young. The roads in every direction were muddy and unimproved. In short, it was a new settlement."

THE HISTORY SINCE 1800.

The Seat of Government was transferred from Philadelphia to Washington in October, 1800.

There were but three thousand inhabitants, and the transition from the populous and comfortable Quaker City was anything but agreeable to the officials. They made no concealment of their discontent, writing letters to the Northern newspapers in which the Capital was spoken of as "a mud-hole almost equal to the great Serbonian bog," "a Capital of miserable huts," "a city of streets without houses," "without one solitary attractive feature."

Notwithstanding, the city grew rapidly. Its population in 1810 was eight thousand, and in 1820 fourteen thousand. Its progress was made in the face of much adverse criticism. Congress sneered at it, and the people generally manifested no interest in its condition. The Presidents did their best, but could not always persuade Congress to grant the necessary money. Jefferson got some appropriations to continue the erection of the public buildings, and had Pennsylvania Avenue opened and planted with trees. Madison did what he could, but was greatly hindered by the war with England.

The invasion of the city by the British, in 1814, was a great calamity. It was rumored during August that the enemy might attack the Capital, but it was supposed that a force could be collected sufficient to repel their advance. But the Americans soon realized that seven thousand raw militia were but ill adapted to contend with four thousand veterans, whose boast it was that for years they had not slept under a roof. General Ross, indeed, made a perilous experiment in marching sixty miles into the heart of an enemy's country, and had the Americans repeated the tactics of Lexington, and fought the British from behind stone walls and hedges, probably few would have escaped. As it was, they risked a pitched battle and were speedily routed. This battle took place at Bladensburg, August 24, 1814.

The British continued their march to Washington, and arrived on the eastern grounds of the Capitol the evening of the same day. Accounts of what followed are somewhat confused. According to the British statement, General Ross had sent in a flag of truce before entering the city, intending to levy a contribution, but not to destroy it. The flag was fired upon, and the destruction of the city followed. The buildings set fire to were the unfinished Capitol, with the contents of the Library of Congress, and many valuable paintings and archives, the Treasury, the White House, the Arsenal, and some private dwellings. Owing to a sudden alarm and subsequent hasty retreat, they could not complete their work, and a heavy rain setting in prevented the complete destruction of the buildings.

According to their own story, when they arrived at the President's House, they found dinner ready, devoured it, and then set the house on fire. Mr. Madison sent a messenger to his wife to bid her flee. She wrote to her sister, ere going: "Our kind friend, Mr. Carroll, has come to hasten my departure, and is in a very bad humor with me because I insist on waiting till the large picture of General Washington is secured, and it requires to be unscrewed from the wall." She finally secured it, and went off in her carriage with her sister, Mrs. Cutts, bearing the original parchment of the Declaration of Independence, which also owes its safety to her. The Federalist papers made plenty of fun of her retreat, and Mr. Lossing has preserved a fragment of one of their ballads in which she says to the President, in the style of John Gilpin:

"Sister Cutts and Cutts and I,
And Cutts's children three,
Shall in the coach, and you shall ride
On horseback after we."

But, on the whole, the lady of the Presidential "palace" carried off more laurels from Washington than most American men.

The news of the burning of Washington was variously received in England. The British *Annual Register* called it "a return to the times of barbarism," but the London *Times* saw in it, on the contrary, the disappearance of the American Republic, which it called by the withering name of an "association." "That ill-organized association is on the eve of dissolution, and the world is speedily to be delivered of the mischievous example of the existence of a government founded on democratic rebellion." But the burning had, on the contrary, just the opposite effect from this. After Washington had fallen, Baltimore seemed an easy prey; but there was a great rising of the people; the British army was beaten off—the affair turning largely on the gallant defence of Fort McHenry by Colonel George Armistead—and General Ross was killed. It was at this time that Key's lyric " The Star-spangled Banner" was written, the author being detained on board the British ship "Minden" during the bombardment.

The loss to the Government was over $2,000,000, and to private citizens about $500,000.

For some time there was much agitation on the subject of removing the Capital, but it died out, and Congress authorized the reconstruction of the public buildings.

The city contined to grow, slowly indeed, but steadily. In 1830 Pennsylvania Avenue was paved, though the work was poorly done. In 1835 the Baltimore and Ohio Railroad built its Washington branch, and in 1836 Long Bridge was opened.

By 1840 the population of the city had increased to twenty-four thousand. In 1844 a very sad accident happened. A number of prominent officials visited the "Princeton," the first screw man-of-war. While a salute was being fired in their honor, one of the guns burst, killing Secretary of State Upshur, Secretary of the Navy Gilmer, and three other persons, and seriously injuring eighteen others. Gilmer, by the way, had been a Western lawyer, and never having seen a ship-of-war before becoming Secretary, was entirely ignorant of its construction. It is said, that while on an official visit to the Norfolk Navy Yard, he was taken on board the line-of-battle ship "Pennsylvania," the largest war vessel built up to that time. Happening to look down the hatchway, he exclaimed: " By ——, the old thing is hollow!"

In 1850 the population had risen to forty thousand, and in 1860 to sixty-one thousand. The city was still, however, a very uncomfortable place to live in. The streets were dirty and unpaved, the private houses mean and insignificant, and the pretentious public buildings, scattered about at great intervals served only to emphasize the general squalid appearance.

During the Civil War, Washington was a busy, bustling city. At the beginning of the conflict, it had no defences against a domestic enemy; Fort Washington, on the Potomac, being intended to stop the advance of a foreign fleet. The Government at once recognized the vital necessity of preserving the Capital from capture by the Confederate forces, and immediately began the construction of forts on all sides of the city. By 1863, there were, south of the Potomac, more than thirty forts and batteries, mounting over four hundred and fifty heavy guns, and on the north, over forty with four hundred guns. The defences were made so complete that, although the enemy on several occasions approached the city and caused some alarm to the inhabitants, there was never any serious danger.

The surrender of General Lee's army at Appomattox Court-House, April 9, 1865, was the virtual close of the War. There was a grand celebration of the event, the public buildings and many private houses being elaborately decorated, and at night brilliantly illuminated. Everywhere men were congratulating each other that at last the cruel War was over, and the North and South would again be in unity.

In the midst of the general rejoicing, an event happened that thrilled with horror the whole civilized world, and dealt a ruthless blow at the fair prospect of peace and fraternity. President Lincoln was assassinated.

On the night of April 14, 1865, the President and his family went to Ford's Theatre to see the play entitled "Our American Cousin." During the third act the audience was startled by the sound of a pistol-shot, but for the moment thought but little of it, doubtless supposing it one of the incidents of the drama. But the sight of a man leaping from the President's box and, with dagger in hand, rushing across the stage shouting, "'Sic Semper Tyrannis': the South is avenged," made them realize that an awful tragedy had happened, while a scream from Mrs. Lincoln at once directed their attention to the murdered President. The greatest excitement prevailed. The audience swarmed on to the stage, surrounding and attempting to enter the box. It was with great difficulty, owing to the confusion and tumult, that the wounded and unconscious President was removed from the theatre to a house opposite. He was carried to the front room on the second floor, and there he lay, never regaining consciousness, until he died on the following morning, April 15, 1865, a few minutes past seven o'clock.

From subsequent investigations it appeared that Booth had entered the box shortly before ten, and, without attracting the attention of any of the occupants, advanced to the back of the President's chair, placed the pistol close to his head, and fired. The President fell forward and the assassin leaped on to the stage and escaped by one of the wings. At a side entrance he had in readiness a fleet horse, and mounting it he hurriedly rode away. He made his way into Maryland and thence into Virginia, hoping to escape to the South and afterwards get out of the country. The pursuit was hot and he soon found his way blocked. On April 26th he was discovered hiding in a barn near Port Royal, Virginia, and was fatally wounded while resisting arrest, dying two hours afterward. Several of his accomplices were afterward arrested and tried for murder, and four of them, among whom was Mrs. Surratt, were hanged.

On the same night that the President was shot an attempt was made to assassinate Secretary of State Seward. A stranger, calling at his residence, asked for an interview, and on the appearance of the Secretary made a violent attack upon him with a knife. He was repulsed, but not before Mr. Seward and his son, who had come to his assistance, received serious wounds, from which, however, they subsequently recovered.

The news of the assassination spread rapidly through the city and excited the most profound sorrow and indignation. The loss the people had sustained was manifested in universal mourning. The public buildings, churches, schools, and many private dwellings were profusely draped with black, not only at Washington but throughout the whole of the North. The body of the President lay in state in the Rotunda until April 20, when the funeral cortège started for Springfield, passing on its way through the great cities of the East and North, and being everywhere received with universal manifestations of sorrow.

The close of the War was finally celebrated by a grand review of the Union troops, April 23d and 24th. The first day was occupied by the parade of the Army of the Potomac, under the command of Major-General George G. Meade; the second day by the march of Sherman's famous army. It was a magnificent sight, and the Nation's brave defenders were received with most enthusiastic cheers. The spectators realized that this was no holiday show. The veterans before them had risked their lives for the cause of their country, and the soiled and faded uniforms showed many a trace of wearisome march and deadly battle. The "boys in blue" were accompanied by their many curious pets, both bird and beast, and, with their battered camp utensils, presented a novel appearance.

During the years immediately following the War the Government had so much to do with settling the matters resulting from the conflict that but little could be done for the city. Nevertheless, it continued to grow in population —and ugliness.

A great change took place in 1871. Alexander R. Shepherd, an able and shrewd business man, residing in the city, believed there was a great future before the Capital if its affairs were conducted with energy and determination. Some Western cities had, moreover, made powerful efforts to change the location and have the Federal City removed to the west of the Mississippi. Quickness and vigor were necessary, or the change would be made. Shepherd persuaded Congress to pass "An Act to provide a Government for the District of Columbia," taking effect June 1, 1871, whereby the old charters, under which the cities of Washington and Georgetown had been governed as ordinary municipalities, were repealed, and a territorial government was created for the whole District. The Act vested all executive power and authority in a Governor and Secretary (appointed by the President, by and with the advice and consent of the Senate), and a Legislative Assembly, consisting of a Council and House of Delegates; provided for the appointment of a Board of Public Works, and authorized the election of a Delegate to represent the District in Congress.

Shepherd was appointed Governor, but was practically absolute, since his strong will easily dominated every department of the District government, and everything was done according to his direction.

A change in the aspect of the city immediately began. Streets were opened, well paved, and planted with trees; swamps were drained; hollows filled up; a vast and admirable system of water-works and sewerage was begun; and everything was done to promote the healthy growth of the city and to make it an attractive place of residence. All this could not, of course, be done without money, and the debt of the city rapidly increased and taxes were high. The citizens became very much dissatisfied, charging Shepherd with being autocratic and extravagant, and petitioned for a change of government. Congress finally acceded to their demands and abolished the territorial government, but not before the new public works had been so far advanced that their utility could be seen and their continuation and completion were assured.

After the abolition of the Shepherd government, the present system was instituted. By "An Act for the government of the District of Columbia, and for other purposes," approved June 20, 1874, the President was directed to appoint, by and with the advice and consent of the Senate, a Board of three Commissioners, who should "exercise all the power and authority now lawfully vested in the Governor and Board of Public Works" of the District. The representation, also, of the District in Congress was to cease with the expiration of the term of the then Delegate.

The chief event in the city's history of late years was the assassination of President Garfield, in 1881. The President was a firm opponent of the old "spoils of office" theory, and his action produced something of a factional quarrel in his party. A rejected office-seeker, Charles J. Guiteau, rendered half-crazy, though not irresponsible, by his disappointment, shot and fatally wounded the President, July 2, 1881. President Garfield was starting on a trip to the East, and had arranged to leave by the Pennsylvania Railroad, whose branch line to Washington is the Baltimore and Potomac, with a station at Sixth and B Streets, N. W. The President was accompanied by Secretary of State Blaine, and, after a short stay in the ladies' waiting-room, started for the train. When about the middle of the room, while leaning on the arm of Mr. Blaine, Guiteau fired several shots at him, one of which entered the back and eventually proved fatal. The wounded President was removed to the White House, where he remained for some weeks, until the physicians thought that his condition might be improved by his removal to the sea-coast. Arrangements were made to take him to Elberon, near Long Branch, and every possible facility was offered by the railroads, a car being fitted up as a hospital and tracks laid to the door of the cottage. Hopes were entertained that he would recover, but, after lingering a few weeks, he died September 19, 1881.

Guiteau had a carriage at the door of the station and endeavored to escape, but was arrested as soon as he reached the pavement. After a most sensational trial at the District Court-House, he was condemned to death, and was hanged at the District Jail.

The population of the city in 1891 was two hundred and forty thousand, and is increasing very rapidly. The great variety of interesting objects, and the presence of many learned and scientific men, make it a delightful home for people of culture. Magnificent houses are being built in the fashionable quarters, and the social life of the city is very gay and attractive, rendered especially so, indeed, by the presence of foreign diplomatists and travellers from all parts of the globe. More and more every year is Washington becoming the Capital of the Union, not only politically, but in literary, scientific, and social life.

THE GENESIS OF THE UNITED STATES OF AMERICA.

THE ALBANY CONFERENCE, 1754.

In 1754 the Lords of Trade ordered Commissioners from the various Colonies and Provinces to meet at Albany and confer in regard to the conduct of the impending French and Indian War. Franklin, the Commissioner from Pennsylvania, proposed a plan of union, but was overruled.

THE FIRST COLONIAL CONGRESS, 1765.

A Congress composed of delegates from nine Colonies (New Hampshire, Virginia, North Carolina, and Georgia being acquiescent but not represented) met at New York, October 7, 1765, to take action in regard to the taxation bills passed by the British Parliament—notably the Stamp Act. This is generally known as the First Colonial Congress.

THE FIRST CONTINENTAL CONGRESS, 1774.

In response to a call, proposed by Virginia and issued by Massachusetts, a Congress assembled at Carpenters' Hall, Philadelphia, September 5, 1774. Delegates were present from all the Colonies except Georgia, which was, however, known to be in thorough sympathy with the movement. It was so thoroughly representative that it is usually known as the First Continental, though sometimes called the Second Colonial, Congress.

After adopting addresses to the King, and to the people of the Colonies, of Quebec, and of Great Britain, it passed a Declaration of Colonial Rights. It also passed Articles of Association, to be signed by the people everywhere, and, in addition, the following Resolution: "That this Congress approve the opposition of the inhabitants of Massachusetts Bay to the execution of the late Acts of Parliament; and if the same be attempted to be carried into execution by force, in such case all America ought to support them in their opposition."

In framing rules for its government, the Congress resolved that in determining questions each Colony or Province should have one vote—a principle afterward embodied in the Articles of Confederation, and still preserved, although in a modified form, in the United States Senate.

After summoning a new Congress, to meet at Philadelphia, May 10, 1775, the First Continental Congress adjourned.

THE SECOND CONTINENTAL CONGRESS, 1775.

When the Second Continental Congress met at Philadelphia, May 10, 1775, the Revolution had already begun. Lexington was fought April 19, 1775, and Ticonderoga captured the very day of the meeting. Still the Colonies adhered to their allegiance to the Crown, as is evidenced by their sending an address to the King, July, 1775, and also in the appointment of a committee, November, 1775, "to maintain intercourse with the friends of the Colonies in Great Britain, Ireland, and elsewhere."

But as it became evident that the King was determined to put down the "rebellion" by force, and as all hope of recognition of their rights by the British Parliament vanished, the feeling in favor of Independence grew stronger, and on June 7, 1776, it was moved by Richard Henry Lee, of Virginia, and seconded by John Adams, of Massachusetts, that the Colonies should declare their independence of Great Britain. A committee was appointed to draw up a declaration in conformity with the resolution, but the resolution itself was not adopted until July 2, 1776, when the Congress passed it as follows:

"*Resolved*, That these United Colonies are, and of right ought to be, Free and Independent States; that they are absolved from all allegiance to the British Crown, and that all political connection between them, and the State of Great Britain, is, and ought to be, totally dissolved."

The DECLARATION OF INDEPENDENCE was agreed to July 4, 1776—the date, according to the decision of the Supreme Court, of the beginning of the existence of the United States of America.

At the time of the Declaration of Independence Congress began preparing a "form of confederation" which should express the relative powers of the State and National Governments. The Articles of Confederation and perpetual Union of the United States of America were agreed to by the delegates of the thirteen original States in Congress assembled, November 15, 1777; subject to the ratification by the Legislatures of the several States. They were ratified by eight States July 9, 1778, and, therefore, bear that date. The last State, Maryland, did not ratify until March 1, 1781.

The Second Continental Congress is considered to have lasted from May 10, 1775, until March 4, 1789, when, in accordance with the resolution of September 13, 1788, adopting the Federal Constitution, which had been previously ratified by the necessary number of States, its existence terminated.

THE THIRTEEN ORIGINAL STATES.

THE FEDERAL UNION, 1789.

The privilege of becoming a member of the Federal Union by the mere ratification of the Constitution was reserved to those States alone that had been parties to the previous Confederation.

By the provisions of the Constitution it was to go into effect when ratified by nine States—the exact date to be determined by Congress. The eleventh State, New York, ratified it July 26, 1788, and Congress, September 13, 1788, appointed the first Wednesday (4th day) of March, 1789, as the date when the new Government should begin. Two of the States, North Carolina (November 21, 1789) and Rhode Island (May 29, 1790) did not ratify the Constitution until after its establishment, yet they were not considered as new States, and their Senators and Representatives were admitted to Congress upon the presentation of their authenticated certificates of ratification.

The Union having been completed, and its Constitution and Government established, the United States, under the Constitution (Art. IV. Sect. 3), reserved to themselves, in Congress assembled, the right and power to admit new States, by declaring that "new States may be admitted, etc." As the Constitution provides that "The United States shall guarantee to every State in this Union a Republican form of Government," it has been deemed requisite that each new State, on applying for admission, shall present with its application a copy of its Constitution, in order that Congress may judge if it be in conformity with the Constitution of the United States.

The Constitution also provides (Art. IV. Sect. 3) that "Congress shall have power to dispose of and make all needful rules and regulations respecting the territory or other property of the United States, etc." Under this clause Congress exercises the power of creating territorial governments, which may, after a time, when possessed of sufficient population and material resources, be admitted as sovereign States.

It is by the operation of these clauses of the Constitution that the number of States has been increased from thirteen in 1790 to forty-four in 1891.

THE THIRTEEN ORIGINAL STATES.

	States	Settled	Ratified the Constitution	Area in square miles	Population in 1890
1	Delaware	1638	Dec. 7, 1787	2,050	168,493
2	Pennsylvania	1682	Dec. 12, 1787	45,215	5,258,014
3	New Jersey	1664	Dec. 18, 1787	7,815	1,444,933
4	Georgia	1733	Jan. 2, 1788	59,475	1,837,353
5	Connecticut	1633	Jan. 9, 1788	4,990	746,258
6	Massachusetts	1620	Feb. 6, 1788	8,315	2,238,943
7	Maryland	1634	April 28, 1788	12,210	1,042,390
8	South Carolina	1670	May 23, 1788	30,570	1,151,149
9	New Hampshire	1623	June 21, 1788	9,305	376,530
10	Virginia	1607	June 25, 1788	42,450	1,655,980
11	New York	1614	July 26, 1788	49,170	5,997,853
12	North Carolina	1650	Nov. 21, 1789	52,250	1,617,947
13	Rhode Island*	1636	May 29, 1790	1,250	345,506

* The official name is The State of Rhode Island and Providence Plantations.

STATES ADMITTED TO THE UNION.

	States	Organized as a Territory	Admitted as a State	Area in square miles	Population in 1890
14	Vermont		March 4, 1791	9,565	332,422
15	Kentucky		June 1, 1792	40,400	1,858,635
16	Tennessee	May 26, 1790	June 1, 1796	42,050	1,767,518
17	Ohio	May 7, 1800	Nov. 29, 1802	41,000	3,672,316
18	Louisiana	March 26, 1804	April 8, 1812	48,720	1,118,587
19	Indiana	May 7, 1800	Dec. 11, 1816	36,350	2,192,404
20	Mississippi	April 7, 1798	Dec. 10, 1817	46,810	1,289,600
21	Illinois	Feb. 3, 1809	Dec. 3, 1818	56,650	3,826,351
22	Alabama	March 3, 1817	Dec. 14, 1819	52,250	1,513,017
23	Maine	June 19, 1819*	March 15, 1820	33,040	661,086
24	Missouri	March 26, 1804	Aug. 10, 1821	69,415	2,679,184
25	Arkansas	March 2, 1819	June 15, 1836	53,850	1,128,179
26	Michigan	Jan. 11, 1805	Jan. 26, 1837	58,915	2,093,889
27	Florida	March 30, 1822	March 3, 1845	58,680	391,422
28	Texas	................†	Dec. 29, 1845	265,780	2,235,523
29	Iowa	June 12, 1838	Dec. 28, 1846	56,025	1,911,896
30	Wisconsin	April 20, 1836	May 29, 1848	56,040	1,686,880
31	California	................‡	Sept. 9, 1850	158,360	1,208,130
32	Minnesota	March 3, 1849	May 11, 1858	83,365	1,301,826
33	Oregon	Aug. 14, 1848	Feb. 14, 1859	96,030	313,767
34	Kansas	May 30, 1854	Jan. 29, 1861	82,080	1,427,096
35	West Virginia	May 13, 1862§	June 31, 1862	24,780	762,704
36	Nevada	March 2, 1861	Oct. 31, 1864	110,700	45,761
37	Nebraska	May 30, 1854	March 1, 1867	77,510	1,058,910
38	Colorado	Feb. 28, 1861	Aug. 1, 1876	103,925	419,198
39	North Dakota	March 2, 1861	Nov. 3, 1889	70,795	182,719
40	South Dakota	March 2, 1861	Nov. 4, 1889	77,650	328,808
41	Montana	May 26, 1864	Nov. 8, 1889	146,080	132,159
42	Washington	March 2, 1853	Nov. 11, 1889	69,180	349,390
43	Idaho	March 3, 1863	July 3, 1890	84,800	84,385
44	Wyoming	July 25, 1868	July 11, 1890	97,890	60,705

* Act of Massachusetts Legislature relating to the separation of the District of Maine.
† Texas declared its independence of Mexico in 1836, and was admitted as an independent State.
‡ California was acquired from Mexico by treaty of Guadalupe Hidalgo, February 2, 1848.
§ Act of Virginia Legislature relating to the formation of the State of West Virginia.

TERRITORIES.

	Organized as a Territory		Area in square miles	Population in 1890
New Mexico	Sept. 9, 1850		122,580	153,593
Utah	Sept. 9, 1850		84,970	207,905
Arizona	Feb. 24, 1863		113,020	59,620
Oklahoma	May 2, 1890		39,030	61,834
Indian	June 30, 1834		31,400	74,997
Alaska	July 27, 1868*		577,390	30,329
District of Columbia	July 16, 1790		64	230,392

* Act of Congress extending certain laws of the United States over the Territory.

THE PRESIDENTS AND VICE-PRESIDENTS.

THE PRESIDENTS OF THE UNITED STATES.

Name	Native State	Citizen of	Served	Dates	Died
1. George Washington	Va.	Va.	8 years.	1789–1797	Dec. 14, 1799
2. John Adams	Mass.	Mass.	4 "	1797–1801	July 4, 1826
3. Thomas Jefferson	Va.	Va.	8 "	1801–1809	July 4, 1826
4. James Madison	Va.	Va.	8 "	1809–1817	June 28, 1836
5. James Monroe	Va.	Va.	8 "	1817–1825	July 4, 1831
6. John Quincy Adams	Mass.	Mass.	4 "	1825–1829	Feb. 23, 1848
7. Andrew Jackson	N. C.	Tenn.	8 "	1829–1837	June 8, 1845
8. Martin Van Buren	N. Y.	N. Y.	4 "	1837–1841	July 24, 1862
9. *William Henry Harrison	Va.	Ohio.	1 month.	1841–1841	April 4, 1841
10. †John Tyler	Va.	Va.	3 years 11 mos.	1841–1845	Jan. 18, 1862
11. James Knox Polk	N. C.	Tenn.	4 years.	1845–1849	June 15, 1849
12. *Zachary Taylor	Va.	La.	1 yr. 4 m. 5 d.	1849–1850	July 9, 1850
13. †Millard Fillmore	N. Y.	N. Y.	2 yrs, 7 m. 23 d.	1850–1853	March 8, 1874
14. Franklin Pierce	N. H.	N. H.	4 years.	1853–1857	Oct. 8, 1869
15. James Buchanan	Pa.	Pa.	4 "	1857–1861	June 1, 1868
16. *Abraham Lincoln	Ky.	Ill.	4 yrs. 1 m. 11 d.	1861–1865	April 15, 1865
17. †Andrew Johnson	N. C.	Tenn.	3 yrs. 10 m.17 d.	1865–1869	July 31, 1875
18. Ulysses Simpson Grant	Ohio.	Ill.	8 years.	1869–1877	July 23, 1885
19. Rutherford Birchard Hayes	Ohio.	Ohio.	4 "	1877–1881	
20. *James Abram Garfield	Ohio.	Ohio.	6 mos. 15 days.	1881–1881	Sept. 19, 1881
21. †Chester Alan Arthur	Vt.	N. Y.	3 yrs. 5 m. 13 d.	1881–1885	Nov. 18, 1886
22. Grover Cleveland	N. J.	N. Y.	4 years.	1885–1889	
23. Benjamin Harrison	Ohio.	Ind.		1889–	

* Died in office. † Elected as Vice-President

THE VICE-PRESIDENTS OF THE UNITED STATES.

Name	Native State	Citizen of	Served	Dates	Died
1. John Adams	Mass.	Mass.	8 years.	1789–1797	July 4, 1826
2. Thomas Jefferson	Va.	Va.	4 "	1797–1801	July 4, 1826
3. Aaron Burr	N. J.	N. Y.	4 "	1801–1805	Sept. 14, 1836
4. *George Clinton	N. Y.	N. Y.	7 yrs 1 m. 16 d.	1805–1812	April 20, 1812
5. *Elbridge Gerry	Mass.	Mass.	1 yr. 8 m. 19 d.	1813–1814	Nov. 23, 1814
6. §Daniel D. Tompkins	N. Y.	N. Y.	8 years.	1817–1825	June 11, 1825
7. ‡John Caldwell Calhoun	S. C.	S. C.	7 yrs. 9 m. 24 d.	1825–1832	March 31, 1850
8. Martin Van Buren	N. Y.	N. Y.	4 years.	1833–1837	July 24, 1862
9. Richard Mentor Johnson	Ky.	Ky.	4 "	1837–1841	Aug. 2, 1850
10. †John Tyler	Va.	Va.	1 month.	1841–1841	Jan. 18, 1862
11. George Mifflin Dallas	Pa.	Pa.	4 years.	1845–1849	Dec. 31, 1864
12. †Millard Fillmore	N. Y.	N. Y.	1 yr. 4 m. 5 d.	1849–1850	March 8, 1874
13. *William Rufus King	N. C.	Ala.	1 m. 14 d.	1853–1853	April 18, 1853
14. John Cabell Breckenridge	Ky.	Ky.	4 years.	1857–1861	May 17, 1875
15. Hannibal Hamlin	Me.	Me.	4 "	1861–1865	July 4, 1891
16. †Andrew Johnson	N. C.	Tenn.	1 m. 11 d.	1865–1865	July 31, 1875
17. Schuyler Colfax	N. Y.	Ind.	4 years.	1869–1873	Jan. 13, 1885
18. *¶Henry Wilson	N. H.	Mass.	2 yrs. 8 m. 18 d.	1873–1875	Nov. 22, 1875
19. William Almon Wheeler	N. Y.	N. Y.	4 years.	1877–1881	June 4, 1887
20. †Chester Alan Arthur	Vt.	N. Y.	6 m. 15 d.	1881–1881	Nov. 18, 1886
21. *Thomas Andrews Hendricks	Ind.	Ind	8 m. 21 d.	1885–1885	Nov. 25, 1885
22. Levi Parsons Morton	Vt.	N. Y.		1889–	

* Died in office.
† Succeeded to the Presidency : John Tyler, April 4, 1841
    Millard Fillmore, July 9, 1850
    Andrew Johnson, April 15, 1865
    Chester Alan Arthur, Sept. 19, 1881

‡ Resigned, John Caldwell Calhoun, December 28, 1832.

§ Originally, Daniel Tompkins. He added the "D" while at school to distinguish himself from another Daniel Tompkins.

¶ Originally, Jeremiah Jones Colbaith. On reaching his majority, he obtained authority from the Legislature to change his name to Henry Wilson.

THE CHIEF JUSTICES.

Appointed by	Name	State	Served		Died
Washington	1. John Jay,	N. Y.	1789–1795	Resigned.	May 17, 1829
	2. John Rutledge,	S. C.	1795	Not confirmed.	July 23, 1800
	3. Oliver Ellsworth,	Conn.	1796–1800	Resigned.	Nov. 26, 1807
Adams	4. John Marshall,	Va.	1801–1835	Died in office.	July 6, 1835
Jackson	5. Roger B. Taney,	Md.	1836–1864	" " "	Oct. 12, 1864
Lincoln	6. Salmon P. Chase,	Ohio.	1864–1873	" " "	May 7, 1873
Grant	7. Morrison R. Waite,	Ohio.	1874–1888	" " "	March 23, 1888
Cleveland	8. Melville W. Fuller,	Ill.	1888–		

THE ASSOCIATE JUSTICES.

Appointed by	Name	State	Served		Died
Washington	Rutledge, John	S. C.	1789–1791	Resigned.	1800
	Cushing, William	Mass.	1789–1810	Died in office.	1810
	Wilson, James	Pa.	1789–1798	" " "	1798
	Blair, John	Va.	1789–1796	Resigned.	1800
	Harrison, Robert H.	Md.	1789–1790	"	1798
	Iredell, James	N. C.	1790–1799	Died in office.	1799
	Johnson, Thomas	Md.	1791–1793	Resigned.	1819
	Paterson, William	N. J.	1793–1806	Died in office.	1806
	Chase, Samuel	Md.	1796–1811	" " "	1811
Adams	Washington, Bushrod	Va.	1798–1829	" " "	1829
	Moore, Alfred	N. C.	1799–1804	Resigned.	1810
Jefferson	Johnson, William	S. C.	1804–1834	Died in office.	1834
	Livingston, Brockholst	N. Y.	1806–1823	" " "	1823
	Todd, Thomas	Ky.	1807–1826	" " "	1826
Madison	Story, Joseph	Mass.	1811–1845	" " "	1845
	Duval, Gabriel	Md.	1811–1836	Resigned.	1844
Monroe	Thompson, Smith	N. Y.	1823–1843	Died in office.	1843
Adams, J. Q.	Trimble, Robert	Ky.	1826–1828	" " "	1828
Jackson	McLean, John	Ohio	1829–1861	" " "	1861
	Baldwin, Henry	Pa.	1830–1844	" " "	1844
	Wayne, James M.	Ga.	1835–1867	" " "	1867
	Barbour, Philip P.	Va.	1836–1841	" " "	1841
Van Buren	Catron, John	Tenn.	1837–1865	" " "	1865
	McKinley, John	Ala.	1837–1852	" " "	1852
	Daniel, Peter V.	Va.	1841–1860	" " "	1860
Tyler	Nelson, Samuel	N. Y.	1845–1872	Resigned.	1873
Polk	Woodbury, Levi	N. H.	1845–1851	Died in office.	1851
	Grier, Robert C.	Pa.	1846–1870	Resigned.	1870
Fillmore	Curtis, Benjamin R.	Mass.	1851–1857	"	1874
Pierce	Campbell, John A.	Ala.	1853–1860	"	1889
Buchanan	Clifford, Nathan	Me.	1858–1881	Died in office.	1881
Lincoln	Swayne, Noah H.	Ohio	1862–1881	Resigned.	1884
	Miller, Samuel F.	Iowa	1862–1890	Died in office.	1890
	Davis, David	Ill.	1862–1877	Resigned.	1886
	Field, Stephen J.	Cal	1863–		
Grant	Stanton, Edwin M.	Ohio	1869	Died in office.	1869
	Strong, William	Pa.	1870–1880		
	Bradley, Joseph P.	N. J.	1870–1890	Died in office.	1892
	Hunt, Ward	N. Y.	1872–1882	Resigned.	1886
	Harlan, John M.	Ky	1877–		
	Woods, William B.	Ga.	1881–1887	Died in office.	1887
	Matthews, Stanley	Ohio	1881–1889	" " "	1889
	Gray, Horace	Mass.	1881–		
	Blatchford, Samuel	N Y.	1882–		
Cleveland	Lamar, Lucius Q. C.	Miss.	1888–		
Harrison, Benjamin	Brewer, David J.	Kan.	1889–		
	Brown, Henry B.	Mich.	1890–		
	Shiras, George, Jr.	Pa.	1892–		

Originally the Supreme Court consisted of a Chief Justice and five Associate Justices. Additional Justices were added as follows: By Act of Feb. 24, 1807, one; March 3, 1837, two; March 3, 1863, one. The Act of April 10, 1869, reduced the number one. At present there are eight Associate Justices.

The "Address to the King" from the Continental Congress of 1774 was sent to "Paul Wentworth, Esq.; Doctr. Benj. Franklin; William Bollen, Esq.; Doctr. Arthur Lee; Thomas Life, Esq.; Charles Garth, Esq.," "the several colony agents, in order that the same may be by them presented to his Majesty." The accompanying letter to the agents was signed by "Henry Middleton, President," "by order and on behalf of Congress." Dr. Franklin, Mr. Bollen, and Dr. Lee took charge of the Address, and presented it to Lord Dartmouth, who laid it before the King.

Under the Articles of Confederation there was an official known as the Secretary of Foreign Affairs. In case the office was vacant, the President of Congress acted as Secretary.

THE SECRETARIES OF FOREIGN AFFAIRS.

LIVINGSTON, ROBERT R , of New York. Qualified October 20, 1781. Resigned June, 1783.

BOUDINOT, ELIAS, of New Jersey. President of Congress, Secretary *ad interim*, June, 1783 to November 3, 1783.

MIFFLIN, THOMAS, of Pennsylvania. President of Congress, Secretary *ad interim*, November 3, 1783, to December 21, 1784.

JAY, JOHN, of New York. December 21, 1784, to March 4, 1789. Continued as Secretary until September 26, 1789.

THE SECRETARIES OF STATE.
(Department created by Act of Congress, September 15, 1789.)

In the administration of	Name	State	Appointed
Washington (1789-1797) . . .	Jefferson, Thomas	Va.	Sept. 26, 1789
	Randolph, Edmund	Va.	Jan. 2, 1794
	Pickering, Timothy	Pa.	Dec. 10, 1795
Adams, John (1797-1801 . . .	Pickering, Timothy	Pa.	Continued.
	Marshall, John	Va.	May 13, 1800
Jefferson (1801-1809)	Madison, James	Va.	March 5, 1801
Madison (1809-1817)	Smith, Robert	Md.	March 6, 1809
	Monroe, James	Va.	April 2, 1811
Monroe (1817-1825)	Adams, John Quincy	Mass.	March 5, 1817
Adams, J. Q. (1825-1829)	Clay, Henry	Ky	March 7, 1825
Jackson (1829-1837)	Van Buren, Martin	N. Y.	March 6, 1829
	Livingston, Edward	La	May 24, 1831
	McLane, Louis	Del.	May 29, 1833
	Forsyth, John	Ga.	June 27, 1834
Van Buren (1837-1841)	Forsyth, John	Ga.	Continued.
Harrison, W. H. (1841 to April 4, 1841	Webster, Daniel	Mass.	March 5, 1841
Tyler (April 4, 1841-1845)	Webster, Daniel	Mass.	Continued.
	Legaré, Hugh S.	S. C.	May 9, 1843
	Upshur, Abel P.	Va.	July 24, 1843
	Calhoun, John C.	S. C.	March 6, 1844
Polk (1845-1849)	Buchanan, James	Pa.	March 6, 1845
Taylor (1849 to July 9, 1850) . . .	Clayton, John M.	Del.	March 7, 1849
Fillmore (July 9, 1850-1853) . . .	Webster, Daniel	Mass.	July 22, 1850
	Everett, Edward	Mass.	Nov. 6, 1852
Pierce (1853-1857)	Marcy, William L.	N. Y.	March 7, 1853
Buchanan (1857-1861)	Cass, Lewis	Mich.	March 6, 1857
	Black, Jeremiah S.	Pa.	Dec. 17, 1860
Lincoln (1861 to April 15, 1865).	Seward, Wm. H.	N. Y.	March 5, 1861
Johnson (April 15, 1865-1869) . . .	Seward, Wm. H.	N. Y.	Continued
Grant (1869-1877)	Washburne, Elihu B.	Ill.	March 5, 1869
	Fish, Hamilton	N. Y.	March 11, 1869
Hayes (1877-1881)	Evarts, William M.	N. Y.	March 12, 1877
Garfield (1881 to Sept. 19, 1881).	Blaine, James G.	Me.	March 5, 1881
Arthur (Sept. 19, 1881-1885). . .	Frelinghuysen, F. T.	N. J.	Dec. 12, 1881
Cleveland (1885-1889)	Bayard, Thomas F.	Del.	March 6, 1885
Harrison, Benjamin (1889-) . .	Blaine, James G.	Me.	March 5, 1889
	Foster, John W.	Ind.	June 29, 1892

PRESIDENTIAL CABINET OFFICERS.

THE SECRETARIES OF THE TREASURY.
(Department created by Act of Congress, September 2, 1789.)

In the administration of	Name	State	Appointed
Washington (1789-1797)	Hamilton, Alexander	N. Y.	Sept. 11, 1789
	Wolcott, Oliver	Conn.	Feb. 2, 1795
Adams, John (1797-1801) .	Wolcott, Oliver	Conn.	Continued.
	Dexter, Samuel	Mass.	Jan. 1, 1801
Jefferson (1801-1809)	Dexter, Samuel	Mass.	Continued.
	Gallatin, Albert	Pa.	May 14, 1801
Madison (1809-1817)	Gallatin, Albert	Pa.	Continued
	Campbell, George W	Tenn.	Feb. 9, 1814
	Dallas, Alexander J.	Pa.	Oct. 6, 1814
	Crawford, Wm. H.	Ga.	Oct. 22, 1816
Monroe (1817-1825) .	Crawford, Wm. H.	Ga.	Continued.
Adams, J Q. (1825-1829)	Rush, Richard	Pa.	March 7, 1825
Jackson (1829-1837) .	Ingham, Samuel D.	Pa.	March 6, 1829
	McLane, Louis	Del.	Aug. 8, 1831
	Duane, Wm. J.	Pa.	May 29, 1833
	Taney, Roger B.	Md.	Sept. 23, 1833
	Woodbury, Levi	N. H.	June 27, 1834
Van Buren (1837-1841)	Woodbury, Levi	N. H.	Continued.
Harrison, W. H. (1841 to April 4, 1841)	Ewing, Thomas	Ohio	March 5, 1841
Tyler (April 4, 1841-1845)	Forward, Walter	Pa.	Sept. 13, 1841
	Spencer, John C.	N. Y.	March 3, 1843
	Bibb, George M	Ky.	June 15, 1844
Polk (1845-1849) .	Walker, Robert J.	Miss.	March 6, 1845
Taylor (1849 to July 9, 1850)	Meredith, Wm. M.	Pa.	March 8, 1849
Fillmore (July 9, 1850-1853).	Corwin, Thomas	Ohio	July 23, 1850
Pierce (1853-1857)	Guthrie, James	Ky.	March 7, 1853
Buchanan (1857-1861) .	Cobb, Howell	Ga.	March 6, 1857
	Thomas, Philip F.	Md.	Dec. 12, 1860
	Dix, John A.	N. Y.	Jan. 11, 1861
Lincoln (1861 to April 15, 1865)	Chase, Salmon P.	Ohio	March 5, 1861
	Fessenden, Wm. P.	Me.	July 1, 1864
	McCulloch, Hugh	Ind.	March 7, 1865
Johnson (April 15, 1865-1869)	McCulloch, Hugh	Ind.	Continued.
Grant (1869-1877) .	Boutwell, George S.	Mass.	March 11, 1869
	Richardson, Wm. A.	Mass.	March 17, 1873
	Bristow, Benj. H.	Ky.	June 2, 1874
	Morrill, Lot M.	Me.	June 21, 1876
Hayes (1877-1881)	Sherman, John	Ohio	March 8, 1877
Garfield (1881 to September 19, 1881).	Windom, Wm.	Minn.	March 5, 1881
Arthur (Sept. 19, 1881-1885).	Folger, Charles J.	N. Y.	Oct. 27, 1881
	Gresham, Walt. Q.	Ind.	Oct. 24, 1884
	McCulloch, Hugh	Ind.	Oct. 28, 1884
Cleveland (1885-1889) .	Manning, Daniel	N. Y.	March 6, 1885
	Fairchild, Charles S.	N. Y.	April 1, 1887
Harrison, Benjamin (1889-)	Windom, Wm.	Minn.	March 5, 1889
	Foster, Charles	Ohio	Feb. 24, 1891

THE SECRETARIES OF WAR.
(Department created by Act of Congress, August 7, 1789.)

In the administration of	Name	State	Appointed
Washington (1789-1797) .	Knox, Henry	Mass.	Sept. 12, 1789
	Pickering, Timothy	Pa.	Jan. 2, 1795
	McHenry, James	Md.	Jan. 27, 1796
Adams, John (1797-1801) .	McHenry, James	Md.	Continued.
	Dexter, Samuel	Mass.	May 13, 1800
	Griswold, Roger	Conn.	Feb. 3, 1801
Jefferson (1801-1809)	Dearborn, Henry	Mass.	March 5, 1801
Madison (1809-1817)	Eustis, William	Mass.	March 7, 1809
	Armstrong, John	N. Y.	Jan. 13, 1813
	Monroe, James	Va.	Sept. 27, 1814
	Crawford, Wm. H.	Ga.	Aug. 1, 1815
Monroe (1817-1825) . . .	Graham, George	Va.	April 7, 1817
	Calhoun, John C.	S. C.	Oct. 8, 1817

PRESIDENTIAL CABINET OFFICERS.

THE SECRETARIES OF WAR—*Continued.*

In the administration of	Name	State	Appointed
Adams, J. Q. (1825–1829)	Barbour, James	Va.	March 7, 1825
	Porter, Peter B.	N. Y.	May 26, 1828
Jackson (1829–1837)	Eaton, John H.	Tenn.	March 9, 1829
	Cass, Lewis	Ohio.	Aug. 1, 1831
Van Buren (1837–1841)	Poinsett, Joel R.	S. C.	March 7, 1837
Harrison, W. H. (1841 to April 4, 1841)	Bell, John	Tenn.	March 5, 1841
Tyler (April 4, 1841–1845)	Bell, John	Tenn.	Continued.
	Spencer, John C.	N. Y.	Oct. 12, 1841
	Porter, James M.	Pa.	March 8, 1843
	Wilkins, William	Pa.	Feb. 15, 1844
Polk (1845–1849)	Marcy, Wm. L.	N. Y.	March 6, 1845
Taylor (1849 to July 9, 1850) . .	Crawford, George W.	Ga.	March 8, 1849
Fillmore (July 9, 1850–1853) . . .	Conrad, Charles M.	La.	Aug. 15, 1850
Pierce (1853–1857)	Davis, Jefferson	Miss.	March 7, 1853
Buchanan (1857–1861)	Floyd, John B.	Va.	March 6, 1857
	Holt, Joseph	Ky.	Jan. 18, 1861
Lincoln (1861 to April 15, 1865) . .	Cameron, Simon	Pa.	March 5, 1861
	Stanton, Edwin M.	Ohio	Jan. 15, 1862
Johnson (April 15, 1865–1869) . . .	Stanton, Edwin M.	Ohio	Continued
	Schofield, John M.	U. S. A.	May 28, 1868
Grant (1869–1877)	Rawlins, John A.	Ill.	March 11, 1869
	Sherman, W.T.*(ad inter.)*	U. S. A	Sept. 9. 1869
	Belknap, Wm. W.	Iowa	Oct. 25, 1869
	Taft, Alphonso	Ohio	March 8, 1876
	Cameron, J. Donald	Pa.	May 22, 1876
Hayes (1877–1881)	McCrary, George W.	Iowa	March 12, 1877
	Ramsey, Alexander	Minn.	Dec. 12, 1879
Garfield (1881 to Sept. 19, 1881). . .	Lincoln, Robert T.	Ill.	March 5, 1881
Arthur (Sept. 19, 1881–1885)	Lincoln, Robert T.	Ill.	Continued.
Cleveland (1885–1889)	Endicott, Wm. C.	Mass.	March 6, 1885
Harrison (1889–)	Proctor, Redfield	Vt.	March 5, 1889
	Elkins, Stephen B.	W. Va.	Dec. 24, 1891

THE ATTORNEYS-GENERAL.

(Duties regulated by the Judiciary Act of September 24, 1789.)
Department re-organized, 1870.)

In the administration of	Name	State	Appointed
Washington (1789–1797)	Randolph, Edmund	Va.	Sept. 26, 1789
	Bradford, William	Pa.	Jan. 28, 1794
	Lee, Charles	Va.	Dec. 10, 1795
Adams John (1797–1801)	Lee, Charles	Va.	Continued.
Jefferson (1801–1809)	Lincoln, Levi	Mass.	March 5, 1801
	Smith, Robert	Md.	March 3, 1805
	Breckenridge, John	Ky.	Aug. 7, 1805
	Rodney, Cæsar A.	Pa.	Jan. 20, 1807
Madison (1809–1817)	Rodney, Cæsar A.	Pa.	Continued.
	Pinckney, William	Md.	Dec. 11, 1811
	Rush, Richard	Pa.	Feb. 10, 1814
Monroe (1817–1825)	Rush, Richard	Pa.	Continued.
	Wirt, William	Va.	Nov. 13, 1817
Adams, J Q. (1825–1829)	Wirt, William	Va.	Continued
Jackson (1829–1837)	Berrien, John M.	Ga.	March 9, 1829
	Taney, Roger B.	Md.	July 20, 1831
	Butler, Benjamin F.	N. Y.	Nov. 15, 1833
Van Buren (1837–1841)	Butler, Benjamin F.	N. Y.	Continued.
	Grundy, Felix	Tenn.	Sept. 1, 1838
	Gilpin, Henry D.	Pa.	Jan. 11, 1840
Harrison, W. H. (1841 to April 4, 1841)	Crittenden, John J.	Ky.	March 5, 1841
Tyler (April 4, 1841–1845)	Crittenden, John J.	Ky.	Continued.
	Legaré, Hugh S.	S. C.	Sept. 13, 1841
	Nelson, John	Md.	July 1, 1843
Polk (1845–1849) .	Mason, John Y.	Va.	March 6, 1845
	Clifford, Nathan	Me.	Oct. 17, 1846
	Toucey, Isaac	Conn.	June 21, 1848

PRESIDENTIAL CABINET OFFICERS.

THE ATTORNEYS-GENERAL—Continued.

In the administration of	Name	State	Appointed
Taylor (1849 to July 9, 1850)	Johnson, Reverdy	Md.	March 8, 1849
Fillmore (July 9, 1850-1853)	Crittenden, John J.	Ky.	July 22, 1850
Pierce (1853-1857)	Cushing, Caleb	Mass.	March 7, 1853
Buchanan (1857-1861)	Black, Jeremiah S.	Pa.	March 6, 1857
	Stanton, Edwin M.	Ohio	Dec. 20, 1860
Lincoln (1861 to April 15, 1865)	Bates, Edward	Mo.	March 5, 1861
	Speed, James	Ky.	Dec. 2, 1864
Johnson (April 15, 1865-1869)	Speed, James	Ky.	Continued
	Stanbery, Henry	Ohio	July 23, 1866
	Evarts, Wm. M.	N. Y.	July 15, 1868
Grant (1869-1877)	Hoar, Ebenezer R.	Mass.	March 5, 1869
	Akerman, Amos T.	Ga.	June 23, 1870
	Williams, George H.	Or.	Dec. 14, 1871
	Pierrepont, Edwards	N. Y.	April 26, 1875
	Taft, Alphonso	Ohio	May 22, 1876
Hayes (1877-1881)	Devens, Charles	Mass.	March 12, 1877
Garfield (1881 to Sept. 19, 1881)	McVeagh, Wayne	Pa.	March 5, 1881
Arthur (Sept. 19, 1881-1885)	Brewster, Benjamin H.	Pa.	Dec. 16, 1881
Cleveland (1885-1889)	Garland Augustus H.	Ark.	March 6, 1885
Harrison (1889–)	Miller, Wm. H. H	Ind.	March 5, 1889

THE POSTMASTERS-GENERAL.

(A Bureau of the Treasury until 1829. In that year became a Cabinet Office.)

In the administration of	Name	State	Appointed
Washington (1789-1797)	Osgood, Samuel	Mass.	Sept. 26, 1789
	Pickering, Timothy	Pa.	Aug. 12, 1791
	Habersham, Joseph	Ga.	Feb. 25, 1795
Adams, John (1797-1801)	Habersham, Joseph	Ga.	Continued.
Jefferson (1801-1809)	Habersham, Joseph	Ga.	Continued.
	Granger, Gideon	Conn.	Nov. 28, 1801
Madison (1809-1817)	Granger, Gideon	Conn.	Continued.
	Meigs, Return J.	Ohio	March 17, 1814
Monroe (1817-1825)	Meigs, Return J.	Ohio	Continued.
	McLean, John	Ohio	June 26, 1823
Adams, J. Q. (1825-1829)	McLean, John	Ohio	Continued.
Jackson (1829-1837)	Barry, Wm. T.	Ky.	March 9, 1829
	Kendall, Amos	Ky.	May 1, 1835
Van Buren (1837-1841)	Kendall, Amos	Ky.	Continued.
	Niles, John M.	Conn.	May 25, 1840
Harrison, W. H. (1841 to April 4, 1841)	Granger, Francis	N. Y.	March 6, 1841
Tyler (April 4, 1841-1845)	Granger, Francis	N. Y.	Continued.
	Wickliffe, Charles A.	Ky.	Sept. 13, 1841
Polk (1845-1849)	Johnson, Cave	Tenn.	March 6, 1845
Taylor (1849 to July 9, 1850)	Collamer, Jacob	Vt.	March 8, 1849
Fillmore (July 9, 1850-1853)	Hall, Nathan K.	N. Y.	July 23, 1850
	Hubbard, Samuel D.	Conn.	Aug. 31, 1852
Pierce (1853-1857)	Campbell, James	Pa.	March 7, 1853
Buchanan (1857-1861)	Brown, Aaron V.	Tenn.	March 6, 1857
	Holt, Joseph	Ky.	March 14, 1859
	King, Horatio	Me.	Feb. 12, 1861
Lincoln (1861 to April 15, 1865)	Blair, Montgomery	D. C.	March 5, 1861
	Dennison, Wm.	Ohio	Sept. 21, 1864
Johnson (April 15, 1865-1869)	Dennison, Wm.	Ohio	Continued.
	Randall, Alex. W.	Wis.	July 25, 1866
Grant (1869-1877)	Creswell, John A. J.	Md.	March 5, 1869
	Jewell, Marshall	Conn.	Aug. 24, 1874
	Tyner, James N.	Ind.	July 12, 1876
Hayes (1877-1881)	Key, David M.	Tenn.	March 12, 1877
	Maynard, Horace	Tenn.	Aug. 25, 1880
Garfield (1881 to Sept. 19, 1881)	James, Thomas L.	N. Y.	March 5, 1881
Arthur (Sept. 19, 1881-1885)	Howe, Timothy O.	Wis.	Dec. 20, 1881
	Gresham, Walter Q.	Ind.	April 3, 1883
	Hatton, Frank	Iowa	Oct. 14, 1884
Cleveland (1885-1889)	Vilas, Wm. F.	Wis.	March 6, 1885
	Dickinson, Don M.	Mich.	Jan. 16, 1888
Harrison, Benjamin (1889–	Wanamaker, John	Pa.	March 5, 1889

THE SECRETARIES OF THE NAVY.

(Department created by Act of Congress, April 30, 1798.)

In the administration of	Name	State	Appointed
Adams, John (1797-1801)	Cabot, George	Mass.	May 3, 1798
	Stoddert, Benjamin	Md.	May 21, 1798
Jefferson (1801-1809)	Stoddert, Benjamin	Md.	Continued.
	Smith, Robert	Md.	July 15, 1801
	Crowninshield, Jacob	Mass.	March 3, 1805
Madison (1809-1817)	Hamilton, Paul	S. C.	March 7, 1809
	Jones, William	Pa,	Jan. 12, 1813
	Crowninshield, Benj. W.	Mass.	Dec. 19, 1814
Monroe (1817-1825)	Crowninshield, Benj. W.	Mass.	Continued.
	Thompson, Smith	N. Y.	Nov. 9, 1818
	Southard, Samuel L.	N. J.	Sept. 16, 1823
Adams, J. Q. (1825-1829)	Southard, Samuel L.	N. J.	Continued.
Jackson (1829-1837)	Branch, John	N. C.	March 9, 1829
	Woodbury, Levi	N. H.	May 23, 1831
	Dickerson, Mahlon	N. J.	June 30, 1834
Van Buren (1837-1841)	Dickerson, Mahlon	N. J.	Continued.
	Paulding, James K.	N. Y.	June 30, 1838
Harrison, W. H. (1841 to April 4, 1841)	Badger, George E.	N. C.	March 5, 1841
Tyler (April 4, 1841-1845)	Badger, George E.	N. C.	Continued.
	Upshur, Abel P.	Va.	Sept. 13, 1841
	Henshaw, David	Mass.	July 24, 1843
	Gilmer, Thomas W.	Va.	Feb. 15, 1844
	Mason, John Y.	Va.	March 14, 1844
Polk (1845-1849)	Bancroft, George	Mass.	March 10, 1845
	Mason, John Y.	Va.	Sept. 9, 1846
Taylor (1849 to July 9, 1850)	Preston, Wm. B.	Va.	March 8, 1849
Fillmore (July 9, 1850-1853)	Graham, Wm. A.	N. C.	July 22, 1850
	Kennedy, John P.	Md.	July 22, 1852
Pierce (1853-1857)	Dobbin, James C.	N. C.	March 7, 1853
Buchanan (1857-1861)	Toucey, Isaac	Conn.	March 6, 1857
Lincoln (1861 to April 15, 1865)	Welles, Gideon	Conn.	March 5, 1861
Johnson (April 15, 1865-1869)	Welles, Gideon	Conn.	Continued.
Grant (1869-1877)	Borie, Adolph E.	Pa.	March 5, 1869
	Robeson, George M.	N. J.	June 25, 1869
Hayes (1877-1881)	Thompson, Rich. W.	Ind.	March 12, 1877
	Goff, Nathan, Jr.	W. Va.	Jan. 6, 1881
Garfield (1881 to Sept. 19, 1881)	Hunt, Wm. H.	La.	March 5, 1881
Arthur (Sept. 19, 1881-1885)	Hunt, Wm. H.	La.	Continued.
	Chandler, Wm. E.	N. H.	April 1, 1882
Cleveland (1885-1889)	Whitney, Wm. C.	N. Y.	March 6, 1885
Harrison, Benjamin (1889-)	Tracy, Benj. F.	N. Y.	March 5, 1889

THE SECRETARIES OF THE INTERIOR.

(Department created by Act of Congress, March 3, 1849.)

In the administration of	Name	State	Appointed
Taylor (1849 to July 9, 1850)	Ewing, Thomas	Ohio	March 8, 1849
Fillmore (July 9, 1850-1853)	McKennan, Thos. M. T.	Pa.	Aug. 15, 1850
	Stuart, Alex. H. H.	Va.	Sept. 12, 1850
Pierce (1853-1857)	McClelland, Robert	Mich.	March 7, 1853
Buchanan (1857-1861)	Thompson, Jacob	Miss.	March 6, 1857
Lincoln (1861 to April 15, 1865)	Smith, Caleb B.	Ind.	March 5, 1861
	Usher, John P.	Ind.	Jan. 8, 1863
Johnson (April 15, 1865-1869)	Harlan, James	Iowa	May 15, 1865
	Browning, Orville H.	Ill.	Sept. 1, 1866
Grant (1869-1877)	Cox, Jacob D.	Ohio	March 5, 1869
	Delano, Columbus	Ohio	Nov. 1, 1870
	Chandler, Zachariah	Mich.	Oct. 19, 1875
Hayes (1877-1881)	Schurz, Carl	Mo.	March 12, 1877
Garfield (1881 to Sept. 19, 1881)	Kirkwood, Samuel J.	Iowa	March 5, 1881
Arthur (Sept. 19, 1881-1885)	Kirkwood, Samuel J.	Iowa	Continued.
	Teller, Henry M.	Col.	April 6, 1882
Cleveland (1885-1889)	Lamar, Lucius Q. C.	Miss.	March 6, 1885
	Vilas, William F.	Wis.	Jan. 16, 1888
Harrison, Benjamin (1889-	Noble, John W.	Mo.	March 5, 1889

THE SECRETARIES OF AGRICULTURE.

(Formerly a Bureau of the Interior. Organized as a Department by Act of Feb. 9, 188'

In the administration of	Name	State	Appointed
Cleveland (1885-1889)	Coleman, Norman J.	Mo.	Feb. 10, 1889
Harrison, Benjamin (1889-) .	Rusk, Jeremiah M.	Wis.	March 5, 1889

THE PRESIDENTIAL SUCCESSION.

The Constitution, Art. II. Sect. 1, provides:
" In case of removal of the President from office, or of his death, resignation, or inability to discharge the powers and duties of the said office, the same shall devolve upon the Vice-President, and the Congress may by law provide for the case of removal, death, resignation, or inability, both of the President and Vice-President, declaring what officer shall then act as President, and such officer shall act accordingly, until the disability be removed, or a President shall be elected."

In accordance with the power given, Congress, by Act approved March 1, 1792, regulated the succession as follows:

"Sect. 9. *And be it further enacted*, That in case of a removal, death, resignation, or inability, both of the President and Vice-President of the United States, the President of the Senate *pro tempore*, and, in case there shall be no President of the Senate, then the Speaker of the House of Representatives, for the time being, shall act as President of the United States, until the disability be removed, or a President shall be elected."

This statute was never satisfactory, and the question of the succession was frequently considered, but without result, for nearly a century. But in 1885, the death of Vice-President Hendricks forced the attention of the people again to this question, and after considerable discussion an Act was passed to regulate the succession. It was approved January 19, 1886.

By its terms, in case of the removal, death, resignation, or inability of both the President and Vice-President, then the Secretary of State shall act as President until the disability of the President or Vice-President is removed or a President is elected. If there be no Secretary of State, then the Secretary of the Treasury shall act; and the remainder of the order of succession is: the Secretary of War, the Attorney-General, the Postmaster-General, the Secretary of the Navy, and the Secretary of the Interior. The acting President must, upon taking office, convene Congress, if not at the time in session, in extraordinary session, giving twenty days' notice. The Act applies only to such Cabinet officers as shall have been appointed by and with the advice and consent of the Senate, and are eligible under the Constitution to the Presidency.

DIRECTORY OF THE CITY, AND GENERAL INFORMATION FOR VISITORS.

THE City of Washington, the Capital of the United States of America, occupies a portion of the District of Columbia, a territory which is under the immediate control of Congress.

The District of Columbia comprises an area of about sixty-five square miles, and lies on the northern bank of the Potomac, one hundred and sixteen miles above its mouth. The greater part of this area is a plateau rising some four hundred feet above the level of the Potomac, and is traversed by two streams, the Anacostia River or Eastern Branch, and Rock Creek. Above the mouth of the Anacostia the edge of the plateau recedes from the bank of the Potomac, and leaves a comparatively low piece of land, about seven square miles in area. It is upon this that the city is built. The suburbs occupy the hills to the north and west, the old city of Georgetown now forming a part of Washington.

The plan of the city is regular and symmetrical. Radiating from the Capitol are three streets, running north, east, and south, and known respectively as North Capitol, East Capitol, and South Capitol Streets. These, together with a broad stretch of public gardens, known as The Mall, on the west, divide the city into four quarters, called the North-East, South-East, South-West, and North-West. The streets run in the cardinal directions, the north and south ones being designated by numbers, and the east and west ones by the letters of the alphabet—the numbers advancing eastward and westward, the letters northward and southward from the Capitol. Besides these streets there is a system of avenues, named from the States, which, for the most part, radiate from the Capitol and White House as centres, and run diagonally to the cardinal points.

This arrangement of avenues makes communication between different parts of the city very direct, while the system of numbering the houses makes it very easy to find any designated locality. The quarter is always given. Thus, 610 Fourteenth Street, N. W., is on the fourteenth street west of the Capitol, a few doors above F Street (the sixth) north.

The various street railways of the city give easy access to all the places of interest. The fare is five cents, or six tickets for twenty-five cents. These are good on all lines, and also on the Herdic coaches running on Pennsylvania Avenue. Exchange tickets are given at many of the junctions, thus enabling the traveller to reach almost any point for a single fare.

The charges for cab and carriage service are regulated by the Board of Commissioners, the Chief of Police having charge. The established rates are given below.

[*Extract from the Police Regulations.*]

HACK RATES.

SECTION 1. Every public vehicle of what kind soever for hire for the conveyance of passengers on the streets, whether engaged by the passenger upon the street or at any livery stable, shall be considered a hack within the meaning and intent of these regulations.

SEC. 2. The charges for hack service within the limits of the District of Columbia shall not exceed those stated in the following schedule, namely:

	Between the hours of 5 o'clock A.M. and 12.30 o'clock P.M.	Between the hours of 12.30 o'clock P.M. and 5 o'clock A.M.
BY THE HOUR.		
For one passenger or two passengers, for the first hour	Seventy-five cents.	One dollar.
For each additional quarter of an hour or part thereof	Twenty cents.	Twenty-five cents.
Provided, That for multiples of one hour the charge shall be at the rate per hour of	Seventy-five cents.	One dollar.
For three or four passengers, for the first hour	One dollar.	One dollar and twenty-five cents.
For each additional quarter of an hour or part thereof	Twenty-five cents.	Thirty-five cents.
Provided, That for multiples of one hour the charge shall be at the rate per hour of	One dollar.	One dollar and twenty-five cents
BY THE TRIP.		
By the trip of fifteen squares or less, for each passenger	Twenty-five cents.	Forty cents.
For each additional five squares or part thereof	Ten cents.	Fifteen cents.
Provided, That for multiples of fifteen squares the charge shall be at the rate, for each fifteen squares, of	Twenty-five cents.	Forty cents.

Provided, That in the case of a two-horse hack engaged at a livery stable, the proprietor or driver thereof may, by special agreement made in advance with the passenger, charge according to such special agreement: *And provided further*, That hacks engaged upon the street, drawn by two horses, and with seats for four passengers, may charge by the hour at rates not to exceed one dollar and fifty cents for the first hour, and twenty-five cents for each additional one-quarter hour: *And provided further*, That a two-horse hack as above shall not be required to take less than two passengers.

In all cases when a hack is not engaged by the hour it shall be considered as being engaged by the trip.

The fare to any point outside of the cities of Washington and Georgetown shall, in all cases, be charged by the hour or part of an hour, and if the hack is dismissed outside the said cities a charge of twenty-five cents additional may be made.

Each passenger shall be entitled to have conveyed, without extra charge, one trunk or other travelling-box or bag: *Provided*, That there be not more

GENERAL INFORMATION FOR VISITORS. 77

than two trunks or other travelling-boxes or bags to be conveyed at any one time for the person or persons hiring the hack. If there be more than two trunks, travelling-boxes, or bags the driver shall be entitled to twenty-five cents for each one additional to the two. Each passenger shall be entitled also to have conveyed, without charge, such other small packages as can be conveniently carried within the hack, and the driver shall load and unload all baggage without charge.

SEC. 3. Every hack shall have permanently affixed to the interior thereof, in a place readily to be seen by the passenger, the foregoing schedule of rates and no other, which schedule shall be printed on heavy white cards, eight by ten inches in size, printed in black ink, with full-face, double primer Roman type, to be furnished by the Major of Police.

SEC. 4. In case of any disagreement between the driver and the passenger of a hack the same may be referred by the passenger to the nearest police station, whither the driver shall convey him without discussion or delay, and the decision of the Lieutenant of Police or other officer in charge of such station shall be conclusive; and in case the passenger is about to leave by railroad, stage, or steamboat, such disagreement shall be summarily decided by the police officer or principal police officer on duty at the station or other place of departure.

The following list shows the location of the Chief Places of Interest, with a reference to the page where a description is given. Places not mentioned may be found by the Index.

All Government Buildings are open from 9 A.M. to 2 P.M., closing at 4 P.M.

AGRICULTURAL DEPARTMENT (p. 107), The Mall, opposite Thirteenth and B Streets, S. W.
ALEXANDRIA, VA. (p. 155), Steamer from Seventh Street Wharf, 10 A.M. Train from Pennsylvania Railroad Station, Sixth and B Streets, N. W.
ARLINGTON, VA. (p. 149). Sunrise to sunset.
ARMORY, NATIONAL RIFLES, G Street, between Ninth and Tenth, N. W.
    "   WASHINGTON LIGHT INFANTRY, Fifteenth Street, south of Pennsylvania Avenue, N. W.
ARSENAL, WASHINGTON (p. 132), foot of Four-and-a-Half Street, S. W. Sunrise to sunset.
BARRACKS, MARINE (p. 132), Eighth and G Streets, S. E. Sunrise to sunset
    "   WASHINGTON (p. 132, *see* Arsenal).
BARTHOLDI FOUNTAIN (p. 20), Botanical Gardens, Pennsylvania Avenue, First to Third Streets, N. W.
BRIDGE, CABIN-JOHN (p. 147), Conduit Road, seven miles from Georgetown.
    "   LONG (p. 32), foot of Fourteenth Street, S. W.
CAPITOL, THE (pp. 37-71), Capitol Hill.
CEMETERIES:
    CONGRESSIONAL (p. 131), Eighteenth and E Streets, S. E.
    OAK HILL (p. 145), end of Twenty-eighth Street, N. W.
COAST SURVEY (p. 133), New Jersey Avenue and B Street, S. E.
CORCORAN ART GALLERY (p. 121), Pennsylvania Avenue and Seventeenth Street, N. W., 10 A.M. to 4 P.M.
COURTS:
    CLAIMS (p. 106), Department of Justice, 1509 Pennsylvania Avenue, N. W.
    SUPREME (p. 57), The Capitol.
COURT-HOUSE, DISTRICT (p. 129), Judiciary Square, D and Four-and-a-Half Streets, N. W.
DEAD-LETTER OFFICE (p. 98), the General Post-Office, Seventh and E Streets, N. W.

GENERAL INFORMATION FOR VISITORS.

DEAF-MUTE COLLEGE, NATIONAL (p. 137), Seventh and M Streets, N. E. Thursdays.
EDUCATION, BUREAU OF (p. 103), Patent Office, F Street, between Seventh and Ninth, N.W.
ENGRAVING AND PRINTING, BUREAU OF (p. 112), Fourteenth and B Streets, S. W.
EXECUTIVE MANSION (p. 73, see White House).
FISH COMMISSION BUILDING (p. 133), Sixth and B Streets, S. W.
FORD'S THEATRE (p. 129), Tenth Street, between E and F, N. W.
GARDENS:
    BOTANICAL (p. 20), Pennsylvania Avenue, First to Third Streets, N. W.
    PROPAGATING, Agricultural Department (p. 108), Fifteenth and B Streets, S. W.
G. A. R. HALL, 1112 Pennsylvania Avenue, N. W.
INDIAN BUREAU (p. 103), Patent Office, F Street, between Seventh and Ninth, N. W.
INSANE, GOVERNMENT HOSPITAL (p. 134), east of the Anacostia. Wednesdays, 2 to 6 P.M.
INTERIOR DEPARTMENT (p. 101, see Patent Office).
JAIL, DISTRICT (p. 132), Ninth and B Streets, S. E.
JUSTICE, DEPARTMENT OF (p. 106), Pennsylvania Avenue, between Fifteenth and Sixteenth Streets, N. W.
LIBRARY, CONGRESSIONAL (p. 54), The Capitol.
    "   "   NEW (p. 111), East Capitol and First Streets, S. E.
LOUISE HOME (p. 135), Massachusetts Avenue and Fifteenth Street, N. W.
MALL, THE (p. 20), west from the Capitol to the Potomac.
MARKET, CENTRE (p. 31), Pennsylvania Avenue and Seventh Street, N. W.
MASONIC TEMPLE (p. 139), Ninth and F Streets, N. W.
MONUMENTS:
    GARFIELD (p. 39), Maryland Avenue and B Street, S W.
    NAVAL (p. 39), Pennsylvania Avenue and B Street, N. W.
    WASHINGTON (p. 29), The Mall, western end.
MOUNT VERNON (p. 159), Virginia. Steamer from Seventh Street wharf, 10 A.M., returning 3.30 P.M.; $1.00.
MUSEUMS:
    ARMY MEDICAL (p. 121), Seventh and B Streets, S. W.
    NATIONAL (p. 118), The Mall, opposite Ninth and B Streets, S. W.
NAVY DEPARTMENT (p. 91), east wing, State, War, and Navy Bldg., Pennsylvania Avenue and Seventeenth Street, N. W.
" YARD (p. 132), foot of Eighth Street, S. E. Sunrise to sunset.
OBSERVATORY, NAVAL (p. 125), Twenty-third and E Streets, N. W.
ODD-FELLOWS' HALL (p. 139), Seventh Street, between D and E, N. W.
PATENT OFFICE (p. 102), F Street, between Seventh and Ninth, N. W.
PENSION BUILDING (p. 101), Judiciary Square, G Street, between Fourth and Fifth, N. W.
POST-OFFICE DEPARTMENT (p. 96), Seventh and E Streets, N. W.
PRINTING OFFICE, GOVERNMENT (p. 128), North Capitol and G Streets, N. W.
REDEMPTION BUREAU, Treasury Department, Pennsylvania Ave. and Fifteenth St., N. W.
SMITHSONIAN INSTITUTION (p. 114), The Mall, opposite Tenth and B Streets, S. W.
SIGNAL OFFICE (p. 126, see Weather Bureau).
SOLDIERS' HOME (p. 142), east of Seventh Street Extension, N. W. Sunrise to sunset.
STATE DEPARTMENT (p. 88), south wing, State, War, and Navy Bldg., Pennsylvania Avenue and Seventeenth Street, N. W.
TREASURY DEPARTMENT (p. 92), Pennsylvania Avenue and Fifteenth Street, N. W.
UNIVERSITIES:
    CATHOLIC (p. 143), Lincoln and Bunker Hill Roads, N. E.
    COLUMBIAN, Fifteenth and H Streets, N. W.
    HOWARD (p. 138), Seventh Street Extension, N. W.
WAR DEPARTMENT (p. 90), north and west wings, State, War, and Navy Bldg., Pennsylvania Avenue and Seventeenth Street, N. W.
WEATHER BUREAU (p. 126), 1725 G Street, N. W.
WHITE HOUSE (p. 73), Pennsylvania Avenue, Fifteenth to Seventeenth Streets, N. W.

The following lists are for the information of strangers in the city. While not containing all names, those places located most conveniently to the Hotels are given:

GENERAL INFORMATION FOR VISITORS. 79

AMUSEMENTS. (*See* Theatres, etc.)
BANKERS AND BROKERS:
  Bateman & Co., 1411 F Street, N. W.
  Bell & Co., 1487 Pennsylvania Avenue, N. W.
  Corson & McCartney, 1419 F Street, N. W.
  Crane, Parris & Co., 1344 F Street, N. W.
  Lilley, Frederick B., 1419 F Street, N. W.
  Pelouze, Frank H., 1335 F Street, N. W.
  Reddington & Co., 1416 F Street, N. W.
  Riggs & Co., Pennsylvania Avenue and Fifteenth Street, N. W.
  Rose & Co., 1417 F Street, N. W.
  Tewksbury, Lewis G. & Co., 1335 F Street, N. W.
BANKS:
  American Security and Trust Co., 1419 G Street, N. W.
  Capital Savings, 804 F Street, N. W.
  Central National, Pennsylvania Avenue and Seventh Street, N. W.
  Citizens' National, 616 Fifteenth Street, N. W.
  Columbia National, 911 F Street, N. W.
  Lincoln National, Ninth and D Streets, N. W.
  National Bank of the Republic, 318 Seventh Street, N. W.
  National Bank of Washington, Seventh and C Streets, N. W.
  National Capital, 314 and 316 Pennsylvania Avenue, N. W.
  National Metropolitan, 613 Fifteenth Street, N. W.
  National Savings, New York Avenue and Fifteenth Street, N. W.
  Traders' National, 918 Pennsylvania Avenue, N. W.
  West End National, 1415 G Street, N. W.
BOOKSELLERS, PUBLISHERS, ETC.:
  Allen, Ed. H., 930 F Street, N. W.
  Appleton, D. & Co., 437 Seventh Street, N. W.
  Boyd, W. Andrew, Directory Co., 810 F Street, N. W.
  Bretano's, 1015 Pennsylvania Avenue, N. W.
  Collier, P. F., 923 F Street, N. W.
  Dunbar, W. (Artistic), New York Avenue and Fifteenth Street, N. W.
  Scribner, Charles & Son, 802 F Street, N. W.
CITY GOVERNMENT OFFICES, First Street, near C, N. W.
CHURCHES:
  BAPTIST:
    Calvary, Rev. Samuel H. Green, Eighth and H Streets, N. W. 11 A.M., 7.45 P.M.
    E Street, Rev. J. J. Muir, E Street near Sixth, N. W. 11 A.M., 7.30 P.M.
    First, Rev. Charles A. Stakely, Sixteenth and O Streets, N. W. 11 A.M., 7.30 P.M. Thursdays, 7.30 P.M.
  CHRISTIAN DISCIPLES (DISCIPLES OF CHRIST):
    Garfield Memorial, Rev. Frederick D. Power, Vermont Avenue near N Street, N. W. 11 A.M, 7.30 P.M. Thursdays, 7.30 P.M.
  CONGREGATIONAL:
    Congregation of the Tabernacle, Rev. L. E. Pangburne, Ninth Street, between B Street and Virginia Avenue, N. W. 11 A.M., 7.30 P.M. Thursdays, 7.30 P.M.
    First, Rev. Stephen M. Newman, Tenth and G Streets, N. W. 11 A.M., 7.30 P.M. Thursdays, 7.30 P.M.
  EPISCOPAL, PROTESTANT:
    *Ascension, Rev. J. H. Elliott, S.T.D., Massachusetts Avenue and Twelfth Street, N. W. 11 A.M., 7.30 P.M.
    Christ, Rev. Gilbert F. Williams, G Street, between Sixth and Seventh, S. E. 11 A.M., 7.30 P.M.
    Epiphany, Rev. R. H. McKim, D.D., G Street near Eighteenth, N. W. 11 A.M., 4 and 7.30 P.M.
    Incarnation, Rev. I. L. Townsend, Twelfth and N Streets, N. W. 7.45 and 11 A.M., 4 P.M.
    St. John's, Rev. George S. Douglass, Sixteenth and H Streets, N. W. 8 and 11 A.M., 4 P.M.
    St. Paul's, Rev. Alfred Harding, Twenty-third Street, between Pennsylvania Avenue and S Street, N. W. 11 A.M., 7.30 P.M.
    Trinity, Rev. James A. Birch, Third and C Streets, N. W. 11 A.M., 7.30 P.M.

GENERAL INFORMATION FOR VISITORS.

CHURCHES—*Continued:*

FRIENDS' MEETING:
(Orthodox), Chapel of Y. M. C. A., 1409 New York Avenue, N. W. 11 A. M.
Meeting-House, 1811 I Street, N. W. 11 A.M.

HEBREW:
Adas Israel Congregation (Orthodox), Leopold Hermann, Sixth and G Streets, N. W. Friday, 5.30 P.M.; Saturday, 10 A.M.
Washington Congregation, L. Stein, Eighth Street, between H and I, N. W. Friday, 7.30 P.M.; Saturday, 10 A.M.

LUTHERAN:
Church of the Fatherland, Rev. A. Hamrighaus, Sixth and P Streets, N. W. 11 A.M. (German), 7.30 P.M (English).
Concordia, Rev. John Müller, Twentieth and G Streets, N. W. 11 A.M., 8 P.M. (German).
Grace, Rev. Emanuel G. Taessel, Thirteenth and Corcoran Streets, N. W. 11 A.M., 7.30 P.M.
Memorial, Rev. J. G. Butler, Fourteenth Street and Vermont Ave., N. W. 11 A.M., 4.30 P.M.
St. Paul's, Eleventh and H Streets, N. W. 10.30 A.M., 7.30 P.M.; Thursday, 7.30 P.M.

METHODIST EPISCOPAL:
Fifteenth Street, Rev. L. A. Thirlkeid, D.D., Fifteenth and R Streets, N. W. 11 A.M., 7.30 P.M.; Thursdays, 7.30 P.M.
Foundry, Rev. O. A. Brown, Fourteenth and G Streets, N. W. 11 A.M., 7.30 P.M.
McKendree, Rev. L. T. Widerman, Massachusetts Avenue near Ninth Street, N. W. 11 A.M., 7.30 P.M.
Metropolitan, Rev. George H. Corey, Four-and-a-Half and C Streets, N. W. 11 A.M., 7.30 P.M.

PRESBYTERIAN:
Church of the Covenant, Rev. T. S. Hamlin, D. D., Connecticut Avenue and Eighteenth Street, N. W. 11 A.M., 8 P.M. Thursdays, 8 P.M.
First, Rev. B. Sunderland, D. D., Four-and-a-Half Street, between C and D Streets, N. W. 11 A.M., 7.30 P.M. Thursdays, 7.30 P.M.
Fourth, Rev. Joseph T. Kelley, Ninth Street, between G and H Streets, N. W. 11 A.M., 7.30 P.M. Thursdays, 7.30 P.M.
New York Avenue, Rev. William A. Bartlett, D. D., New York Avenue, between Thirteenth and Fourteenth Streets, N. W. 11 A.M., 7.30 P.M. Thursdays, 7.30 P.M.

REFORMED:
First, Rev. Gustav Facius, Sixth and N Streets, N. W. 11 A.M., 7.30 P.M.
Grace, Rev. A. Th. G. Apple, Fifteenth and P Streets, N. W. 11 A.M., 7.30 P.M. Thursdays, 7.30 P.M.

ROMAN CATHOLIC:
Immaculate Conception, Rev. S. F. Ryan, Eighth and C Streets, N. W. Sundays: 7, 9, 10.30 A.M., 4 P.M. Week days: 6.30 and 7 A.M.
St. Matthew's, Rev. P. L. Chapelle, D.D., Fifteenth and H Streets, N. W. Sundays: 7, 9, 11 A.M., 4 P.M. Week days: 7 and 9 A.M.
St. Patrick's, Rev. J. A. Walter, Tenth Street near F Street, N. W. Sundays: 7, 9, 11 A.M., 4 P.M.

SWEDENBORGIAN:
New Jerusalem, Rev. Frank Sewell (temporary), 1801 Massachusetts Avenue, N. W. 11 A.M., 5 P.M.

UNITARIAN:
All Souls', Rev. Rush R. Shippen, Fourteenth and L Streets, N. W. 11 A.M., 7.30 P.M.

UNIVERSALIST:
Church of Our Father, Prof. S. A. Whitcomb, Thirteenth and L Streets, N. W. 11 A.M., 7.30 P.M.

DRUGGISTS, HOMŒOPATHIC, 1007, H Street, N. W.

EXPRESS COMPANIES:
Adams, 921 Pennsylvania Avenue, N. W., and 1425 F Street, N. W.
Union Transfer, 1239 Pennsylvania Avenue, N. W., and 1413 E Street, N. W.
United States, 819 Market Square, N. W., and 613 Fifteenth Street, N. W.

GENERAL INFORMATION FOR VISITORS. 81

FOREIGN LEGATIONS:
ARGENTINE REPUBLIC:
Señor Don Vincente G. Quesada, Envoy Extraordinary and Minister Plenipotentiary. Absent.
Señor Don Roque Casal Carranza, Chargé d'Affaires *ad interim*, First Secretary of Legation, The Arno.
Office of the Legation, The Arno.
AUSTRIA-HUNGARY:
Chevalier de Tavera, Envoy Extraordinary and Minister Plenipotentiary, 1537 I St., N. W.
Mr. de Mezey, Counsellor of Legation, 1708 H Street, N. W.
BELGIUM:
Mr. Alfred Le Ghait, Envoy Extraordinary and Minister Plenipotentiary, 1336 I Street,N.W.
Count Gaston d'Arschot, Counsellor of Legation, 1211 K Street, N. W.
BRAZIL:
Senhor Salvador de Mendonça, Envoy Extraordinary and Minister Plenipotentiary, 1761 Massachusetts Avenue, N. W.
Office of the Legation, 1761 Massachusetts Avenue, N. W.
CHILE:
Señor Don Pedro Montt, Envoy Extraordinary and Minister Plenipotentiary. Absent.
Señor Anibal Cruz, First Secretary of Legation and Chargé d'Affaires *ad interim*, 1019 Connecticut Avenue, N. W.
CHINA:
Mr. Tsui Kwo Yin, Envoy Extraordinary and Minister Plenipotentiary, Dupont Circle.
Mr. Pung Kwang Yu, First Secretary, Dupont Circle.
COLOMBIA:
Señor Don José Marcelino Hurtado, Envoy Extraordinary and Minister Plenipotentiary, 1903 N Street, N. W.
Señor Don Julio Rengifo, Secretary of Legation, 1807 H Street, N. W.
Office of the Legation, 1903 N Street, N. W.
COSTA RICA:
Señor Don Joaquin Barnardo Calvo, Chargé d'Affaires *ad interim*, 1616 Nineteenth St., N.W.
Office of the Legation, 1616 Nineteenth Street, N. W.
DENMARK:
Count de Sponneck, Envoy Extraordinary and Minister Plenipotentiary, 2 Iowa Circle.
FRANCE:
Mr. J. Patenôtre, Envoy Extraordinary and Minister Plenipotentiary, 1400 Massachusetts Avenue, N. W.
Mr. Paul Desprez, Counsellor, 1110 Connecticut Avenue, N. W.
Office of the Legation, 1400 Massachusetts Avenue, N. W.
GERMANY:
Mr. Theodore von Holleben, Envoy Extraordinary and Minister Plenipotentiary, 734 Fifteenth Street, N. W.
Mr. Alfons Mumm von Schwarzenstein, Secretary of Legation, 734 Fifteenth Street, N. W.
GREAT BRITAIN:
Sir Julian Pauncefote, G.C.M.G., K.C.B., Envoy Extraordinary and Minister Plenipotentiary, British Legation, Connecticut Avenue, Corner of F Street, N. W.
Hon. Michael H. Herbert, Secretary of Legation, 1228 Connecticut Avenue, N. W.
GUATEMALA:
Señor Don Antonio Batres, Envoy Extraordinary and Minister Plenipotentiary. Absent.
Señor Don Antonio Valenzuela, Attaché, The Elsmere, 1408 H Street, N. W.
HAITI:
Mr. Hannibal Price, Envoy Extraordinary and Minister Plenipotentiary, New York.
Mr. John Hurst, Secretary of Legation.
HAWAII:
J. Mott Smith, Envoy Extraordinary and Minister Plenipotentiary, The Arlington.
ITALY:
Baron de Fava, Envoy Extraordinary and Minister Plenipotentiary.
Marquis Imperiali di Francavilla, Secretary of Legation, 1015 Connecticut Avenue, N. W.
Office of the Legation, 1015 Connecticut Avenue, N. W.

FOREIGN LEGATIONS—*Continued:*

JAPAN:
    Mr. Gozo Tateno, Envoy Extraordinary and Minister Plenipotentiary, 1310 N Street, N.W.
    Mr. Durham White Stevens, Counsellor of Legation, 1416 N Street, N. W.

KOREA:
    Mr. Pak Chung Yang, Envoy Extraordinary and Minister Plenipotentiary. Absent.
    Mr. Ye Cha Yun, Secretary of Legation and Chargé d'Affaires *ad interim*, 1500 Thirteenth Street, Iowa Circle.
    Office of the Legation, 1500 Thirteenth Street, Iowa Circle.

MEXICO:
    Señor Don Matias Romero, Envoy Extraordinary and Minister Plenipotentiary, Mexican Legation, 1413 I Street, N. W.
    Señor Don Cayetano Romero, First Secretary of Legation, 1332 I Street, N. W., The Franklin.
    Office of the Legation, 1413 I Street, N. W. (entrance by side street).

NETHERLANDS:
    Mr. G. de Weckherlin, Envoy Extraordinary and Minister Plenipotentiary, 1013 Fifteenth Street, N. W.

NICARAGUA:
    Señor Don Horacio Guzmán, Envoy Extraordinary and Minister Plenipotentiary, 1625 Massachusetts Avenue, N. W.
    Señor Don Román Mayorga, Secretary of Legation, 1837 Corcoran Street, N. W.

PERU:
    Dr. Don Pedro A. del Solar, Envoy Extraordinary and Minister Plenipotentiary. Absent.
    Dr. Don José Maria Yrigoyen, Secretary of Legation and Chargé d'Affaires *ad interim*, 1839 Corcoran Street, N. W.
    Office of the Legation, 1839 Corcoran Street, N. W.

PORTUGAL:
    Senhor Thomaz de Souza Roza, Envoy Extraordinary and Minister Plenipotentiary, 1103 Sixteenth Street, N. W.

RUSSIA:
    Mr. Charles de Struve, Envoy Extraordinary and Minister Plenipotentiary, 1705 K Street, N. W.
    Mr. Alexandre Greger, First Secretary of Legation, 1705 K Street, N. W.

SALVADOR:
    Dr. Manuel Morales, Envoy Extraordinary and Minister Plenipotentiary, The Arlington.
    Señor Federico Mora, Secretary of Legation, The Arlington.

SPAIN:
    Señor Don Miguel Suarez Guanes, Envoy Extraordinary and Minister Plenipotentiary. Absent.
    Señor Don José Felipe Sagrario, First Secretary and Chargé d'Affaires *ad interim*, 1431 Q Street, N. W.

SWEDEN AND NORWAY:
    Mr. J. A. W. Grip, Envoy Extraordinary and Minister Plenipotentiary. Absent.
    Baron H. J. Beck-Friis, Chargé d'Affaires *ad interim*, Secretary of Legation, 806 Eighteenth Street, N. W.
    Office of the Legation, 2011 Q Street, N. W.

SWITZERLAND:
    Mr. Alfred de Claparède, Envoy Extraordinary and Minister Plenipotentiary, 1761 Q Street, N. W.
    Dr Charles C. Tavel, Secretary of Legation, 1823 I Street, N. W.
    Office of the Legation, 1761 Q Street, N. W.

TURKEY:
    Mavroyeni Bey, Envoy Extraordinary and Minister Plenipotentiary, 1015 Connecticut Avenue, N. W.
    Mgrditch Effendi Norighian, First Secretary of Legation, 1631 Q Street, N. W.
    Office of the Legation; 1015 Connecticut Avenue, N. W

GENERAL INFORMATION FOR VISITORS. 83

FOREIGN LEGATIONS—*Continued:*
VENEZUELA:
  Señor Don Nicanor Bolet-Peraza, Envoy Extraordinary and Minister Plenipotentiary, 1754 M Street, N. W.
  Señor Don Leopoldo Terrero, First Secretary, 1754 M Street, N. W.

HOTELS:
  The American House, Pennsylvania Avenue and Seventh Street, N. W. Duffy & Leannards, Proprietors. Capacity, 250. $2.00 per day. $10.00 to $14.00 per week.
  The Arlington, Vermont Avenue, H and I Streets, N. W. T. E. Roessle. Proprietor. Capacity, 400. $4.00 and upwards per day.
  The Ebbitt House, Fourteenth and F Streets, N. W. Burch & Gibbs, Managers. Capacity, 500. $4.00 and upwards per day. $21.00 and upwards per week.
  Hotel Fredonia, H Street, between Thirteenth and Fourteenth, N. W. G. H. La Fetra, Proprietor. Capacity, 200. $2.50 to $4.00 per day. $15.00 to $25.00 per week. Rooms, $1.00 to $2.00 per day.
  The Hamilton, Fourteenth and K Streets, N. W. William L. Gilson, Proprietor. Capacity, 150. $2.50 to $3.00 per day. $17.50 to $21.00 per week.
  The Howard House, Pennsylvania Avenue and Sixth Street, N. W. John B. Scott, Proprietor. $2.50 per day. $14.00 per week.
  La Normandie, Fifteenth and I Streets, N. W. Horace M. Cake, Proprietor. Capacity, 250. $5.00 and upwards per day. European plan, $2.00 and upwards per day.
  Metropolitan Hotel, Pennsylvania Avenue, between Sixth and Seventh Streets, N. W. W. H. Selden, Proprietor. Capacity, 350. $3.00 to $5.00 per day.
  National Hotel, Pennsylvania Avenue and Sixth Street, N. W. F. Tenney & W. H. Crosby, Proprietors. Capacity, 500. $2.50 and upwards per day. Rooms, $1.00 and upwards per day.
  Hotel Oxford, New York Avenue and Fourteenth Street, N. W. Walter Burton, Manager. Capacity, 150. $2.50 and upwards per day. $15.00 and upwards per week.
  The Randall, Pennsylvania Avenue and Fifteenth Street, N. W. John T. Trego, Proprietor. Capacity, 300. $3.00 and upwards per day. $20.00 and upwards per week. Special Rates to Tourist Parties.
  Riggs House, Fifteenth and G Streets, N. W. Gasherie De Witt, Proprietor. Capacity, 400. $4.00 and $5.00 per day. $25.00 and upwards per week. Strictly American plan.
  The St. James, Pennsylvania Avenue and Sixth Street, N. W. H. T. Wheeler, Manager. 120 Rooms. $1.00 and upwards per day.
  Temple Hotel, 604 and 606 Ninth Street, N. W. Mrs. S. H. Martin, Proprietress. Capacity, 100. $1.50 to $2.00 per day. $7.00 to $10.00 per week. Special Rates for Parties.
  Welckers' Hotel, 721-727 Fifteenth Street, N. W. Th. Felter, Proprietor. Capacity, 200. $1.50 to $15.00 per day. $10.00 to $100.00 per week. European plan.
  Willard's, Pennsylvania Avenue and Fourteenth Street, N. W. O. G. Staples, Proprietor. Capacity, 600. $3.50 to $5.00 per day. $21.00 and upwards per week.
  Hotel Windsor, New York Avenue and Fifteenth Street, N. W. Mrs. M. J. Colley, Proprietress. Capacity, 150. $2.50 per day. $15.00 per week.
  Wormley Hotel, Fifteenth and H Streets, N. W. James T. Wormley, Proprietor. Capacity, 125. $4.00 and $5.00 per day.
  The Arno, Sixteenth between I and K Streets, N. W. W. E. Prall, Proprietor. Capacity, 150. $4.00 to $5.00 per day. European plan, $2.00 to $3.00 per day.
  The Belvedere, Pennsylvania Avenue and Third St., N. W. D. E. Hoadley & Son, Proprietors. Capacity, 200. $2.00 to $3.00 per day. European plan, $1.00 and upward per day.
  The Cochran, Fourteenth and K Streets, N. W. W. F. Paige, Proprietor. Capacity, 250. $5.00 per day.
  The Congressional, New Jersey Avenue and B Street, S. E. Henry Brock, Proprietor. Capacity, 100. $2.50 and $3.00 per day.
  Hillman House, North Capitol near C Street, N. W. N. J. Hillman, Proprietor. Capacity, 150. $2.00 to $3.00 per day. $10.00 and upward per week.
  The Shoreham, Fifteenth and H Streets, N. W. John T. Devine, Proprietor. Capacity, 275. $5.00 and upward per day. American or European plan.

INFORMATION:
  Boyd's Bureau. United States Directory Exchange. Guides and Guide-books furnished. 810 F Street, N. W.

PHOTOGRAPHERS:
  Bell, Ch. M., 463 Pennsylvania Avenue, N. W., and 701 Fifteenth Street, N. W.
  Brady, Matt. B., Pennsylvania Avenue and Thirteenth Street, N. W.
  Jarvis, John F., 135 Pennsylvania Avenue, N. W., and 219 G Street, N. W.
  Prince, George, 403 Eleventh Street, N. W.
  Pullman Galleries, 935 Pennsylvania Avenue, N. W.
  Rice, Moses P., 1217, 1219, and 1225 Pennsylvania Avenue, N. W.
POLICE COURT, Sixth and D Streets, N. W.
  Headquarters, Fifth and D Streets, N. W.
POST-OFFICE, CITY, Louisiana Avenue, between Sixth and Seventh Streets, N. W.
  Money Order Office, open 9.00 A.M. to 5.00 P.M., except Sunday.
  Special Delivery Messengers, 7.00 A.M. to 11.00 P.M.
  BRANCHES:
    Senate Wing, The Capitol.
    House Wing, The Capitol.
    C, 1113 F Street, N. W.
    D, Fourteenth and Corcoran Streets, N. W.
    F, 1921 Pennsylvania Avenue, N. W.
    G, Connecticut and Louisiana Avenues, N. W.
    H, 2007 H Street, N. W.
    P, Fourteenth and Stoughton Streets, N. W.
PUBLISHERS. (*See* Booksellers.)
RAILROADS:
  Baltimore and Ohio Railroad Station, New Jersey Avenue and C Street, N. W. Trains for Baltimore, Philadelphia, New York, and the East; for Pittsburg, Cincinnati, Indianapolis, St. Louis, Chicago, and the West. Offices, 619 and 1351 Pennsylvania Avenue, N. W.
  Pennsylvania Railroad Station, Sixth and B Streets, N. W. Trains for Baltimore, Philadelphia, New York, Boston, and the East; for Harrisburg, Erie, Rochester, Buffalo, and the North; for Pittsburg, Cincinnati, Indianapolis, St. Louis, Chicago, and the West; for Alexandria, Norfolk, Richmond, Atlanta, New Orleans, Texas, the South and South-West. Office, 1239 Pennsylvania Avenue, N. W.
STEAMERS:
  For Alexandria and Mount Vernon daily (except Sunday), from Seventh Street Wharf, at 10.00 A.M.
  For Chesapeake Bay, Norfolk, Philadelphia, New York, and Boston, from Seventh Street Wharf.
TELEGRAPH COMPANIES, ETC.:
  Mutual District Messenger, 1428 F Street, N. W.
  Postal Telegraph Cable, 1416 F Street, N. W.; 511 Pennsylvania Avenue, N. W.; 923 B Street, N. W.; Government Departments, and Capitol.
  Western Union Telegraph, 541 Fifteenth Street, N. W.
  Long Distance Telephone, 613 Fifteenth Street, N. W.
THEATRES, ETC.:
  Albaugh's Grand Opera House, Fifteenth and E Streets, N. W.
  Bijou, 1108 D Street, N. W.
  Cyclorama Building, Ohio Avenue and Fifteenth Street, N. W.
  Kernan's New Washington, Eleventh and C Streets, N. W.
  Lincoln Music Hall, Ninth and D Streets, N. W.
  New National, E Street near B Street, N. W.
TOURIST AGENCY:
  Choate, Warren & Co., 730 Eleventh Street, N. W.
WOMEN'S CHRISTIAN ASSOCIATION HOUSE, 1719 Thirteenth Street, N. W.
YOUNG MEN'S CHRISTIAN ASSOCIATION, 1409 New York Avenue, N. W.
YOUNG WOMEN'S CHRISTIAN HOME, 404 Sixth Street, N. W.

INDEX.

ADAMS, President John, occupies the White House, 75
   portrait of, 80
Adams, Mrs. John, account of the White House, 75
Adams, President John Quincy, death of, 64
   design for tympanum of Capitol, 41
Adams, Samuel, statue of, 65
Agriculture, Department of, 107
Alabama room at Mount Vernon, 164
Alexandria, 155-158
   Carlyle House, 158
   Christ Church, 157
   Conference of Governors, 158
   funeral ceremonies of Washington reported in the *Times and Advertiser* of, 184
   newspapers, 155, 184
   stone in the Washington monument, 157
   Washington's connection with, 155-157
   Washington relics, 157
Allen, Ethan, statue of, 66
Allen, Gov. William, statue of, 66
Almanac, Nautical, 92
"America, The Genius of," tympanum of the Capitol, 41
"America," statuary group of, 118
   statue (Naval Monument), 39
"American Civilization," Senate tympanum, 43
American Daily Advertiser, Claypole's, proof of Washington's Farewell Address, 167
Analostan Island, 149
Ancestry of Washington, 186 *et seq.*
Anecdotes, John Custis, 150
   Jackson, 92
   Marshall, 58
   Senator Preston, 125
   Washington, 155-157
Angelo, Michael, statue of, 123
"Apotheosis of Washington," painting of, 46
Apron made by La Marquise de Lafayette, 157
Aqueduct, 35, 147
   (Conduit) Road, 147
   Bridge, 149
Architects. (See Artists *et al.*)
Archives and Indexes, Bureau of, 89
Arlington, 149-155
   Cemetery, 153
   Custis Family, 149-152
   estate, 149
   mansion, 151
   relics, 152
   sale, 152
   tombs, Mr. and Mrs. Custis, 154
      Sheridan, 153
      Unknown Dead, 153
Arms and accoutrements, War Department, 90
Army, Commanders-in-Chief, portraits, 91
   Head-Quarters, 91
Army of the Cumberland, statues erected by the Society of, (Garfield) 39, (Thomas) 21
   of the Tennessee, statue erected by the Society of, (McPherson) 25

Arsenal. (See Barracks.)
Arthur, President, improvements made to the White House, 76
Artists, architects, engineers, painters, sculptors, Andrews. E. F., 78
Bailey, James, 28
Baldwin, E. F., 144
Ball, Thomas, 29
Bartholdi, 20
Bell, John, 118
Bierstadt, 67, 68
Bracquemond, 118
Brown, H. K., 23, 28
Brumidi, 46, 47, 61, 68, 69
Buberl, C., 120
Capellano, 42, 48, 49
Carpenter, F. B., 68
Casey, Gen. S., 112
Causici, 48, 49, 63
Chapman, John G., 49
Cluss, Adolph, 107
Crawford, Th., 43, 44, 46, 66, 123
D'Angers, 66
Falquiere, 21
Flannery, Lot, 27
Franzoni, 64
Gavelot, 48
Green, B. R., 112
Greenough, Horatio, 40, 42
Hadfield, Geo., 129
Hall, 126
Hoban, James, 73, 74
Houdon, 22, 66
Hoxie, Mrs. Vinnie Ream, 25, 66
Hunt, R. M., 145
Huntingdon, 79
Lambdin, 165, 167
Latrobe, 33, 56, 63
Lentze, Emanuel, 68
Meigs, Gen., 121
Mercie, 21
Mills, Clark, 21, 22
Mills, Robert, 94, 97
Moran, 62
Mullett, A. B., 88
Olmstead, Fred. L., 37
Peale, Rembrandt, 61, 165
Pelz, 111
Persico, 41, 42
Powell, W. H., 49, 62
Powers, Hiram, 62, 68, 124
Renwick, James, 122
Rietschel, 24
Robisso, Louis T., 26
Rogers, Randolph, 643
Scheffer, Ary, 67
Schulze, 121
Simmons, Franklin, 39
Smithmeyer, 111
Stone, Horatio, 63, 66
Story, W. W., 117
Struthers, John, 162
Stuart, Gilbert, 78, 79, 165

85)

Artists, etc.
  Thompson, Launt, 22, 143
  Troye, 69
  Valperti, 63
  Vanderlyn, John, 49, 67
  Walker, James, 63
Attorney-General, office of the, 106
  portraits of, 106
Auvergne, chair from the Chateau of Charagnac, Lafayette's birthplace, 166
Avenue, Pennsylvania, 19
Avenues, 18

BACCHUS, painting of, 70
  Baird, Spencer F., Secretary Smithsonian Institution, 117
Baker, Col. Ed. D., death of, 66
  statue of, 66
Ball, inauguration, 106
Ball, Mary (the mother of Washington), 172, 190
Ball's Bluff, battle of, death of Kearney, 66
Baltimore and Potomac R. R. Station, scene of Garfield's assassination, 28
Baltimore, Lord, dining-table of, 147
Barracks, Washington, 132
Barron, Commodore, duel with Decatur, 141
Bartholdi fountain, 20
Basement of the Capitol, 69, 70
  adventure of a lady, 70
Bassett, Col., bedstead of, 168
Bastile, key of, 164
  model of, 166
Bayard, Hon. Thomas F., oration of, 23
Beall, Ninian, Georgetown, 146
Belhaven (Alexandria), 155
Belvoir, estate of the Fairfax family, 172
Benevolent institutions, 133, 134
"Bivouac of the Dead," poem by Theodore O'Harra, 154
Bladen, Gov. Thomas, founding of Bladensburg, 141
Bladensburg, battle of, 141
  foundation of, 141
Blaine, Hon. James G., house of, 23
  present at Garfield's assassination, 28
Blodgett's Hotel, session of Congress in 1814, 130
Boards, Public Works, 19
  Regents of the Smithsonian Institution, 116
Boone, Daniel, conflict with Indians, sculpture, 48
Booth, John Wilkes, assassination of Lincoln, 129
  burial of, 133
  relics of, 91
Boreas, painting of, 70
Botanical Gardens, 20
Braddock, General, at Alexandria, 158
  landing-place of, 125
Bradford, Thomas, gift of land of, 33
Bridges, Aqueduct, 149
  Cabin-John, 147
  Chain, 148
  Long, 32
Brington, Great, church of, tombs of the Washingtons in, 189
  painting of, 166
Brington, Little, Washington cottage at, 188
  painting of, 166
British, evacuation of New York, 174
  invasion of Washington, 55, 75, 130, 141
  Legation, 23
"Brother Jonathan," Gov. Jonathan Trumbull, statue of, 64
Burgoyne, Surrender of, painting of, 52
Burning of Washington, 55, 75, 130
Burns, David, cabin of, 140

Butler, Jane, married Augustine Washington, 172

CABINET officers of the, 87
  commissions, 88
  Washington's, portraits of, 61
Cabot, medallion of, 49
Calhoun, John C., death of, 131
  portrait of, 62
California, Settlement of, painting of, 67
Calvert, Nelly, married to John Parke Custis, 151
Canal, Chesapeake and Ohio, 148
Cannon, captured, Cornwallis, Cortez, 132
  used for statues, 21, 24, 26
Cannon, manufactured, Naval Gun-Foundry, 132
Canopy of the Rotunda, "Apotheosis of Washington," painting of, 46
Canova, lions of, 123
  mantel at Mount Vernon, 165
  statue of, 123
Capitol, The, 37, 41 et seq.
  basement of, 69, 70
  canopy of Rotunda of, 46
  committee rooms of, 68, 69
  dome of, 45
  view from, 46, 70
  doors, Rogers, 43
    Crawford, 44
  galleries, House, 68
    Senate, 62
    whispering, 46
  grounds of, 37
  historical paintings of, 49-54
  House of Representatives, 67
  "Liberty," statue of, 47, (cast) 63
  Library of Congress, 54
  lobby, House, 68
    Senate, 60
  Mace, the Speaker's, 67
  marble room, Senate, 60
  porticos of, 41, 43
  restaurants of, 70
  Rotunda of, 42
  staircases of, 61, 68
  Senate, 59
  Statuary Hall, 63
  Supreme Court, 56
  Trumbull paintings in, 49-54
  Tympanum, central, 41
    Senate, 43
Carlyle House (Alexandria), Braddock's headquarters, 158
Carroll of Carrollton, Charles, portrait of, 66
  relics of, 168
  signature of, 88
Carroll, Daniel, house of, 140
Carroll, Rt. Rev. John, founder of Georgetown College, 146
"Carthagena, Admiral Vernon before," painting of, 166
Cash-room, Treasury, 44
Catholic University, 143
Cemeteries, Arlington, 153
  Congressional, 131
  Glenwood, 143
  National Military, 144
  Oak Hill, 145
  Rock Creek, 144
Cenotaphs of Congressmen, 131
Ceres, painting of, 73
"Chapultepec, Storming of," painting of, 63
Chase, Chief Justice, 59
  grave of, 146
Chastellux, General, visit to Mount Vernon, 176
Childs, George W., gift to Mount Vernon, 167

Chinese Legation, 23
Chippewa chief, bust of, 68
Churches, Christ Church, 83
  Christ Church, Alexandria, 157
  Christian Disciples (Garfield Memorial), 34
  St. John's, 33
  St. Paul's (Rock Creek), 33
Cincinnatus, painting of, 69
Circles, Dupont, 22
  Iowa, 24
  Thomas, 23
  Washington, 22
City Hall. (See Court House.)
"Civilization, American," sculpture of, Senate tympanum, 43
  statuary group of, 42
Clark Bros., opticians, makers of the great equatorial telescope, 126
Clay, Henry, house of, 22
  portrait of, 62
Claypole, *American Daily Advertiser*, proof of Washington's Farewell Address, 167
Clement XIII., Lions of Canova at the tomb of, 123
Cleveland, President, house of, "Oak View," 145
  inauguration ball, 106
  marriage of, 80
Clinton, Vice-President, grave of, 131
  statue of, 65
Clocks, House of Representatives, 68
  Statuary Hall, 64
Coast and Geodetic Survey, 133
Coat-of-arms, Washington's, 191
Cogswell, Dr., drinking-fountain of, 28
Collamer, Jacob, statue of, 66
Collections, Agricultural, 108
  National Museum, 119
  Ordnance Museum, 124
  Smithsonian, 118
  Tayloe (Art), 123
Colleges. (See Universities.)
Colorado, Cañon of the, painting of, 62
Columbian Mirror and Alexandria Gazette, early newspaper at Alexandria, 155
Columbian University, 137
Columbus, Landing of, painting of, 49
  medallion of, 49
  scenes from life, Rogers bronze door, 43
  statue (group), 42
Committee Rooms, 68, 69
Concerts, Marine Band, 76, 132
Conduit Road, 147
Congressmen, monuments to, 131
Congress, Houses of, 59, 67
  resolutions on the death of Washington, 185
Conrad, Mrs., grave of, 162
Conservatories, Agricultural, 108
  Botanical Gardens, 20
  White House, 77
Constitution of U. S., original draft of, 89
Convent of the Visitation, 139, 146
Copyright law, 56
Corcoran, W. W., Gallery of Art, 121
  gifts of, 121, 135, 137, 145, 146
  life of, 135
  Louise Home, 135
  medallion of, 123
  tomb of, 145
Cornwallis, cannon captured from, 132
  Surrender, painting of, 53
Correspondence of the early Presidents in the archives of the State Department, 89
Cortez, cannon used by, 132
Cottage, the President's, Soldiers' Home, 143
Counterfeits, specimens of, Treasury Department, 94

Courts, Claims, 107
  District, 27
  Supreme, 56
Crawford, Thomas, bust of, 65
  statue of, 123
Crypt of the Rotunda, 54
Culpepper, Lord, patent issued to John Washington, 172
Cumberland, Society of the Army of the, statues erected, (Garfield) 39, (Thomas) 24
Cunningham, Miss Ann Pamela, "The Southern Matron," exertions in behalf of Mount Vernon, 160
  portraits of, 166, 167
Curiosities. (See Relics.)
Curtis, George Ticknor, on the character of Washington, 177
Custis Family, 149-152
  death of John Parke Custis, 168
Custis, Nelly, adopted by Washington, 169
  grave of, 162
  harpsichord of, 164
  letters of, 166
  marriage of, 151
  portrait of, 165
  room at Mount Vernon, 168

DANDRIDGE, Martha (Martha Washington), 150
Da Vinci, statue of, 123
Dead-Letter Office, 98
  Museum of, 100
Deaf-Mute College, 137
Decatur, Commodore, duel with Commodore Barron 141
  house of, 22
  relics of, 147
D'Estaing, Count, statue of, 21
De Grasse, Count, statue of, 21
De Lancey, Gov., conference at Alexandria, 158
De Soto, Discovery of the Mississippi, painting of, 49
Diagram, principal story of the Capitol, 71
Dining-table of Lord Baltimore, 143
Dinners, State, White House, 81
Dinwiddie, Gov., conference at Alexandria, 158
Diplomatic intercourse, 89
  reception-room, State Department, 89
District of Columbia, area of, 17
  Court-House, 27, 129
  government, 35
  location of, 17
Discovery of the Hudson, painting of, 67
  the Mississippi, painting of, 49
"Discovery," statue of (group), 42
Dix, General, portrait of, 62
Dome of the Capitol, 45
  view from, 46, 70
Doors of the Capitol, Crawford, 44
  Rogers, 43
Douglass, Hon. Fred., oration by, 29
Houlton & Co., gift of, 118
Duddington Manor, (house of Daniel Carroll), 110
Duel, Decatur and Barron, 141
"Dumbarton, Rock of," (Georgetown), 146
Dupont, Admiral, Circle, 22
  statue of, 22
Importail, General, statue of, 21
Dürer, Albert, statue of, 123

EATON, General, grave of, 146
  Education, Bureau of, 103
Educational institutions. (See Universities, etc.)

Egg-rolling, Easter custom at the White House, 76
Electric time-service, 126
Electoral Commission, painting of, 62
Ellsworth, Chief Justice, 58
Emancipation, Signing of the Proclamation, painting of, 68
 statue of (group), 29
Emigration, John and Lawrence Washington, 190
Encke's comet, connection with Naval Observatory, 125
Engineers. (See Artists et al.)
Engraving and Printing, Bureau of, 112
Epitaphs, John Custis, 150
 Unknown Dead, 153
Etting, Col. Frank, gift to Mount Vernon, 168
Eulogy of Washington, Gov. Henry Lee, 41, 185
Evacuation day, 174
Evans, W. W., gift to Mount Vernon, 165
Everett, Edward, gift to Mount Vernon, 161
Ewing, Thomas, Secretary of the Interior, 101
Executions, Booth, Guiteau, Mrs. Surratt, Lincoln conspirators, 132, Wirz, 131
Executive Departments, 87 et seq.
Executive Mansion. See White House
Exploring expedition, Wilkes, 119

FAIRFAX, Anne, marriage to Lawrence Washington, 172
Fairfax, Lord, employs Washington, 155
 portrait of, 157
Fairfax, Col. William, 172
Falls of the Potomac, 148
 painting of, 166
Farewell Address, Washington's, corrected proof of, 167
 published, 179
Farewell to his officers, Washington's, Tallmadge's account of, 175
Farragut, Admiral, Square, 25
 statue of, 25
Fillmore, Mrs. President, selects the library of the White House, 82
Finishing notes, Treasury, 95
Fish Commission, 133
Fitzhugh, Mary Lee, married to G. W. P. Custis, 152
Flag, American, 191
Flora, painting of, 70
Florida Purchase, 85
Force, Peter, library acquired by the Government, 55
Ford's Theatre, assassination of Lincoln, 129
Forts, Du Quesne, Washington's march to, 158
 Foote, 160
 Myer, 155
 Washington, 160
Fountains, Bartholdi, 24
 Cogswell, 28
France, treaty with, 89
Franklin, Benjamin, bon-mot, 88
 chair of, 168
 commission as postmaster, 100
 public school, 34
 Square, 26
 statues of, 27, 62
Franklin, Sir John, expedition in search of, 83
Freneau, Philip, attacks upon Washington, National Gazette, 179
Fuller, Chief Justice, 59
Fulton, Robert, portrait of, 69
 statue of, 66
Funeral of Washington, 157
 account in Alexandria Times, 184
 Lear's account, 181
 ceremonies, 185
 oration, 185

GALLAUDET, Ed. M., instructor at Deaf Mute College, 137
Gallaudet, Dr. Thom. H., first instructor of deaf-mutes, 137
Galleries, House of Representatives, 68
 Senate, 62
Gallery, Corcoran Art, 121
Gardens, Botanical, 20
 Mount Vernon, 171
Garfield, President, assassination of, 28
 Memorial Church, 31
 Hospital, 134
 memorial tablets to, 28, 31
 monument of, 39
 statue of, 66
 "Genius of America," sculpture on Capitol tympanum, 42
Georgetown, 146
Georgetown College, 146
Georgia room at Mount Vernon, 166
Gerry, Vice-President Elbridge, grave of, 131
Ghent, signing of the treaty by President Madison, 76
 picture of the signing, 69
Gillis, Lieut., appropriation for the Naval Observatory, 125
"Golden Gate, The," painting of, 68
Gonzaga College, 139
Gordon, Commodore, tolls his ship's bell while passing Mount Vernon, 160
Gould, Jay, gift to Mount Vernon, 161
Governors of five States in conference with Braddock at Alexandria, 158
Grant, General, portrait of, 90
Graves, Vice-President Clinton, 131
 Mrs. Conrad, 162
 Corcoran family, 145
 G. W. P. Custis and wife, 154
 Nelly Custis, Custis family, 162
 General Eaton, 146
 Elbridge Gerry, 131
 Prof. Henry, 146
 Tobias Lear, 131
 Lewis family, 162
 Napoleon, hydrangea brought by Lafayette from, 172
 John Howard Payne, Bishop Pinckney, Admiral Rogers, 146
 Sheridan, 153
 Stanton, 146
 Van Ness family, 145
 Washington and wife, 161
 Washington family, 162
"Greek Slave, The," statue of (Powers), 124
Greene, Gen. Nathaniel, Square, 28
 statue of, 28
Guiteau, assassination of Garfield, 28
 trial of, 129
 execution of, 132
Gun-Foundry, Naval, 132

HALL, Prof., discovers the moons of Mars, 126
Hamilton, Alexander, portrait of, 61
 statue of, 66
Hancock, John, signature of, 88
 statue of, 63
Harrison, Mrs. Constance Cary, on Life at Mount Vernon, 173, 176
Harrison, Gov. Benj., chairs at Mount Vernon, 169
Harrison, President and Mrs., improvements to the White House, 76
"Hartford, The," statue of Farragut made from the propeller of, 25
Harvests, ancient and modern, paintings of, 69
Haviland, Henry & Co., gift of panel of Limoges faience, 118

INDEX. 89

Hayes, President, Chairman of the Committee on the Library of Congress, 55
Hayes, Mrs. President, portrait of, 79
Heights of great buildings, 31 (note)
Henry, Prof. Joseph, Secretary of the Smithsonian Institution, 117
  grave of, 146
  statue of, 117
"History," statue (Naval Monument), 39
Hodgkins, Th. G., gift to the Smithsonian Institution, 116
Homes, For the Aged, 134
  Louise, 135
Homestead laws, 104
Hospitals, Children's, Freedmen's, Garfield Memorial, Insane (Government), Providence, 134
  Naval, 132
Hospitality, Southern, Mrs. Constance Cary Harrison on, 176
Houses, historic, Calhoun (death of), 131
  Clay, Decatur, Seward, Van Buren, Webster, 22
  "Duddington Manor," 140
  Lincoln, 130
  "Octagon," 76, 140
  Van Ness, 140
House of Representatives, 67
Howard, Gen. O. O., 138
  University, 138
Hudson, Discovery of the, painting of, 67
Hunting Creek, 150
Hydrographic Office, 92

ILLINOIS, room at Mount Vernon, 166
  Inauguration of the Presidents, 43
  ball, 106
Indian Bureau, 103
  schools, 103
"Indian Races, Decadence of the," sculpture, Senate tympanum, 43
Indians, statues of (groups), 42
  Chippewa Chief, bust of, 68
Independence, The Declaration of, original, 88
  signing of, painting of, 50
Insane, Government Hospital for, 134
Interior, Department of, 101
Iowa Circle, 24
Ironclads, battle of, painting of, 62

JACKSON, anecdote of, 92
  statue of, 21
Jail, District, 132
Japan, swords from, treaty with, 79
Jay, Chief Justice, 58
Jefferson, Thomas, Secretary of State, 88
  library of, 55
  portraits of, 61, 66
  trees presented to Washington, 172
  statues of, 66, 68
"Jonathan, Brother," Gov. Jonathan Trumbull, statue of, 64
Jones' Point, 159
Josephine, Empress, maize from Analostan Island planted at Malmaison, 149
Judicial circuits, 56
Judiciary Square, 26
Justice, Department of, 106
"Justice," painting of, 61
Justices, Chief, 58, 59

KEARNEY, General, death of, 66
  statue of, 66
Kendall, Amos, founds the Deaf-Mute College, 137
Kendall Green, 137

King, Gov. William, statue of, 66
Knox, Gen. Henry, Secretary of War, 90
Kosciusko, bust of, 66

LADIES' ROOM, Senate, 63
  Lands, Public, office of, 104
  settlement of, 104
Langley, Samuel P., Secretary of the Smithsonian Institution, 117
  Fish Commissioner, 133
La Salle, medallion of, 49
Lafayette, chair from the birthplace of, 166
  hydrangea planted at Mount Vernon, 172
  memorial of, 21
  portrait of, 67, 157
  room at Mount Vernon, 168
  Square, 20
  visit to the United States, 163
Lafayette, La Marquise de, Masonic apron used by Washington, 168
Lear, Tobias, account of Washington's death, 180
  grave of, 131
Lee family, the, 152
Lee, Gov. Henry, eulogy of Washington, extracts, 41, 131
L'Enfant's plan of Washington, 17
Leinster, Duke of, palace at Dublin like the White House, 73
Legations, British, 23
  Chinese, 23
Letters, Nelly Custis, Washington, 166
Lexington, battle of, painting of, 69
Libraries, Agricultural Department, 107
  Army Medical Museum, 121
  Congress, 54, 55
  New Congress, 111
  Peter Force, 55
  Jefferson, 55
  Navy Department, 92
  Patent Office, 103
  Smithsonian, 55, 117
  War Department, 91
  White House, 88
  Washington's, 167
"Liberty, The Goddess of," painting of, 61
  statues of, 46, 63
Limoges Faience, panel presented to the Smithsonian Institution, 118
Lincoln, assassination of, 129
  relics of, 91
  bust of, 66
  model of a boat, 103
  Park, 28
  Signing of the Emancipation Proclamation, painting of, 68
  portraits of, 66, 79
  statues of, 27, 29, 66
Lions, Canova's 123
Little Falls of the Potomac, 148
Livingston, Chancellor Robt. R., statue of, 65
Lobby, House, 68
  Senate, 60
Logan, Gen. John A., grave of, 144
  oration of, 26
  statue of, 24
Louis XVI., portrait of, 166
Louisiana Purchase, 85, 104
Luther, statue of, 24
Lyman, Hon. Theodore F., gift to Mount Vernon, 167

MACE, the Speaker's, 67
  Macerating machine, destroying worn-out notes, 95
McPherson, Gen. James B., Square, 25
  statue of, 25

90 INDEX.

Madison, President, signs the Treaty of Ghent, 76
Madison, Mrs., 130
  the interrupted dinner, 75
  saves the picture of Washington, 75
  president of the City Orphan Asylum, 133
Marble room, Senate, 60
Marine Band Concerts, 77, 132
Marine barracks, 132
Markets, 32
Marriages, President Cleveland, 80
  General Lee, 152
  Washington, 150, 173
  Mrs. Washington, 150, 173
Marshall, Chief Justice, 58
  anecdote of, 58
  statue of, 40
Mars, discovery of the moons of, 126
Mars, statue of (Naval Monument), 39
Mason, General John, Analostan Island, 149
Mason, John Y., Confederate Commissioner, captured by Capt. Wilkes, 149
Masons, 189
Masonic Temple, 139
Massachusetts, room at Mount Vernon, 167
Matthews, Hon. Stanley, oration of, 24
Maynard, Hon. Horace, oration of, 25
Medical School, Columbian University, 137
Memorial stones in the Washington monument, 31, 157
Memorial tablets, Garfield, 28, 34
  John Quincy Adams, 64
Mexico, City of, money collected by General Scott, 142
"Miantonomoh," model of the, 91
Military Affairs, committee-room, 68
Military Justice, Bureau of, Booth relics, 91
"Mississippi, Discovery of the," painting of, 49
Models, Lincoln's boat, 103
  Museum (Patent Office), 103
  naval vessels, 91
Money-Order Office, 101
Monroe, President, lives in the "Octagon House," 76
"Monterey," model of the, 91
Monuments, Congressmen, 131
  Garfield, 39
  Naval, 39
  Payne, John Howard, 146
  Washington, 29
  Society, 32
  Washington family, 162
Morrill, Senator, suggests Statuary Hall, 64
Morris, Gov., conference at Alexandria, 158
Morris, Robert, frame made from tree on estate of, 166
Mount Vernon Ladies' Association, 160
Mount Vernon, 159-186
  Alabama room, 164
  banqueting hall, 164
  barn, 163
  cupola, 171
  destruction threatened, 174
  dining-room, 167
  garden, 171
  Georgia room, 166
  green room, 168
  hall, 161
  history, 172-186
  hydrangea planted by Lafayette, 172
  Illinois room, 166
  Lafayette's room, 168
  library, 167
  life at, 173, 176
  kitchens, 171
  mansion, 163
  Maryland room, 168
  Massachusetts room, 167
  monuments, 162

Mount Vernon—*continued.*
  Mrs. Washington's bedroom, 170
  music-room, 164
  Nelly Custis' room, 168
  monument, 162
  New York room, 164
  New Jersey room, 168
  Ohio room, 164
  old tomb, 162
  out-buildings, 171
  Pennsylvania room, 168
  piazza, 163
  Rhode Island, gift of citizens of, 171
  river room, 163
  "rose, the Mary Washington," 172
  sale, 161, 186
  sitting-room, 166
  South Carolina room, 167
  souvenirs, 172
  stairway, 168
  sun-dial, 171
  tolling of the bell by passing vessels, 160
  tomb, 161
  trees planted by Washington, 171, 172
  Virginia room, 169
  visits to, Lafayette, 168, 172
  Rochambeau and Chastellux, 176
  Washington's bedroom, 169
  West Virginia room, 168
Muhlenberg, William, statue of, 66
Museums, Agricultural, 107
  Army Medical, 121
  Dead-Letter Office, 100
  Models (Patent Office), 103
  National, 118
  Navy Yard, 132
  Ordnance, 124
  Postal, 100
Murillo, statue of, 123

NAPOLEON, hydrangea from the grave of, 172
National Museum, 118
National Gazette, Freneau's attacks upon Washington, 179
Naval Monument, 39
  Observatory, 125
  new, 145
Navy, building, 87
  bureaus of, 92
  Department, 91
  gun-foundry and yard, 132
Neptune, statue of (Naval Monument), 39
New Jersey room at Mount Vernon, 168
New Orleans, battle of, 21
Newspapers, old, *Alexandria Times and Advertiser,* 184
  Claypole's *American Daily Advertiser,* 167
  Columbian Mirror and Alexandrian Gazette, 155
  Freneau's *National Gazette,* 179
New York room at Mount Vernon, 164

OAK View, President Cleveland's house, 145
Observatory, Naval, 125
  new, 145
Octagon House, 76, 140
Odd-Fellows, 139
Officers of the Cabinet, 89
Official Gazette, Patent Office, 102
O'Harra, Col. Theodore, poem, "Bivouac of the Dead," 154
Orphan asylums, 133, 134
Orations, Hon. Th. F. Bayard (Dupont statue), 23
  Hon. Fred. Douglass (Emancipation statue), 29

Orations—*continued.*
  Gov. Henry Lee (eulogy of Washington), 185
  Gen. Logan (McPherson statue), 26
  Hon. Stanley Matthews (Thomas statue), 24
  Hon. Horace Maynard, Hon. Daniel W. Voorhees (Farragut statue), 25
  Hon. Robert C. Winthrop (Washington monument), 32
Osgood, Samuel, 91
  portrait of, 61

PAINTERS. See Artists *et al.*
  Paintings, portraits, etc., John Adams, 80
  Apotheosis of Washington, 46
  Attorneys-General, 106
  Bacchus, 70
  Boreas, 70
  Boston Massacre, 67
  Great Brington church, 166
  Burgoyne, Surrender of, 52
  Calhoun, 62
  California, Settlement of, 67
  Carroll, Charles, 66
  Ceres, 70
  Chapultepec, 63
  Chief Justices, 59
  Cincinnatus, 69
  Clay, 62
  Colorado cañon, 62
  Columbus, Landing of, 49
  Commanders-in-Chief of U. S. Army, 91
  Cornwallis, Surrender of, 53
  Miss Cunningham, 166, 167
  Nelly Custis, 165
  De Kalb, 167
  De Soto, Discovery of the Mississippi, 49
  Gen. Dix, 52
  "Discovery," 61
  Electoral Commission, 62
  "Executive Power," 61
  "Exploration," 61
  Fairfax, Lord, 157
  Flora, 70
  frieze of the rotunda, 47
  Fulton, 69
  Golden Gate, The, 68
  Grant, 90
  Great Falls of the Potomac, 167
  Hamilton, 61
  harvests, ancient and modern, 69
  Mrs. Hayes, 79
  "History," 61
  Hudson, Discovery of the, 67
  Independence, Signing of the Declaration of, 50
  ironclads, battle of, 62
  Jefferson, 61, 66, 69, 70, 79, 157
  "Justice," 62
  Knox, 61
  Lafayette, 67
  "Legislation," 61
  Lexington, Battle of, 69
  "Liberty," 61
  Lincoln, 66, 68, 78, 79
  Marion, 169
  Moultrie, 169
  Osgood, Samuel, 61
  "Peace," 61
  Perry's Victory on Lake Erie, 62
  Gen. Pickens, 167
  Pilgrims, Embarkation of, 49
  "Plenty," 61
  Pocahontas, Baptism of, 49
  Mrs. Polk, 79
  Presidents, 82, 83
  "Prudence," 61
  Putnam, 69

Paintings, portraits, etc.—*continued*
  Randolph, Edmund, 61
  "Religion," 61
  Revolutionary generals, 166
  Rittenhouse, 166
  Scott, 68
  Secretaries, Navy, 91
    State, War, 90
  Sheridan, 90
  Sherman, 90
  Speakers of the House of Representatives, 68
  "Strength," 61
  Sulgrave Manor, England, 166
  Sumner, 62
  Sumter, 167
  Taylor, 80
  "Temperance," 61
  Treaty of Ghent, Signing of the, 69
  Mrs. Tyler, 79
  Valley Forge, 69
  Van Buren, 80
  Wakefield, Washington's birthplace, 169
  "War," 61
  Washington, 46, 54, 61, 66, 67, 68, 69, 70, 77, 78, 157, 165
  Washington, Mrs., 78
  Washington cottage, at Little Brington, England, 166
  Washington family, 166
  Webster, 62
  Benj. West, 66
  "Westward Ho!" 68
  Gen. Wooster, death of, 69
  Yellowstone cañon, 62
Payne, John Howard, grave of, 146
Payne, Lewis, assassination (attempted) of Secretary Seward, 22
Patent Office, 102
  Museum of Models, 103
  Official Gazette, 102
Parks, Lincoln, 28
  National, 144
  Zoölogical, 145
Penn, Treaty with the Indians, sculpture of, 48
Pennsylvania Avenue, 19
  room at Mount Vernon, 168
"Pennsylvania," model of the, 91
Pension building, 105
  office business, 104
Perry, Victory on Lake Erie, painting of, 62
Pews, Christ Church, Alexandria, 157
  Garfield's, 34
  Trinity Church, New York, 166
Phidias, statue of, 123
Pinckney, Bishop, grave of, 146
Pilgrims, Embarkation of the, painting of, 49
  Landing of the, sculptured panel, 48
Pocahontas, Baptism of, painting of, 49
  saving Capt. John Smith, sculpture of, 48
Poem, "Bivouac of the Dead," 154
Polk, Mrs., portrait of, 79
Pompeii, relic from, 92
Population of Washington, 17
Porter, Admiral, design for Naval Monument, 39
Portraits. See Paintings.
Postmaster-General, 97
Post-Office Department, 96
  growth and statistics of, 98
Presidents, summer cottage of the, 143
  portraits of, 82, 83
  receptions, 79, 85
  room in the Capitol, 62
Printing, Bureau of Engraving and, 112
  Government Office, 128
  notes and securities, 112, 113
Prison, Old Capitol, 131

Public lands, 104
Public schools, 31
Purleigh, England, Lawrence Washington, rector of, 188
Putnam Leaving the Plough, painting of, 69

QUARTERS of the city, 18, 19

RALEIGH, Sir Walter, medallion of, 49
Randolph, Edmund, Attorney-General, 106
  portrait of, 69
Randolph, John, support of the Library of Congress, 55
Raphael, statue of, 123
Rathbone, Mrs. Elizabeth, gift to Mount Vernon, 163
Rawlins, Gen. John A., statue of, 27
Reception rooms, Diplomatic, State Department, 89
  library of the Navy Department, 92
  Senate, 61
Receptions, The President's, 79, 85
  President and Mrs. Washington's, 177, 178
Record and Pension Division, War Department, 130
Redemption, Bureau of, Treasury, destruction of old notes, 95
Relics, curiosities, etc., Arlington, 152
  arms and accoutrements, 90
  Booth, 91
  Decatur, 147
  National Museum, 119
  Navy Yard, 132
  Secret Service Division, Treasury, 94
  Smithsonian, 118
  State Department, 88
  War Department, 90
  Washington, 88, 119, 157, 164 et seq.
Rembrandt, statue of, 123
Reservoirs, 143, 147
"Resolute," British ship, table for the President, presented by the British Government, 93
Restaurants in the Capitol, 70
Rhode Island, gift of citizens of Rhode Island to Mount Vernon, 171
Rittenhouse, David, portrait of, 166
River Road, 149
Rochambeau, Count de, statue of, 21
  visit to Mount Vernon, 176
Rogers, Admiral, grave of, 146
"Rogues' Gallery," Treasury Department, 94
Rooms. See Mount Vernon, 164-171
  White House, 77-85
Rose, The Mary Washington, 172
Rotunda of the Capitol, 46
Rubens, statue of, 123
Rush, Hon. Richard, obtains the Smithsonian bequest, 116
Rusk, Jeremiah M., Secretary of Agriculture, 108
Rutledge, Chief Justice, 58

SALARIES, Cabinet Officers, 87
  Justices of the Supreme Court, 59
Scott, Charlotte, first subscription toward the Emancipation statue, 29
Scott, General, suggests the Soldiers' Home, 142
  portrait of, 68
  statues of, 23, 143
  Square, 23
Sculptors. See Artists et al.
Sculptures. See Statues, etc
Seals, Treasury, 95
  United States, 89

Secretaries of the Executive Departments, 87
  Agriculture, 108
  Interior, 101
  Navy, 91
  State, 88
  Treasury, 94
  War, 90
Smithsonian Institution, 117
Secret Service Division, Treasury, "Rogues' Gallery," 94
Senate chamber, 59
  old, 56
Settlement of public lands, 104
"Settlement of America," statue of (group), 42
Seward, attempt to assassinate Secretary, 22
  house of, 22
Sharpe, Gov., conference at Alexandria, 158
Shepherd, Alex. R., Governor of D. C., 19
Sheridan, General, portrait of, 90
  tomb of, 153
Sherman, Roger, statue of, 64
Sherman, General, portrait of, 90
Shirley, Gov., conference at Alexandria, 158
Signal Office, 126
Signatures, Declaration of Independence, 88
  President's, 88
  Secretary of State, 88
Signing, Acts of Congress, 60
  Declaration of Independence, painting of, 50
  Emancipation Proclamation, painting of, 68
  Treaty of Ghent, painting of, 69
    by President Madison, 76
Slave, statue of (Emancipation), 29
Slidell, Confederate Commissioner, 149
Smith, Captain John, Pocahontas saving the life of, sculptured panel, 48
Smithson, James, 115
  bequest of, 116
  relics of, 118
Smithsonian Institution, 115
  building, 114
  library, 117
  publications, 117
Soldiers' Home, 142
  President's cottage, 143
South Carolina, room at Mount Vernon, 167
"Southern Matron, The," Miss Ann Pamela Cunningham, 160
Souvenirs of Government paper, 95
Speakers of the House of Representatives, portraits of, 68
Staircases, Capitol, 61, 68
  State, War, and Navy building, 88
Standard time, 126
Stanton, Secretary, grave of, 146
  Place, 28
State Department, 88
  curiosities, 89
State, War, and Navy building, 87
Station, Baltimore and Potomac Railroad, (Pennsylvania R. R.) 28
Statistics of the Post-Office Department, 97
Statues, sculptures, etc.
  Adams, Samuel, 65
  Allen, Ethan, 66
  Allen, Gov. William, 66
  "America" (Naval Monument), 39
    group, 118
  America, Settlement of (group), 42
  "America, Genius of," 41, 42
  American eagle, 63
  American Civilization and Decadence of the Indian Races, 43
  Angelo, Michael, 123
  Baker, Col. Edward D., 66
  Boone in Conflict with Indians (panel), 48
  Canova, 123

INDEX. 93

Statues, sculptures, etc.—*continued*.
  Chippewa chief (bust), 68
  "Civilization," 42
  Clinton, Vice-President, 65
  Clock, Statuary Hall, 64
  Collamer, Jacob, 66
  Columbia, the Protectress of Science and Industry, 120
  Columbus (Discovery of America, group), 42
  Corcoran, W. W. (medallion of), 123
  Crawford, Thomas (bust), 66, 123
  Da Vinci, 123
  D'Estaing, Count, 21
  De Grasse, Count, 21
  Discovery of America (group), 42
  Dürer, Albert, 123
  Duportail, General, 21
  "Emancipation" (group), 28, 29
  Farragut, Admiral, 25
  Franklin, 26, 62
  Fulton, Robert, 66
  Garfield, 39, 66
  Greene, General Nathaniel, 28, 66
  "Greek Slave, The," 124
  Hamilton, 66
  Hancock, John, 60
  Henry, Prof. Joseph, 117
  "History" (Naval Monument), 39
  Jackson, 27
  Jefferson, 66, 68
  Kearney, General, 66
  King, Gov. William, 66
  Kosciusko (bust), 66
  Lafayette, 21
  "Liberty," 46, 63
  Lincoln, (Emancipation, group) 28, 29, 66
    (bust), 66
  Lions, Canova, 123
  Livingston, Chancellor Robt. R., 65
  Logan, Gen. John A., 24
  Luther, 24
  McPherson, General, 25
  Marshall, Chief Justice, 40
  Murillo, 123
  "Peace" (Naval Monument), 39
  Penn making the Treaty with the Indians (panel), 48
  Phidias, 123
  Pilgrims, Landing of the (panel), 48
  Pocahontas Saving the Life of Capt. John Smith (panel), 48
  Raphael, 123
  Rawlins, General, 27
  Rembrandt, 123
  Rochambeau, Count de, 21
  Rubens, 123
  Scott, General, 23, 143
  Sherman, Roger, 64
  Stockton, Richard, 66
  Titian, 123
  Thomas, General, 23
  Trumbull, Gov. Jonathan, 64
  "War," 42
  Washington, 22, (Greenough's) 40
    (crowned with laurel), 42
    (Houdon's, cast), 66
  Williams, Roger, 64
  Wilson, Vice-President (bust), 61
  Winthrop, Gov. John, 65
"Stewart Castle," Chinese Legation, 23
Stockton, Richard, statue of, 66
Stony Point, Storming of, painting of, 69
Streets of Washington, 18
Sumner, Charles, house of, 22
  portrait of, 63
Sumter, General, painting of, 167
Supreme Court, 56–59
  chamber, 56
  old, 56

Supreme Court—*continued*.
  Chief Justices, 58, 59
  procedure of, 57, 58
Surratt, Mrs., execution of, 132

TALLMADGE, Col. Benjamin, account of Washington's Farewell to his Officers, 175
Taney, Chief Justice, 58
Tayloe, Col. John, art collection of, 123
  house of, 140
Taylor, President, portrait of, 80
Thomas, General, Circle, 23
  statue of, 23
Thompson, Mrs. Mary E., gift to the Government, 68
Time-ball, Navy Department, 88
  Naval Observatory, 126
Time, Standard, sent from the Naval Observatory, 126
Titian, statue of, 123
Tolling of the bell by ships passing Mount Vernon, 160
Tombs, Corcoran family, 145
  English Washingtons, 187
  Sheridan, 153
  Unknown Dead, 153
  Van Ness family, 145
  Washington, 161, 162
Treasury Department, 92, 96
  cash-room, 94
  Redemption Bureau and destruction of worn-out notes, 95
  "Rogues' Gallery," 95
  vaults, 95
Treaties preserved in the State Department, 89
  Ghent, 69, 76
Tripolitan cannon, 132
Trumbull, Gov. Jonathan, statue of, 64
Trumbull, Col. John, historical paintings by, 49–54
Tyler, Mrs., portrait of, 79
Tympanum, Eastern Portico of the Capitol, 41
  Senate wing, 43

UNDERCROFT of the Rotunda, 69
Universities, colleges, etc., Carlisle, 142
  Columbian, 137
  Deaf-Mute, 137
  Georgetown, 117
  Gonzaga, 139
  Howard, 138
  Visitation, Academy, 139
    Convent, 146
  Wayland Seminary, 138
Unknown Dead, tomb at Arlington, 153

VALLEY FORGE, Washington at, painting of, 69
Van Buren, President, house of, 22
  portrait of, 145
Van Ness, house of, 140
  tomb of, 145
Van Ness, Mrs., 133, 140
Vaults of the Treasury, 95
Vernon, Admiral, before Carthagena, painting of, 166
  Mount Vernon named from, 172
"Vesuvius," model of the, 91
Vice-Presidents, room in the Capitol, 61
  presiding officer of the Senate, 60
  Henry Wilson, death of, 61
  bust of, 61
Virginia room at Mount Vernon, 169
Voorhees, Hon. Daniel W., oration of, 25

WAITE, Chief Justice, 59
"Wakefield," the birthplace of Washington, picture of, 169
War Department, 90-92
  building, 87
  curiosities of, 90, 91
  library of, 91
  offices of, 90
Washington City, aqueduct, 35
  area of, 17
  arsenal, barracks, 132
  benevolent institutions, 133, 134
  location of, 17
  parks of, 20, 28, 144, 145
  plan of, 17
  population of, 17
  quarters of, 17
  streets of, 17
  trees of, 17
  West End, 19
Washington Family, 186, 192
  ancestry of, 186 et seq.
  coat-of-arms of, 187, 188, 191
  emigration of, 189
  English, 177, 188
  house at Sulgrave, 188
    at Little Brington, 188
      painting of, 166
  tombs of, 161, 162, 188
  Virginia, 189, 190
Washington, George, agent rebuked, 174
  Alexandria, connection with, 155, 157
  ancestry, 186 et seq.
  attacks upon by Freneau, 179
  bedroom of, 165
  birth of, 190
  birthplace of, 189
    picture of, 169
  Braddock, accompanies, 158
  Cabinet, painting of, 61
  character, article by George Ticknor Curtis, 177
  coat-of-arms, 191
  Commander of the American Army, 174
  commission, resignation of, 175
    painting of, 54
  Congress, resolutions on hearing of his death, 185
  correspondence preserved in the State Department, 89
  Custis, adoption of the children of John Parke, 169
  death of, 180
    Lear's account of, 180 et seq.
  Delegate to the Continental Congress, 174
  elm planted in the Capitol grounds, 37
  eulogy delivered by Gov. Henry Lee, extracts from, 40, 185
  Farewell Address, proof of, 167
    published, 179
  farewell to his officers, account of by Col. Benj. Tallmadge, 175
  funeral, 157, 184, 185
  Greenough's statue of, 10
  Houdon's statue of, (cast) 66
  illness, Lear's account of, 180 et seq.
  inherits Mount Vernon, 173
  letters preserved at Mount Vernon, 166
  marriage of, 151, 155, 173
  life at Mount Vernon, 173, 176, 179
  life at Philadelphia, 178
  medical treatment, 181, 182
  mother of, 190
  paintings of, 66, 69, 77, 78, 157, 165, 168
  pedigree, table of, 192

Washington, George—continued.
  property of, 186
  rebukes his agent, 174
  relics of, Alexandria, 157
    Arlington, 152
    State Department, 89
    Mount Vernon, 164 et seq.
  swords of, 89, 164
  tombs of, 161, 162
  will of, 186
Waters, Henry F., researches in regard to the ancestry of Washington, 187
Wayland Seminary, 138
Weather Service, 127
Webster, Daniel, house of, 22
  portrait of, 62
Weights and measures, standard, 133
Welles, Albert, pedigree of Washington, 187 (note).
West, Benjamin, portrait of, 66
West End of the City, 19
West Virginia room at Mount Vernon, 168
"Westward Ho!" painting, 68
Whispering Gallery of the Rotunda, 46
White House, The, 73-85
  architect, 73, 74
  bedrooms, State, 85
  Blue room, 79
  Cabinet room, 84
  Cleveland, marriage of President, 80
  concerts of the Marine Band, 76
  conservatories, 77
  destroyed by the British, 75
  dining room, family, 82
    State, 80
  dinners, State, 81
  East room, 78
  egg-rolling at Easter, 76
  erection, 73, 74
  Green room, 79
  improvements, 75, 76
  library, 82
  name, reason for, 75
  occupied by Pres. Adams, 75
  portraits in, 77-80
  reconstruction, 76
  Red room, 80
  vestibule, 77
  visitors to the President, 85
Wight, Isle of, tiles used at Mount Vernon, 163
Wilkes, Captain, capture of Confederate Commissioners, 149
  exploring expedition, relics of, 119
Williams, Roger, statue of, 64
Wilson, Vice-President, bust of, 61
  death of, 61
Winthrop, Gov. John, statue of, 65
Winthrop, Hon. Robert C., oration of, 32
Wirz, Henry, execution of, 31
Women's National Temperance Union, picture of Mrs. Hayes, presented by, 79
Works, Board of Public, 19
Wooster, General, death of, painting of, 69

YELLOWSTONE, Cañon of the, painting of, 62
Youn Men's Christian Association, 134

ZOOLOGICAL Park, 145

www.ingramcontent.com/pod-product-compliance
Lightning Source LLC
Chambersburg PA
CBHW032120230426

43672CB00009B/1803